Scottish Law of Leases

Scottish Law of Leases

An Introduction

Second Edition

Angus McAllister MA, LLB, Solicitor
Lecturer in Law, University of Paisley

Edinburgh
Butterworths
1995

United Kingdom	Butterworths, a Division of Reed Elsevier (UK) Ltd, 4 Hill Street, EDINBURGH EH2 3JZ and Halsbury House, 35 Chancery Lane, LONDON WC2A 1EL
Australia	Butterworths Pty Ltd, SYDNEY, MELBOURNE, BRISBANE, ADELAIDE, PERTH, CANBERRA and HOBART
Canada	Butterworth Canada Ltd, TORONTO and VANCOUVER
Ireland	Butterworth (Ireland) Ltd, DUBLIN
Malaysia	Malayan Law Journal Sdn Bhd, KUALA LUMPUR
New Zealand	Butterworths of New Zealand Ltd, WELLINGTON and AUCKLAND
Puerto Rico	Butterworths of Puerto Rico Inc, SAN JUAN
Singapore	Malayan Law Journal Pte Ltd, SINGAPORE
South Africa	Butterworth Publishers (Pty) Ltd, DURBAN
USA	Michie, CHARLOTTESVILE, Virginia

ISBN 0 406 04495 3

Typeset by Phoenix Photosetting, Chatham, Kent.
Printed and bound in Great Britain by Redwood Books, Kennett House, Trowbridge, Wiltshire

Preface

In the six years since the first edition changes in the law have been gradual, but have had a considerable cumulative effect. New statutes affecting leases, either directly or indirectly, include the Term and Quarter Days (Scotland) Act 1990, the Agricultural Holdings (Scotland) Act 1991, the Leasehold Reform, Housing and Urban Development Act 1993 and the Requirements of Writing (Scotland) Act 1995. Case law, too, has continued to develop: in particular, rent reviews alone account for more than half of the new decisions, and the law of irritancy continues to be controversial. As a result, the text has grown somewhat in length, although some savings were achieved by cutting the coverage of regulated tenancies, which are now much less prevalent.

I would like to thank my colleagues June Hyslop and Andrew McCowan for their help with certain parts of the book.

The law is stated as at 1 August 1995.

Angus McAllister,
September 1995

Bibliography

(a) General texts on landlord and tenant

1. Gloag and Henderson *Introduction to the Law of Scotland* (10th edn, 1995), ch 41
2. *The Laws of Scotland, Stair Memorial Encyclopaedia*, Vols 1 & 13
3. Gordon *Scottish Land Law* (1989), ch 19
4. Paton and Cameron *The Law of Landlord and Tenant in Scotland* (1967)
5. Rankine *A Treatise on the Law of Leases in Scotland* (3rd edn, 1916)

(b) Other books on landlord and tenant

6. Duncan and Hope *The Rent (Scotland) Act 1984* (1986)
7. Duncan *The Agricultural Holdings (Scotland) Act 1991* (1991)
8. Gill *The Law of Agricultural Holdings in Scotland* (2nd edn, 1990)
9. Halliday *Conveyancing Law and Practice*, Vol III, *Leases and Heritable Securities* (1987)
10. Robson *Residential Tenancies* (1994)
11. Robson *The Housing (Scotland) Act 1988* (1989)
12. Ross and McKichan *Drafting and Negotiating Commercial Leases in Scotland* (2nd edn, 1993)
13. Watchman *The Housing (Scotland) Act 1987* (1991)

(c) Other relevant textbooks

14. Gloag *The Law of Contract* (2nd edn, 1929)
15. Himsworth *Public Sector Law in Scotland* (4th edn, 1994)
16. McBryde *The Law of Contract in Scotland* (1987)
17. Walker *The Law of Contracts and Related Obligations in Scotland* (3rd edn, 1995)
18. Woolman *Contract* (2nd edn, 1994)
19. Reid *The Requirements of Writing (Scotland) Act 1995* (1995)
20. Rennie and Cusine *The Requirements of Writing* (1995)

List of Abbreviations

AC	Appeal Cases (Law Reports)
All ER	All England Law Reports
CA	Court of Appeal
Ch	Chancery (Law Reports)
Cr App R	Criminal Appeal Reports
CLY	Current Law Year Book
D	Dunlop (Court of Session Reports, 2nd Series, 1838–62)
EG	Estates Gazette
EGCS	Estates Gazette Case Summaries
EGLR	Estates Gazette Law Reports
F	Fraser (Court of Session Reports, 5th Series, 1898–1906)
FLR	Family Law Reports
FSR	Fleet Street Reports
GWD	Green's Weekly Digest
HL	House of Lords
HLR	Housing Law Reports
HMSO	Her Majesty's Stationery Office
Hume	Baron Hume's Reports of Decisions, 1781–1822
JLS	Journal of the Law Society of Scotland
KB	King's Bench (Law Reports)
LJ	Law Journal Newspaper
M	Macpherson (Court of Session Reports, 3rd Series, 1862–73)
Mor	Morison's Dictionary of Decisions
P & CR	Property and Compensation Reports
QB	Queen's Bench (Law Reports)
R	Rettie (Court of Session Reports, 4th Series, 1873–98)
RVR	Rating and Valuation Reporter

S	Shaw (Court of Session Reports, 1st Series, 1821–38)
SC	Session Cases
SCCR	Scottish Criminal Case Reports
Sc Jur	Scottish Jurist
SCLR	Scottish Civil Law Reports
SCOLAG	Journal of Scottish Legal Action Group
Sh Ct Rep	Sheriff Court Reports
SI	Statutory Instrument
SLCR	Scottish Land Court Reports
SLR	Scottish Law Reporter
SLT	Scots Law Times
SN	Session Notes
Sol Jo	Solicitors' Journal (England)
TLR	Times Law Reports
WLR	Weekly Law Reports

Contents

Table of Cases

Table of Statutes

1 Introduction

There must be few people in Scotland, whatever their position in life, who have not encountered a lease at some point. Many are tenants of dwellinghouses, having leased them either from private landlords or a public authority, probably the local council. Many others are tenants of business premises, whether they be shops, offices or factories. It is also common for a farmer to be the tenant of the holding he cultivates. Landlords too come in many guises, from large financial institutions, such as banks, insurance companies or pension funds, which have bought property as an investment, to the private individual who leases out his house for a few years while he is absent abroad.

Not only is a lease one of the commonest types of agreement now, but it is also one of the oldest: we will see shortly that statutes going back as far as the fifteenth century are still good law.

Indeed, so familiar is the concept of a lease, that to spend too much time on a definition might be to run the risk of making the basic idea seem less straightforward than it actually is. However, it is necessary to take a brief look at its main features, so as to properly mark out our field of study.

1. MAIN CHARACTERISTICS OF LEASES[1]

A lease is a contract by which a person, known as a tenant, is allowed to occupy someone else's property for a finite period. In return for this he pays to the person granting this right (ie his landlord) a periodical payment known as rent. Rent usually takes the form of money, but may also (though not commonly) be paid in goods.

Several points arise from this that require to be developed:

1 Rankine *Leases* (3rd edn, 1916) Introduction; Paton & Cameron *Landlord and Tenant* (1967) pp 3–5.

1

(1) Subject matter of leases

The subject matter of a lease is **heritable property**. This means, broadly speaking, land and buildings and rights pertaining to them. In a strict sense it means land and its pertinents, including buildings and any other fixtures attached to the land; however, although it is subsidiary in legal theory, it is often a building rather than its site which is the most valuable element in a lease, and therefore the main subject of the contract. Heritable property is the equivalent (though not the exact equivalent) of the English concept of real property. Where moveable property is rented, the contract in strict law is not one of lease but of **hire**, although the term lease is sometimes loosely used in connection with the hire of some moveables.

(2) Exclusive right of occupation

The tenant (or tenants where there is a joint tenancy) normally must be given an exclusive right to occupy the subjects of let. Where the landlord has reserved the right to share occupation in some way, the contract may not be a lease at all but a mere licence. This is an important distinction which we will return to later in the chapter. However, there are certain exceptional types of contract which do not involve exclusive occupation by the tenant, but nevertheless have been traditionally considered to be leases. These include leases of shooting rights, salmon fishings and the right to extract minerals, and are also briefly considered later in the chapter.

(3) Occupation finite

A lease may confer only a temporary right of occupation or its duration may be much longer. In either case the right of ownership remains with the landlord and possession will normally revert to him at the expiry of the lease. The expiry or termination date of a lease is known in Scotland as the 'ish'.

(4) Lease as a contract

A lease is a contract. This means that, as well as the special legal rules relating to landlord and tenant, the general law of contract also applies to leases. It is not within the scope of this book to look in any detail at the law of contract, for which there are several excellent textbooks at various levels[1]. However, reference to contract law will be made from time to time where relevant.

(5) Lease as conferring a right of property

While it is right to regard a lease as a contract for the reasons stated above, this does not tell the full story. It is appropriate for leases of short duration, which may seem to be not unlike other types of business contract. However, where a lease is of long duration the rights conferred on a tenant may be much more substantial than one would normally expect from a mere contract. In some cases the tenant may seem to be enjoying not just a temporary right of occupation, but something much more like a right of property or ownership. There are several ways in which a tenant's rights may transcend those enjoyed under a contract:

(a) *A lease confers a real right*[2]. Generally we would expect a contract only to bind legally the original parties to it. However, if the ownership of a property which is tenanted changes hands, the new owner will normally have to recognise the leases of any sitting tenants, even though he was not a party to them.

(b) *Security of tenure.* We have already noted that the duration of a lease may be of some length. In theory, a lease may even be of perpetual duration, as in the old case of *Carruthers v Irvine*[3] where a lease was stated to endure 'perpetually and continually as long as the grass groweth up and the water runneth down'. In practice, a perpetual lease is something of an anachronism and extremely rare, though leases of 99 or 120 years, or even of 999 years, are not uncommon. In such a case, the tenant may supply some or all of the buildings at his own expense. Even where he has not, and the lease is not quite so long (eg 20 or 30 years), the tenant's legal interest under the lease, because of his lengthy period of tenure, will acquire a capital value and become a marketable asset; in other words, a tenant may be able to charge a substantial sum of money for an assignation (ie transfer) of his lease to a new tenant. In many cases such a transaction will resemble an outright sale of heritable property.

---

1 Gloag *The Law of Contract* (2nd edn, 1929); McBryde *The Law of Contract in Scotland* (1987); Woolman *Contract* (2nd edn, 1994); Walker *The Law of Contracts and Related Obligations in Scotland* (3rd edn, 1995).
2 See ch 2, pt 4 below.
3 (1717) Mor 15195.

(c) *Recorded leases.* A lease of more than 20 years may be recorded in the Register of Sasines or (depending upon the area in which the property is located) registered in the Land Register of Scotland. These are public registers of deeds relating to heritable property, including the deeds (ie a disposition or feu charter) which confer ownership. Recording (or registering) his lease strengthens a tenant's rights considerably; in particular it allows him to use his legal interest as a tenant as security for a loan[1].

(d) *Statutory protection.* There are a number of statutes which (depending on the type of lease) may strengthen further a tenant's rights. These will be noted as we go along. In particular, we will see that in agricultural and residential tenancies a tenant may have statutory security of tenure, ie the right to stay on in the leased property even though the termination date in his lease has arrived and the landlord wants him out[2]. Generally, such statutory rights cannot be contracted out of, ie any provision in the lease document purporting to deprive the tenant of them will not be given effect by the courts.

2. ENGLISH LEASE LAW

Although Scotland still has a separate legal system, there has been a tendency since the Union of the Parliaments in 1707 for the law of the two countries to converge. Nowadays many areas of law are governed by statutes that apply to both Scotland and England, eg employment legislation or company law. In other areas there are separate Scottish and English Acts, but with substantially identical provisions, eg the statutes relating to town and country planning or compulsory purchase and compensation. However, in the realm of landlord and tenant there are still many important differences between the laws of the two countries. It is true that many common principles of contract law underpin lease law on either side of the border; however, Scotland and England traditionally have quite distinct systems of land tenure and this has tended to create a fundamental divergence that is still very much with us.

One manifestation of this is found in the English distinction between freehold and leasehold tenure. In England when one 'buys' a property by paying a capital sum, it is sometimes acquired

1 See ch 6, pt 2 below.
2 See chs 10–14 below.

outright and the purchaser becomes the owner of the freehold. In many instances, however, what is being bought is only the tenant's interest in the unexpired portion of a very long lease, perhaps for 99 years or 120 years or even longer. A nominal amount of rent may be payable, but the main consideration is the capital sum, and the transaction will externally resemble an outright sale. A form of 'leasehold' tenure was traditionally possible in Scotland, but was much less common, particularly in the case of residential property. This was because the Scottish system of feudal tenure allowed landowners to obtain a similar type of monetary return without granting leases: thus an owner could grant a right of perpetual ownership to another person while retaining the right of superior, enabling him to charge the new owner (now his vassal) an annual feuduty. The amount of the feuduty would have been comparable to the rent payable under a long English lease and in both cases a capital sum might or might not have changed hands when the property was first disposed of; this would probably depend upon whether the site already had buildings or whether these were to be provided by the new owner or tenant.

Nowadays, long leases are common in Scotland in the case of commercial and industrial properties, where there has been much English influence. However, long leases of dwellinghouses (always comparatively rare) have now been expressly forbidden in Scotland for periods of more than twenty years[1]. In England, on the other hand, long leases of residential property remain widespread.

Despite the English influence on Scottish commercial and industrial leases, it is here that we find another fundamental difference between the countries. In landlord and tenant law generally, much of Scots common law has been supplemented and in some areas virtually replaced by statute. This is particularly true in the case of residential and agricultural leases, where Scottish and English tenants are both protected by separate but substantially similar legislation. In England, tenants of business premises are similarly protected by a substantial statutory code; for example, under the Landlord and Tenant Act 1954 a tenant often has the right to renew his lease, even where his landlord wants him to move out. In Scotland, with one minor exception[2], there is no such statutory regulation and the parties enjoy virtual freedom of contract.

There are many other differences, the more important of which will be referred to when they arise. Nevertheless, there are enough

1 Land Tenure Reform (Scotland) Act 1974, ss 8–10; see ch 6, pt 4 below.
2 See ch 8 below.

common areas for it to be expedient to quote English cases where there is no equivalent Scottish authority. This is particularly so in the chapter on rent reviews, where the sparse Scottish authority is almost swamped by the deluge of English decisions. Such English authority, however, should always be treated with some caution; English cases may often be highly persuasive, but are never totally binding in Scotland.

3. TYPES OF LEASE

Not all of the following categories are mutually exclusive and there is some overlap between them:

Urban and rural leases

The distinction between urban and rural leases in Scots law is traditional, operating independently of the other classifications described below. It does not mean, as the words might suggest, that one kind is found in the town and the other in the country, though that is a possibility. Where the main subject of let is a building, and there is either no land attached or the land is subsidiary (eg garden ground), we have an **urban** lease. However, where the main subject is land it is a **rural** lease. A lease of an agricultural holding is therefore a rural lease: there may be farm buildings, but they are subsidiary to the land as part of the subjects of let. The distinction between urban and rural leases is still important in some cases where we have to apply the common law of landlord and tenant. For example, whether or not a lease is an urban or rural one may determine whether or not it can be assigned without the landlord's consent[1]. Other incidences will be noted as they arise.

Commercial and industrial leases

Commercial and industrial leases are urban leases, as they relate to the let of buildings. 'Commercial lease' is the term generally applied to leases of shops or offices. An 'industrial lease', as the name suggests, is the lease of a factory. In England, they all may be encountered under the term 'business leases'. As noted above, commercial and industrial leases in Scotland (though not in

1 See ch 5, pt 1 below.

England) are almost free of statutory regulation. Commercial and industrial subjects are generally the most valuable types of heritable property, and are commonly acquired by large financial institutions for the purpose of investment. It is in this area, because of the amount of money that is often at stake, that the complex law relating to rent reviews is most alive[1].

Agricultural leases

Agricultural leases are, naturally, rural leases. Leases of farmland are closely regulated by the Agricultural Holdings (Scotland) Act 1991, which confers many important rights upon tenants; these include the right to claim security of tenure (ie to stay on after the expiry date stated in the lease) or, where that is denied, the right to be compensated for improvements which the tenant has made to the holding. In the case of smaller holdings, the lease may instead be governed by the legislation relating to crofts and small landholdings, but the type of protection enjoyed by the tenant is similar[2].

Residential leases

Residential leases are leases of dwellinghouses, including flats, and they are of course urban leases. Like agricultural leases, they are extensively regulated by statute. Until early in this century, the most common types of residential let were those from private landlords. Such leases have for many years been governed by a series of statutes, the most recent being the Housing (Scotland) Act 1988[3]. Over the course of the present century, the incidence of private house lets has gradually decreased in proportion to the rise in public sector tenancies, mainly in the form of local authority housing. However, there are still many private residential leases, notably in the realm of bedsits and other short furnished lets. Statutory regulation has more recently been extended to the public sector itself, in a separate series of Acts giving a tenant, among other things, security of tenure and the right to buy the house he occupies from his landlord[4].

---

1 See ch 10 below.
2 See ch 12 below.
3 See ch 13 below.
4 See ch 14 below.

Leases of certain uses of land

Scots law has traditionally given the status of lease to certain types of agreement under which the tenant does not have an exclusive right to occupy the property, but the right to use it for certain purposes only. Many of these have fallen into disuse in modern times, but others still occur, mainly in rural areas. They include **mineral leases**, which logically should really be regarded as a type of sale, as the subjects are gradually removed by the tenant. For this reason, instead of rent, the mineral tenant generally pays a lordship or royalty, based on the amount of minerals taken. Other special uses of land that may be leased include **salmon fishings** and other **sporting rights**. Readers who wish to explore the above in greater depth, or to investigate some of the more rare and exotic varieties, will have to consult other references[1]. Finally, it should be noted that in deciding whether or not these, or any other borderline cases, should be called leases is no empty exercise. It will determine whether, in addition to the general law of contract, the special legal rules relating to leases will apply; in particular, it will decide whether the tenant will enjoy the benefits conferred by the Leases Act 1449[2].

Long leases

There is no prescribed length that determines whether a lease should be regarded as a long lease or not. Twenty years is perhaps as good a figure as any, as it is the maximum length for leases of residential property and the limit above which leases may be recorded in the Register of Sasines or registered in the Land Register. Long leases of commercial and industrial property are common, as institutional landlords want the financial security of having a tenant committed over a long period, and business tenants have to rely on the lease contract to give them the security of tenure enjoyed by their English counterparts under statute. A common type of long lease is the **ground lease** whereby the landlord leases the ground only, for a relatively modest rent, and the tenant either buys the buildings outright or provides them at his own expense; obviously, a tenant will agree to this only if he is given a reasonable

1 See *Paton & Cameron* pp 73–84.
2 See ch 2, pt 4 below.

length of tenure (eg ninety-nine years) which will at least match the
useful life of his buildings. The various implications of long leases
are sufficiently important to merit a chapter on their own[1].

Other types of lease tenure

The rich and variegated Scottish legal tradition has bequeathed to
us certain special types of lease tenure which, although rare, are
still to be found in certain areas.

The Crown's kindly tenants of the four towns of Lochmaben. This is a
strictly local phenomenon found in Dumfriesshire near the border,
originating historically from grants by King Robert the Bruce to
vassals on the lands of his castle there. It is a strange hybrid of tenancy and ownership, under which the 'tenants' have a potentially
perpetual right along with an absolute right to sell, but can be
removed if they don't pay their rent.[2] Eventually transfers of kindly
tenancies will be registered in the Land Register of Scotland, which
will have the effect of making the tenants proper owners, and
absorbing them into the general system[3]. However, this will happen
only when the area becomes operational for registration of title,
which has not yet occurred[4].

Tenancy at will. This tenure is a little more common. It is an informal type of ground lease to be found particularly in fishing and
rural villages on the north-east coast, in highland villages, and in a
mining village in Lanarkshire[5]. The tenant rents the land from the
landowner in order to build his own house, but is given no formal
title and can be removed for non-payment of rent. This rather insecure position has been somewhat alleviated by statute and the tenant at will now has the right, if he wishes, to purchase his landlord's
interest[6].

---

1 See ch 6 below.
2 *Rankine* ch VII; *Paton & Cameron* pp 69–70.
3 Land Registration (Scotland) Act 1979, s 2(1)(a)(v), s 3(3)(c).
4 See ch 2, pt 4 below.
5 *Paton & Cameron* pp 68–69.
6 Land Registration (Scotland) Act 1979, ss 20–22; see also *McCann v Anderson,
More v Anderson* 1981 SLT (Lands Tr) 13, *Ferguson v Gibbs* 1987 SLT (Lands
Tr) 32.

Licences[1]

A licence is not in fact a lease at all, but may resemble one, and it is sometimes difficult to tell the difference between them. The concept of a licence is less developed in Scotland than in England, though even there determining the difference between licence and lease can still lead to litigation[2].

A licence is defined by *Paton & Cameron* as 'a contract, falling short of a lease, whereby not the heritage itself but a right to use a particular part of it or to put a particular part of it to some use is granted'[3]. The criteria for identifying a licence include:

(1) The express terms of the agreement (eg whether the document calls itself a lease or a licence) or by the customary relation set up by it, or both taken together[4].

(2) Whether the occupant has exclusive possession. If the landlord retains possession rights, the contract may be a licence[5].

(3) Whether the contract lacks some other essential requirement of a lease, eg a rent[6].

The presence of only one of these criteria may not be conclusive. In *Scottish Residential Estates v Henderson*[7] the occupant had exclusive possession of the property, but the terms of the agreement made it clear that the parties intended it to be a licence. And while that case seems conclusive authority for the proposition that the terms of the agreement will determine the matter, the opposite may be the case where the attempt to create a licence is an obvious sham designed to avoid the legal consequences of being a lease. For example, in *Brador Properties Ltd v British Telecommunications plc*[8], the tenants of office premises were refused consent by their landlords (which was required by the lease terms) to sublet the property. Instead the tenants created a number of agreements with third

---

1 *Paton & Cameron* pp 12–15; 13 *Stair Memorial Encyclopaedia* para 120.
2 See eg *Monmouth Borough Council v Marlog* [1994] 44 EG 133; the leading English authority on licenses is *Street v Mountford* [1985] AC 809, [1985] 2 All ER 289, HL.
3 *Paton & Cameron* p 12.
4 *Paton & Cameron* p 12; see also *Scottish Residential Estates Development Co v Henderson* 1991 SLT 490.
5 *Broomhill Motor Co v Assessor for Glasgow* 1927 SC 447; *Chaplin v Assessor for Perth* 1947 SC 373.
6 *Mann v Houston* 1957 SLT 89; see also ch 2, pt 2 below.
7 1991 SLT 490.
8 1992 SLT 490.

parties which granted them possession of office rooms, but which were stated not to be leases. The tenants reserved a right of entry to the properties and also the right, on giving notice, to change the rooms allocated to any of the occupants. It was held that the agreements were not licences but sublets. The court was required to scrutinise such agreements closely and was entitled to consider whether they were delusive devices to defeat the terms of the principal lease.

Finally, as we have already noted, there can be a lease without exclusive possession if it falls within certain traditionally-recognised categories, eg mineral leases or leases of sporting rights[1].

Though the precise definition may be a little blurred at the edges, licence agreements are often used for subjects such as advertisement sites, small units in shopping centres or in other situations where the occupation may be temporary and/or non-exclusive. However, such properties may also be the subject of leases, and the situation in any particular case will depend on the circumstances.

Determining whether a contract is a lease or a licence may be important. For example a lease (though not a licence) will bind a new owner if the property changes hands[2], will entitle the landlord to powerful traditional remedies, such as the right of hypothec for recovery of rent[3], and (particularly in agricultural holdings and residential tenancies) may give the tenant some measure of statutory protection[4]. For the last of these reasons it used to be common (particularly in England) for landlords to attempt to create licences of residential properties; however, since the Housing (Scotland) Act 1988 (and its English equivalent, the Housing Act 1988), which significantly weakened the rights of residential tenants, landlords have had less motivation to employ this device.

Occupation without title

As in the case of a licence, there is no lease involved in the above situation, but we are once more in an anomalous area on the fringe of lease law. Where someone occupies another person's property without the benefit of a lease or on any other apparent legal basis, the onus is on him to show that he is entitled to occupy gratuitously (in which case, as we saw above, there would be a licence). If he is

1 See section above on 'Leases of certain uses of land'.
2 See ch 2, pt 4 below.
3 See ch 4, pt 2 below.
4 See chs 12–14 below.

unable to demonstrate a right to gratuitous occupation, he will be obliged to pay the owner a reasonable sum representing the annual worth of the property[1].

Such a situation can come about in several ways: there may have been negotiations for a lease which have broken down[2], the occupant may have had a lease and stayed on after its termination[3] or he may simply be occupying the property[4].

While the authorities are clear about the occupant's obligation to pay money, they are less so about the legal basis on which this happens. One suggestion is that it is a matter of implied contract, another that it derives from a principle known as *recompense*; the latter is an equitable doctrine whereby, if one person has been enriched at another's expense, he will have to account to the other to the extent that he has been enriched[5]. Recompense comes under the area of law known as quasi contract, ie where there is no contractual relationship, but obligations arise which resemble contractual ones.

The legal basis of the obligation to pay may depend upon whether or not the owner ever agreed to the occupation, however informally. If he did it may be a case of implied contract, if not, one of recompense[6].

4. TERM AND QUARTER DAYS

The four quarter days in Scotland are Candlemas, Whitsunday, Lammas and Martinmas. Whitsunday and Martinmas are also known as term days. The traditional dates for these were 2 February (Candlemas), 15 May (Whitsunday), 1 August (Lammas) and 11 November (Martinmas), but were changed by the Term and Quarter Days (Scotland) Act 1990 to the 28th day of the month in each case. The change applies for the purpose of any enactment or rule of law and in relation to any lease agreement or undertaking. The purpose of the change was to divide up the year more evenly and also to sort out the confusion caused by certain

---

1 13 *Stair Memorial Encyclopaedia* para 118.
2 *Shetland Islands Council v BP Petroleum Development Ltd* 1990 SLT 82.
3 *Rochester Poster Services Ltd v AG Barr plc* 1994 SLT (Sh Ct) 2.
4 *GTW Holdings v Toet* 1994 SLT (Sh Ct) 16.
5 See Walker *The Law of Contracts and Related Obligations in Scotland* (3rd edn, 1995) paras 35.8–35.11.
6 See *Shetland Islands Council v BP Petroleum Development* 1990 SLT 82 at 92 per Lord Cullen.

statutes which, for their own limited purposes, had already defined Whitsunday and Martinmas as the 28th of the month[1].

Although the new definitions apply generally and may affect any type of legal document, they are particularly important in relation to leases, which have always made wide use of the term and quarter days. For example, it is common in commercial, industrial and agricultural leases for the rent to be payable quarterly at the traditional quarter days, and for the expiry date (or ish) to be specified as one of these days. And where leases contain provisions for periodic rent reviews, it is normal for the review dates to be Whitsunday or Martinmas in stated years.

It is therefore essential in any lease using the term and quarter days for there to be no ambiguity regarding which days are meant. And it is equally important to avoid any confusion resulting from the transition from the old to the new definitions, since there are still, and will be for some time, many leases in force that were entered into prior to the Act. In such cases (for example) should the Martinmas rent be paid at 11 or 28 November? Should a notice to quit be sent 40 days prior to 15 or 28 May? Such questions are particularly vital in relation to rent reviews where (as we will see later) the narrow missing of a deadline can sometimes have disastrous consequences for either a landlord or tenant[2].

The 1990 Act tackles the problem by operating retrospectively, and also by allowing its effect to be contracted out of. This means that where a lease refers to Candlemas, Whitsunday, Lammas or Martinmas, without assigning a date to these expressions, they will each be the 28th day of the appropriate month, whether the lease was entered into before or after the Act came into force. On the other hand, if a lease (and this also applies to those entered both before and after the operative date) specifically assigns the traditional dates (or any other dates) to the term and quarter days, then it is these substituted dates which will take effect. Thus if a lease (old or new) merely refers to Whitsunday, this will be 28 May, but if it refers to 'Whitsunday (15 May)', then the latter date will apply.

In order to make the transition easier, the Act did not come into force until a year after it had been passed (ie until 13 July 1991). Until then, the parties to a lease could apply to the sheriff court to have any anomalies resolved. For example, in *Provincial Insurance plc v Valtos Ltd*[3], where a lease referred to Martinmas twice, once as

1 Eg the Removal Terms (Scotland) Act 1886, s 4.
2 See ch 10 below.
3 1992 SCLR 203.

11 November and once without any date being assigned, the sheriff held that both references should be interpreted as 11 November. However, it would appear that this period of rectification was intended to provide temporary alleviation only, during the year that followed the passing of the Act; in other words, if a lease were to turn up now, similarly worded to that in the *Provincial Insurance* case, it would be stuck with two definitions of Martinmas!

5. LEASES AND THE COMMON LAW

We have already seen that for certain types of lease, mainly those relating to farmland and dwellinghouses, the common law of landlord and tenant has been greatly modified by statute. In the field of commercial and industrial leases, there is not the same statutory presence, but the common law, unlike many statutory provisions, can generally be contracted out of, and often is; this means that the legal relationship between the parties is mainly governed by the terms of the lease document itself.

However, the common law of landlord and tenant remains important for a number of reasons. Some common law requirements are so fundamental that no lease can feasibly be without them, and these are considered in the next chapter. The common law will also be required to fill in any gaps that occur when statute law or the terms of the lease document are silent. Thirdly, the party most likely to try and contract out of the common law is the landlord, who is generally in the stronger negotiating position when the lease contract is being drawn up; however, it is unlikely that he will readily give up the powerful traditional rights he enjoys against his tenants, such as irritancy or hypothec[1]. Finally, it is salutary for parties drawing up lease documents to have in mind what might be the consequences of failing to create a clear and unambiguous contractual agreement, covering all important areas. The common law is liable to plug any gap with something that may be confused or ambiguous or contrary to modern lease trends. A good example of the latter is the common law provision which confers significant repairing obligations upon a landlord, the general modern practice in commercial and industrial leases being to pass these on to the tenant – a phenomenon usually known as the FRI (tenant's full

---

1 See ch 4, pt 2 below.

repairing and insuring) lease. Therefore, if a tenant is to be responsible for all repairs, this must be clearly stated in the lease, or much
of the repairing obligation will revert back to the landlord. This is
not the sort of thing likely to make a large financial institution
investing in property very happy with its legal advisers: if the rent
has been fixed on the basis that the tenant does the repairs, the
amount of money at stake might be quite considerable.

The early part of this book will therefore be mainly devoted to a
consideration of the Scottish common law of landlord and tenant.
Then, since the common law is so often contracted out of, we will
take a brief look at the sort of lease terms we are likely to encounter
in practice. Slightly longer consideration will be given to two somewhat problematical clauses, those relating to rent reviews and service charges; rent reviews in particular pose a number of complex
problems in modern lease law. Finally we will consider the main
areas of statutory control of lease contracts.

2 Basic Legal Requirements

1. FORM OF LEASE

Need for writing

Subject to an important qualification which we will consider below, it is and always has been the case that a lease, if it is for more than a year, should be in writing. However, the law has recently changed regarding the precise form such writing should take. For leases and other contracts signed on or after 1 August 1995, the relevant law is contained in the Requirements of Writing (Scotland) Act 1995. However, since that Act does not apply to documents subscribed before 1 August 1995[1] (of which many examples will be around for some time), we will need to consider the earlier position as well.

The 1995 Act

Under the Requirements of Writing (Scotland) Act 1995, the general rule is that contracts do not require to be in writing[2]. However, as was the case before, there are certain special categories of contract for which writing *is* required and (also as before) leases belong to one of these categories. Writing is required for the creation, transfer, variation or extinction of an interest in land, or for the constitution of a contract in relation to any of these[3]. An 'interest in land' does not include tenancies for a year or less[4], but writing will be required to constitute a lease for more than a year.

A lease should be signed by both the landlord and the tenant[5].

---

1 Requirements of Writing (Scotland) Act 1995, s 14(3).
2 Ibid s 1(1).
3 Ibid s 1(2).
4 Ibid s 1(7); see also section below on 'Leases for a year or less'.
5 Ibid s 2(1).

This can take the form of an offer signed by either the landlord or the tenant, followed by an acceptance in a separate document, signed by the other party[1]. The signature or signatures should appear at the end of the last page of the relevant document[2]. Neither signature will require to be witnessed merely to constitute the lease, but if it is to be recorded in the Register of Sasines or registered in the Land Register for Scotland, one witness will be required for each signature[3]. An annexation to the lease (eg an appendix, schedule or plan) also has to be signed, and has to be referred to in the main document, and identified on its face as being the annexation referred to[4].

The above requirements apply *inter alia* to leases subscribed on or after 1 August 1995.

Old law

Contracts relating to heritable property traditionally belonged to a category known as the *obligationes literis*[5]. This meant that they had to be entered into in writing, had to be signed by the parties concerned and, in addition, certain formalities had to be observed. The latter requirement was satisfied if the writing took *one* of the three following forms:

(1) *An attested document.* This was a formal deed, which had to be signed by both landlord and tenant on the last page, each before two witnesses who signed opposite the main party's signature. An attested deed was known as a *probative document*, ie one which proved itself.

(2) *A holograph document.* This was a document written entirely in the handwriting of the party concerned and signed by him. A holograph lease, therefore, might consist of an offer handwritten and signed by the landlord followed by an acceptance handwritten and

---

1 Requirements of Writing (Scotland) Act 1995, s 2(2).
2 Ibid s 7(1).
3 Ibid s 6(1) and (2); see also ch 6, pt 2 below.
4 Ibid s 8(2).
5 See Gloag *The Law of Contract* (2nd edn, 1929) pp 162–179; Walker *The Law of Contracts and Related Obligations in Scotland* (3rd edn, 1995) para 13.22 et seq; Halliday *Conveyancing Law and Practice* (1985) Vol 1, ch 3; McBryde *The Law of Contract in Scotland* (1987) ch 27; Woolman *An Introduction to the Scots Law of Contract* (2nd edn, 1994) pp 60–70.

signed by the tenant. Such a lease would be perfectly valid but, for obvious reasons, professionally drawn-up lease documents did not normally take this form.

(3) *A document adopted as holograph.* This was a variant of (2). The document was not in the handwriting of the party concerned, but was handwritten by someone else or, more commonly, printed or typewritten. The party signed it, writing above his signature the words 'adopted as holograph'. This meant that he was accepting the document as if it were in his own handwriting and, as a result, it had the same legal effect as a holograph document.

If a lease was signed *before* 1 August 1995, it will normally need, in order to be valid, to have observed one of the above three *alternative* formalities. In respect of leases (or any other documents) subscribed on or after that date, any privileges conferred on the expressions 'holograph' or 'adopted as holograph' have been abolished[1].

Normal forms of lease

There are certain practices regarding the forms a lease may take, which should only be partially affected by the change in the law. If a lease is of relatively short duration and/or the rent is relatively low, it is likely to take the form of *missives of let*, ie an offer signed by either the landlord or the tenant followed by an acceptance signed by the other party. It is common for either the offer or acceptance, or both, to be signed by a solicitor as agent for the party concerned. In the past, missives of let were generally adopted as holograph, but this is no longer necessary. It is common for residential leases to be constituted by missives of let.

For a lease of longer duration and/or higher rental value (which will normally be the case with commercial or industrial leases) missives of let will commonly only be used as a temporary measure, to hold the parties contractually bound until a more formal document is drawn up. The latter will be a formal deed, signed by both landlord and tenant on the last page. This would formerly have been an attested document (see above), but witnesses will still be necessary if the deed is to be recorded in the Register of Sasines or registered in the Land Register for Scotland; however, in such a case, the

---

1 Requirements of Writing (Scotland) Act 1995, s 11(3).

number of witnesses for each subscriber has now been reduced from two to one.

A lease may have to be enforced by either the landlord or the tenant, and so it is good practice (though not legally essential) that each of them should have the documentation necessary to achieve this. This may be done by having the lease signed in duplicate, so that both the landlord and the tenant can have their own principal copy. Alternatively, the lease may be registered for preservation in the Books of Council and Session; the original will then be retained and, for the appropriate fee, the parties can each be issued with an extract (official photocopy) which is legally equivalent to the original deed[1]. As with the Register of Sasines and Land Register, the signatures of the parties will require to be witnessed before a document can be registered in the Books of Council and Session[2]. The Books of Council and Session may also be used in connection with the landlord's remedy of summary diligence, and are discussed in more detail in chapter 4[3].

Informal leases

Under the old law, if a lease for more than a year (or any other contract relating to heritable property) was entered into without observing one of the required formalities, it was considered defective in form and (theoretically) either party was entitled to back out of the contract[4]. Under the 1995 Act there are fewer formalities to be overlooked, but it is still possible for parties to enter into a landlord and tenant situation (eg where the tenant takes possession of the property and pays rent) without the requirements of the Act having been observed. For example, the document may be improperly signed, or not signed at all (eg if a draft has been drawn up but not finalised), or the parties may have gone ahead without there being anything in writing at all. In such a situation, the lease may still be enforceable because the parties have demonstrated by their actions that they want the contract to continue.

The 1995 Act provides for a situation where a contract has not been constituted in a written document that complies with the statutory requirements, but one of the parties to the contract has acted or refrained from acting in reliance on the contract. In such a

---

1 *Halliday* para 4.53.
2 Requirements of Writing (Scotland) Act 1995, s 6(1).
3 See ch 4, pt 2 below.
4 See eg *Goldston v Young* (1868) 7 M 188.

case the other party (provided that he knew and acquiesced in the situation) is not entitled to withdraw from the contract, and the contract will not be regarded as invalid[1]. However, it is necessary that the party who acted or refrained from acting on the strength of the contract has been affected to a material extent, or would be so affected if the other party withdrew[2]. Such a situation could arise, for example, if a tenant took possession of a property and, under the impression that he had a lease for a number of years, spent a substantial amount of money improving the property; in such circumstances, it would obviously be unjust if the landlord could take the property back because of a technical flaw.

Under the old law, a very similar doctrine operated in the form of principles known as *rei interventus* and homologation (actings of the parties that could validate an informal contract)[3]. These principles have been replaced by the new statutory doctrine (though only in relation to the constitution of a contract and certain other matters covered by the Act)[4]. *Rei interventus* and homologation are aspects of the equitable doctrine of *personal bar* (the equivalent of the English doctrine of estoppel).

There have been many cases in the past of informal leases being validated by the actings of the parties. For example, in *Wight v Newton*[5] a draft lease of a farm, approved by both parties but unsigned, was held to constitute a valid lease because the tenant had entered into possession. In *Forbes v Wilson*[6] an offer by the tenant which was not accepted in writing by the landlord was held to be sufficient, having been followed by actings of the tenant that amounted to *rei interventus*.

It was clear from the authorities cited above that a lease for more than a year could not be validated by *rei interventus* or homologation unless there was something in writing, however informal, and even if the writing was only by one of the parties. There appears to be no such requirement for the new statutory doctrine introduced by the 1995 Act[7]. However, if a lease is entered without writing it

---

1 Requirements of Writing (Scotland) Act 1995, s 1(3).
2 Ibid s 1(4).
3 *Gloag* pp 167–175; *Walker* paras 13.32–13.49; *McBryde* paras 27.37–27.56; *Woolman* pp 63–70.
4 Requirements of Writing (Scotland) Act 1995, s 1(5).
5 1911 SC 762, 1911 1 SLT 335.
6 (1873) 11 M 454, 45 Sc Jur 276; see also *Errol v Walker* 1966 SC 93, 1966 SLT 159 and *Ferryhill Property Investments Ltd v Technical Video Productions* 1992 SCLR 282.
7 Requirements of Writing (Scotland) Act 1995, s 1(3).

will be difficult to prove that it was intended to be for more than a
year, unless there is clear parole evidence (ie by word of mouth) to
this effect. If all we have is a situation where a tenant has taken possession and started paying rent, it seems unlikely that this will constitute a lease for more than a year.

Leases for a year or less

Under the 1995 Act, a tenancy for a year or less is excluded from
the definition of an interest in land, which means that it does not
have to be constituted in writing[1].

Such leases have traditionally been in a privileged position and,
under the old law, could be entered either orally or by an informal
document[2].The existence of a lease for a year or less could be
inferred from the actings of the parties (amounting to *rei interventus*
or homologation) even where these actings were the only evidence
that an agreement had been reached[3].On the other hand, if the circumstances precluded the possibility of there having been an agreement, it has been held that there is no lease, eg where a landlord
continued to accept rent from a deceased tenant's son and his wife
without knowing that the original tenant had died. In that case it
was held that a new lease with the deceased tenant's successors
could not be implied from the continued acceptance of rent alone[4].

The above authorities continue to be relevant to leases entered
into prior to 1 August 1995. Their influence on the interpretation
of the new statutory provisions remains to be seen.

Leases for a year or less may continue for much longer than that
by the operation of a principle known as *tacit relocation*[5]. It need
hardly be said that it is good practice to have a written lease, even
in the case of leases for a year or less.

2. ESSENTIAL ELEMENTS IN LEASES

Having seen the form that a lease should take, let us now look
briefly at its content. A modern lease is typically a complex and

---

1 Requirements of Writing (Scotland) Act 1995, s 1(7).
2 Rankine *Leases* (3rd edn, 1916) pp 116–119; Paton & Cameron *Landlord and
Tenant* pp 19–21.
3 *Morrison-Low v Paterson* 1985 SLT 255, HL see also *Nelson v Gerard* 1994 SCLR
1052.
4 *Pickard v Ritchie* 1986 SLT 466.
5 See ch 7, pt 2 below.

lengthy document, almost as formidable to the lawyer as to the lay-
man. In order to constitute a valid lease at common law, however,
only four essential elements are required[1]. These are (1) the parties; (2) the subjects; (3) the rent; and (4) the duration, and are
implicit in the very concept of a lease. It is difficult to think of a
lease, as we have described it, without all of these basic ingredients;
without the first two (the people involved and the subject matter),
it is difficult to envisage having any kind of contract at all:

(1) The parties

It is so fundamental as to be self-evident that a lease must have
both a landlord and a tenant. Not only must they both be named,
but they also must be designed (ie properly identified) usually by
the addition of an address. Either landlord or tenant may be an
individual or two or more individuals acting jointly, eg where a husband and wife are joint tenants. Also, either a landlord or tenant
may be a group of people having separate legal identity, eg a limited company or other corporate body.

On the other hand, the parties need to be distinct from one
another. For example, in *Kildrummy (Jersey) Ltd v Commissioners of
Inland Revenue*[2], where the tenant company was a trustee and nom-
inee of the landlords, it was held that the lease was a nullity, as this
was the equivalent of a person contracting with himself. It has also
been held that co-proprietors cannot grant a lease to one of their
number, unless the tenant first expressly divests himself of his
rights as co-proprietor; indeed, there is some doubt whether even
the latter precaution would make such a transaction competent[3].

The landlord must have a legal right to grant a lease. The most
obvious and common example of a person with this right is the
owner of the property. However, other parties can have a right to
grant leases, such as a tenant who grants a sublease. Another example is the right of a heritable creditor under a standard security,
when his debtor is in default, to enter into possession of the security subjects and lease them out, as a method of recouping part of
his loss[4].

---

1 *Rankine* pp 114–116; *Paton & Cameron* pp 5–8.
2 1991 SCLR 498.
3 *Clydesdale Bank v Davidson* 1994 SCLR 828; see also *Bell's Executors v Inland
  Revenue* 1987 SLT 625.
4 Conveyancing and Feudal Reform (Scotland) Act 1970, Sch 3, para 10(3) and
  (4).

(2) The subjects

It is equally fundamental that there must be some property that is being leased. Furthermore, the subjects of let must be properly identified. Sometimes the postal address may be all that is necessary, except in the case of flatted properties where several subjects may share the same address. It is usually better, however, to describe the property at greater length and to provide a plan. This is particularly desirable in the case of a long lease, if it is to be recorded in the Register of Sasines or registered in the Land Register[1].

If the subjects of let are not properly identified, this is not necessarily fatal, as it is possible that they can be established by other evidence of what the parties have agreed or, if the tenant is already in occupation, by the extent of his possession[2]. However, this should not be relied upon as a method of identification. Finally, as we saw in the previous section, where the formal document *is* clear about the extent of the subjects, it would not normally be possible to use extrinsic evidence to alter it.

(3) Rent

Without the above two elements, we would arguably have nothing that could be called a contract at all. However, it is possible to create a legally binding contract allowing a person to occupy a property rent free. Unfortunately, as well as appealing only to philanthropists and tenants, such a contract would not be a lease, but merely a licence[3]. This means that it would not enjoy the benefit of any of the special legal rules relating to leases, notably the provisions of the Leases Act 1449[4].

(4) Duration

The period of the lease should be stated. However, if it is omitted for any reason (usually by accident), this may not be fatal. Provided that there is agreement on the other three essential elements

---

1 See ch 6, pt 2 below.
2 *Piggott v Piggott* 1981 SLT 269; see also *Andert Ltd v J & J Johnston* 1987 SLT 268, where not only the subjects but also the rent and duration were allegedly uncertain.
3 *Mann v Houston* 1957 SLT 89; see also ch 1, pt 3 above.
4 See pt 4 below.

mentioned above, and provided that the tenant has entered into possession or expressly agreed to enter into possession of the subjects, a duration of one year will be implied[1]. Thereafter, if neither party takes steps to terminate the lease, it can be continued indefinitely on a year to year basis by the principle of **tacit relocation** (silent renewal)[2]. Since both landlords and tenants frequently want the other to be committed to a period of more than one year, it is, needless to say, desirable to include the duration rather than to rely upon this legal safety net.

In *Shetland Islands Council v BP Petroleum Development Ltd*[3], the parties had agreed on the main terms of a long lease of over 20 years, with the exception of the rent, and the tenants were in possession of the property. It was argued on behalf of the landlords that, since the other three essential elements were present, the court could apply a similar rule to the above one (where there was no duration) and fix the rent. It was held that the court could not fix a rent for a long lease (such as the one being negotiated), but might fix a rent for an annual tenancy.

The *ratio* of this case is not entirely clear, but seems to be authority for a rule that, where rent is the only essential element not agreed, a lease for a year may be created, irrespective of the proposed duration, at a rent fixed by the court. This situation (where the parties intended there to be a rent, but failed to agree about its amount) should be distinguished from the one mentioned above where the parties agreed that there should be no rent; as we saw, in the latter case we do not have a lease but a licence.

3. OTHER REQUIREMENTS UNDER THE LAW OF CONTRACT

It naturally follows from the fact that a lease is a contract that its validity depends on the same common law rules as any other contract. There must be *consensus in idem* (agreement as to the same thing), and for a contract to be valid there must be no circumstances, when it was entered into, indicating that this consent was not present.

For example, the parties must have contractual capacity. A contract may be challenged if either party, at the time of entering it,

1 *Gray v Edinburgh University* 1962 SC 157, 1962 SLT 173.
2 *Cinema Bingo Club v Ward* 1976 SLT (Sh Ct) 90; see also ch 7, pt 2 below.
3 1990 SLT 82.

was under sixteen[1], was drunk, or was insane. Also, neither party must have entered into the contract under duress, or confused by an error as to what was agreed, either because of accident or induced by the other party's fraud or negligence. All these factors undermine the consent of the parties that is fundamental to the validity of a lease, or any other contract. For a full account of the general requirements for contractual validity, the reader is referred to the standard authorities[2].

4. ACQUISITION OF A REAL RIGHT BY A TENANT

Leases Act 1449

We noted in chapter 1 several respects in which a lease could confer upon a tenant rights beyond those normally enjoyed under a contract[3]. One of these derives from an important early enactment, the Leases Act 1449. Compared with most modern statutes, the 1449 Act is admirably concise, and is worth quoting in full:

> 'Of Takis of Landis for Termes
> Item it is ordanit for the sauftie and fauour of the pure pepil that labouris the grunde that thai and al vtheris that has takyn or sal tak landis in tym to cum fra lordis and has termes and yeris thereof that suppose the lordis sel or analy thai landis that the takeris sal remayn with thare tackis on to the ische of thare termes quhais handis at euer thai landis cum to for sik lik male as thai tuk thaim of befoir.'

In case the meaning of the above is not immediately self-evident, let us attempt to clarify. 'Analy' means 'alienate' (transfer ownership). A 'tack' is the old Scottish term for a lease. 'Ische' (or 'ish') means 'expiry date'. 'Male' (or 'Maill') means 'rent'.

It may also help to look at the underlying theory. By its very nature, a contract usually creates only *personal* rights and obligations, ie ones which affect only the parties entering into it and not third parties. We would therefore expect the landlord and the tenant to be the only people bound by a lease; after all why should

---

1 Age of Legal Capacity (Scotland) Act 1991.
2 *Gloag* ch 5 and pt III; *Walker* ch 5 etc; *McBryde* chs 8–12; *Woolman* pp 53–55, ch 5.
3 See ch 1, pt 1 above.

someone else be obliged to observe an agreement that he did not enter into? However, in the context of leases, the application of this theory could have unfortunate consequences. If a landlord granted a lease for (say) five years, then sold the property after two years, there would be no reason in theory why the new owner could not evict the tenant immediately, without waiting until the expiry of the lease; since he was not a party to the original lease agreement, he would not be bound by it. The tenant would be entitled to sue the original owner for damages for breach of contract, but he would have no right to remain in occupation of the property.

This may be the theory, but the practice has been averted by the 1449 Act. The Act's effect is that, where a property subject to a sitting tenancy changes hands, the new owner will require to recognise the lease and allow the tenant, not only to remain in possession until his expiry date, but to do so at the original rent. Thanks to the Act, the tenant has obtained not just *personal* right, enforceable against the original landlord, but a *real* right, enforceable against the original landlord's *singular successors*. A singular successor is someone who becomes the owner of heritable property by any means other than inheritance, the most obvious example being that of a purchaser. Another example of a singular successor is a creditor with a right in security over heritable property which he is forced to realise to repay the debt owing to him. Someone who inherited the property on the landlord's death, although not classed as a singular successor, would also be bound to recognise the rights of sitting tenants, by virtue of the 1449 Act, and probably under the law of contract as well[1].

Criteria for application

In the centuries since the 1449 Act was passed, it has naturally come before the courts for interpretation on many occasions. As a result, it has been established that several conditions, implicit in the Act's wording, must be fulfilled before it applies and a real right is conferred upon the tenant[2]:

(1) *The lease, if for more than a year, must be in writing.* This is, in fact, the same as the common law rule applying to all leases.

---

1 *McBryde* para 24.01 et seq.
2 *Rankine* ch 5; *Paton & Cameron* ch 7.

(2) *The subjects of the lease must be land.* This has been extended to include all kinds of heritable property, including buildings. Leases which only give the tenant a right to certain uses of land, eg sporting leases, may not qualify, though the case authority on this is complex[1].

(3) *There must be a specific, continuing rent.* As we saw above, this is also a basic common law requirement for all leases. It makes no difference, as long as there is a rent, if a capital sum (grassum) is also payable; however where a grassum is payable, but there is no rent, the Act does not apply[2].

(4) *There must be an ish,* ie a term of expiry of the lease.

(5) *The tenant must have entered into possession.* This condition is satisfied not only if the tenant physically occupies the property himself (natural possession), but also where someone else legitimately occupies it instead of him (civil possession). For example, where a property has been sublet, it is not necessary for a tenant to be in physical occupation, provided that the subtenant is. However, in a case where an owner granted a lease and then sold the property prior to the date of entry, it was held that the new owner was not bound to recognise the lease, even though the tenant had been allowed to occupy part of the property a week before the entry date[3].

(6) *The landlord, if he is the owner of the property, must be infeft.* For a landlord to be infeft (ie for the property to be legally vested in him as owner), a title deed in his favour (eg a feu charter or disposition) must have been recorded in the Register of Sasines or, where applicable, registered in the Land Register. Under this rule, the landlord should be infeft at the time the lease was granted, although if a deed in the landlord's favour is recorded after the lease has begun, the lease will be validated retrospectively under the principle of *accretion*. The requirement for infeftment does not apply where the landlord is not the owner, the most obvious case being where he is himself a tenant who has sublet the property.

---

1 See *Paton & Cameron* pp 105–106; see also the section below on the effects of registration.
2 *Mann v Houston* 1957 SLT 89.
3 *Millar v M'Robbie* 1949 SC 1, 1949 SLT 2.

(7) *Effect of registration*. A real right is also conferred upon a tenant where a lease has been registered in the Register of Sasines or in the Land Register of Scotland, which is gradually superseding the Registor of Sasines under the new system of registration of title[1]. In such a case, therefore, it is not essential for the conditions of the 1449 Act to be complied with. In particular, registering a lease in the Register of Sasines or Land Register is legally equivalent to possession (see condition (5) above). This means, for example, that a creditor who has a security right over a lease need not take physical possession of the property but will acquire a real right provided that the lease and the standard security (the deed securing the loan granted by the creditor) have both been registered in the Register of Sasines or Land Register.

Registration may confer a real right upon a tenant in cases (eg sporting leases) where the 1449 Act does not apply, or where there is some doubt as to whether it applies[2].

In those areas where registration of title is now operational and the lease is of twenty years or more, registration in the Land Register is now the only way for a tenant to acquire a real right[3]. In such cases, therefore, the 1449 Act has been superseded. The areas which have so far become operational are the countries of Renfrew, Dunbarton, Lanark, Glasgow, Clarkmannan, Stirling, West Lothian and Fife, and over the next few years the Land Register will gradually replace the Register of Sasines, area by area, over the rest of Scotland. In due course, therefore, the 1449 Act will cease to apply in respect of all registrable leases[4].

Transmission of conditions

When the 1449 Act has operated, it will not only have the effect of compelling the landlord's singular successors to recognise the existence of a lease, but the conditions of the lease will generally transmit as well. In other words, they will become real conditions and will run with the land, ie they will apply not only to the original landlord and tenant but to their successors under the same lease. However, for this to be so, the conditions must be of the sort normally found in a lease. If they are personal in nature, they will not transmit and will bind only the original parties. Examples of such

1 For more about registration of leases see ch 6, pt 2 below.
2 *Palmer's Trustees v Brown* 1989 SLT 128.
3 Land Registration (Scotland) Act 1979, s 3(3).
4 For more on registration of leases, see ch 6, pt 2 below.

personal conditions include the right of a farm tenant to take peat from a moss in another part of his landlord's estate, a rent abatement in return for personal services by the tenant to the landlord, and a right by the tenant of a 999-year lease at any time to demand a feu charter of the property from his landlord (ie to be granted ownership)[1].

1 *Paton & Cameron* pp 95–97; see also *Bisset v Magistrates of Aberdeen* (1898) 1 F 87.

3 Rights and Obligations of the Parties

At common law, the landlord and tenant under a lease each owe the other a number of implied obligations[1]. All of these automatically apply unless the lease document specifically states otherwise. Some of them are commonly reinforced by inclusion in the lease document, whereas others are often contracted out of. The obligations of the tenant, of course, correspond to the rights of the landlord and vice versa.

1. OBLIGATIONS OF THE TENANT

(1) To enter into possession, to occupy and use the subjects

One might have thought that a tenant would have no reason to pay rent for a property which he is not going to occupy, but in the case of *Graham and Black v Stevenson*[2] the tenant of a hotel took the lease of another nearby hotel purely with the object of closing it down and eliminating competition. It was held that he was not entitled to do this. Likewise, one might ask why the landlord would object to non-occupation, provided that the rent was still being paid; one reason is that an empty property is likely to be neglected and fall into disrepair. In the case of *Blair Trust Co v Gilbert*[3] the tenant of a farm was sent to prison for three years for culpable homicide. It was held that his resulting non-occupation of the property was a material breach of contract which entitled the landlord to rescind, ie back out of the contract. In that particular case, the obligation was actually written into the lease, which is quite

---

1 Rankine *Leases* (3rd edn, 1916) chs 10 and 11; Paton & Cameron *Landlord and Tenant* (1967) ch 9.
2 (1792) Hume 781.
3 1940 SLT 322, 1941 SN 2.

common with this obligation. The tenant will also be liable for any damage to the property caused by his non-occupation[1].

If the landlord does not want to rescind from the lease (eg because there would be a problem finding another tenant), compelling the tenant to re-occupy or continue to occupy the property may be legally difficult to achieve[2].

(2) To use the property only for the purpose for which it was let

If the tenant uses the property for a purpose other than the purpose for which it was let, he is said to **invert the possession,** and the landlord may raise an action of interdict to have the unauthorised use stopped. For example, in *Leck v Merryflats Patent Brick Co*[3] a tenant who had been leased a property for making bricks was stopped from using part of it as a private railway unconnected with the brickwork. And in *Bayley v Addison*[4], the tenant of a meal mill was interdicted from using it as a mill for grinding sawdust.

Although implied at common law, this obligation of the tenant is invariably written into leases in a clause known as the **use clause** (or user clause, as it is generally called in England)[5].

(3) To take reasonable care of the property

Irrespective of whether repairs are the landlord's or the tenant's responsibility under a lease, the tenant will be liable for damage caused by his own negligence. In the case of *Mickel v M'Coard*[6], where a tenant left a house empty during the winter without turning off the water or giving notice to the landlord of his intentions, it was held that he was liable for damage caused by burst pipes.

The tenant's duty of care towards the property may not automatically end along with the lease. In *Fry's Metals Ltd v Durastic Ltd*[7], factory and office premises were broken into and vandalised, after the lease had terminated but before the tenants had returned

1 *Smith v Henderson* (1897) 24 R 1102, 5 SLT 96; *Mickel v M'Coard* 1913 SC 896, 1913 1 SLT 463.
2 See ch 4, pt 1 below: 'Specific implement and interdict'.
3 (1868) 5 SLR 619.
4 (1901) 8 SLT 379; see also *Duke of Argyle v M'Arthur* (1861) 23 D 1236.
5 See ch 9 below.
6 1913 SC 896, 1913 1 SLT 463.
7 1991 SLT 689.

the keys to the landlords. It was held that the damage was caused by the tenants' negligence in having the alarm systems disconnected prematurely, and they were liable to the landlords in damages.

(4) To pay the rent when it becomes due

Although implied, the obligation to pay the rent when it becomes due is also invariably written into the lease. If a rent is *not* stated, the onus will be on the tenant to prove that no payment of rent was intended, otherwise he will be obliged to pay what the property is worth[1]. Invariably the lease will also state the date when the rent is due; this is called the conventional term, ie the term of payment which the parties have agreed to. It is common for leases to state that rent will be payable in advance, either monthly or quarterly. If no conventional term of payment is stipulated in the lease, a term of payment is implied (the legal term). When this would be depends on the type of lease involved and the relevant common law rules are somewhat complex. It is a matter of minor practical importance, since leases invariably state a conventional term of payment, and it would take more space than is available here to explain the legal terms of payment in a comprehensible fashion; however, readers of a masochistic tendency are referred to the authorities cited[2].

(5) To plenish the subjects

The tenant is obliged to stock the subjects of let with sufficient moveable property to provide security for the rent[3]. This is to enable the landlord, if required, to exercise his right of hypothec, which gives him the right to sell off moveable property on the subjects of let in order to recover the rent[4]. The landlord can enforce this obligation by applying to the court for a plenishing order; this is a precautionary measure, which may be taken irrespective of whether or not the tenant is actually in rent arrears. A plenishing order is competent even if it is required only because the tenant's

1 *Glen v Roy* (1882) 10 R 239, 20 SLR 165; though in such a situation there may be doubt as to whether a lease actually exists – see section on 'Occupancy without title' in ch 1, pt 3 above.
2 *Rankine* pp 341 et seq; *Paton & Cameron* pp 139–141.
3 *Rankine* pp 399–401; *Paton & Cameron* pp 212–213.
4 See ch 4, pt 2 below.

moveables have just been sold off in order to recover rent arrears[1]. In fact, when a landlord raises an action of sequestration for rent (the court action used to enforce the landlord's right of hypothec) it is usual for the initial writ to include a request for a plenishing order, to follow after the sale of the seized property.

The obligation to plenish does not apply to agricultural subjects, as they are not subject to the right of hypothec[2].

2. OBLIGATIONS OF THE LANDLORD

(1) To place the tenant in full possession of the subjects let and to allow him to remain there for the duration of the lease[3]

The tenant must not only be given possession of the property, but possession of *all* of the property. Possession must also be given at the agreed date of entry and not later. If, therefore, there is someone else already in occupation (eg a prior tenant) it is up to the landlord to have him removed in good time. If the landlord fails in this obligation to a material extent, the tenant may be able to rescind from the lease; otherwise, he will be entitled to damages in the form of an abatement of rent.

(2) Not to derogate from his grant

Once the tenant is in the property, the landlord must not do anything that would deprive, or partially deprive, the tenant of possession; to do so would be to derogate from his grant to the tenant[4]. However, a landlord can be liable in damages for derogation of his grant only as a result of deliberate or voluntary behaviour on his part. In *Chevron Petroleum (UK) Ltd v Post Office*[5], because of the negligence of contractors, the subtenants of a basement suffered flooding from an escape of water from their landlords' premises

---

1 *Macdonald v Mackessack* (1888) 16 R 168, 26 SLR 124.
2 Hypothec Abolition (Scotland) Act 1880, s 1.
3 *Rankine* p 200 et seq; *Paton & Cameron* pp 127–130.
4 *Huber v Ross* 1912 SC 898, 1912 1 SLT 399; *Lomond Roads Cycling Club v Dunbarton County Council* 1967 SLT (Sh Ct) 35; *Golden Sea Produce Ltd v Scottish Nuclear plc* 1992 SLT 942.
5 1987 SLT 588, 1987 SCLR 97; see also *Owlcastle Ltd v Karmik Ltd* 1993 GWD 33–2157.

above. It was held that the landlords (ie the principal tenants) had
not derogated from their grant and were not liable in damages.

(3) To provide subjects that are reasonably fit for the purpose for which they are let

The property should be in a reasonable condition, but not necessarily fit for a particular kind of business; as to the latter, the tenant
must satisfy himself. For example, in the case of *Glebe Sugar
Refining Co v Paterson*[1] a warehouse was let to a sugar refining company who used it to store sugar. A month after they took entry the
warehouse collapsed, and the tenants sued the landlords claiming
that, because of insecure foundations, the building was unsuitable
for the purpose of the let. It was held that, within the practice in
their own trade, the tenants had overloaded the warehouse. They
had therefore failed to ascertain for themselves the suitability of the
subjects for their business, and *they* were held liable to the *landlords*
in damages. It was in fact a case of the tenants failing in their
implied obligation to take reasonable care of the property.

If the condition of the property makes it substantially unsuitable,
this will be a material breach of contract entitling the tenant to
rescind. Rankine quotes the case of *Kippen v Oppenheim*[2]. 'Thus,
where on entry to a dwelling-house the tenant found it to be over-
run to a great extent and in every part with cockroaches; to be
infested with bugs; to have an offensive smell; and one of the bedrooms to be too damp to be safely used, the Court held that the
condition of the house was such as to render a tenant's life "substantially uncomfortable".' In that case, the tenant was entitled to
rescind (or, as they quaintly put it in those days, to 'throw up' the
lease).

The landlord's implied obligation to provide suitable subjects
applies only to buildings and other artificial structures (as opposed
to land), and in any case applies only to urban rather than rural
leases, ie in leases where buildings are the main subjects of let.
However, in rural leases which are agricultural holdings, the landlord has certain statutory obligations regarding farm buildings and
other equipment provided by him[3].

---

1 (1900) 2 F 615, 7 SLT 374.
2 (1847) 10 D 242; *Rankine* p 245.
3 See ch 12, pt 2 below.

(4) To carry out repairs

Nature of obligation. The obligation to carry out repairs is really the corollary of (3). Once the tenant has moved into premises that are reasonably fit for the purpose of the let, he is entitled to stay on in premises that remain so. The landlord's obligation in urban leases is to uphold the property in a tenantable and habitable condition during the currency of the lease[1]. This includes, but is not confined to, an obligation on the landlord's part to keep the premises wind and water tight so as to be proof against the ordinary attacks of the elements[2]. This has been interpreted quite narrowly to include water penetration through the roof and walls, but not through the floor. In the case of *M'Gonigal v Pickard*[3], the floor of the premises collapsed as a result of deterioration caused by dampness, precipitating the tenant and the bed on which she was lying into the basement. The landlord was held not to be liable, as it was an exceptional encroachment of water due to a cause other than the ordinary attacks of the elements. This decision seems rather strange in view of the landlord's broader obligation, a view reinforced by the more recent case of *Gunn v National Coal Board*[4], where rising damp had caused dampness and mould in the house concerned. The tenant was held to be entitled to damages because the landlord was in breach of his general obligation to keep the premises in a habitable condition.

Scope of landlord's obligation. There are two major exceptions to the landlord's repairing obligation, ie (a) where the damage is caused by *damnum fatale* (Act of God), eg a flood or hurricane[5], and (b) where it is caused by the action of a third party or parties. The latter point is illustrated by the case of *Allan v Roberton's Trs*[6], where subsidence rendered a house uninhabitable because of mineral workings by a coal company which had encroached without permission upon the landlord's minerals. It was held that the landlord was not liable either to restore the house or to pay damages to the tenant, because the house had been destroyed by the fault of others for whom he was not responsible.

---

1 *Rankine* p 241; *Paton & Cameron* p 131.
2 *Wolfson v Forrester* 1910 SC 675, 1910 1 SLT 318.
3 1954 SLT (Notes) 62.
4 1982 SLT 526; see also *McArdle v City of Glasgow District Council* 1989 SCLR 19.
5 *Rankine* p 242; *Sandeman v Duncan's Trs* (1897) 4 SLT 336, 5 SLT 21.
6 (1891) 18 R 932, 28 SLR 726; see also *North British Storage & Transit Co v Steele's Trs* 1920 SC 194, 1920 1 SLT 115.

Also, the landlord is not liable for damage to the leased premises caused by a defect in nearby premises owned by him. In *Golden Casket (Greenock) Ltd v BRS (Pickfords) Ltd*[1], the subjects of let were flooded because of a blocked drain on the landlords' adjoining premises. It was held that the landlords were not liable. A fault in property other than the leased subjects did not give rise to a breach of the lease contract and the landlords had not been negligent in any way that would have founded a claim under delict.

It should be noted that such absence of liability on the landlord's part does not automatically mean that the tenant will be liable instead. In the case of *damnum fatale*, no-one is liable and in the case of third party damage, the third party may be liable, either to the tenant or to the landlord, or to both. A wise landlord, of course, may be well advised to repair the property in order to protect the value of his investment; he will probably also arrange for such disastrous eventualities to be covered by insurance. However, at common law he is not legally obliged to do any of this. This illustrates how the common law may often be inadequate. It shows the need for a well-drawn lease agreement covering all foreseeable possibilities; a common solution, of course, is to pass all liability for repairs on to the tenant.

Another exception to the landlord's obligation is where the damage has been caused by the tenant's own negligence. Here, of course, the tenant *is* liable, as we saw earlier in this chapter when looking at the tenant's duty to take reasonable care of the property.

A final point about the landlord's common law repairing obligation is that it does not amount to a warranty; in other words, the landlord is not guaranteeing against the property falling into disrepair. This means in effect that the landlord's obligation does not arise until the tenant has drawn the need for the repair to his attention; the landlord is not therefore in breach of contract merely because the repair has become necessary, but only after he has been notified and has failed to act[2]. This point may explain the decision in *M'Gonigal v Pickard*, as the tenant in that case had not reported the need for repairs to the landlord; however, that does not emerge as a reason for the decision in the rather truncated case report.

Once a need for repairs *has* been intimated to the landlord, he will be in breach of contract if he fails to carry them out, or does not carry them out within a reasonable time. In the case of *Scottish*

---

1 1972 SLT 146.
2 *Wolfson v Forrester* 1910 SC 675, 1910 1 SLT 318.

Heritable Security Co Ltd v Granger[1], the landlord took a little over two months to repair drains after the defects had been pointed out by the tenant. In the meantime, the tenant had moved out. It was held that the landlord had committed a material breach entitling the tenant to rescind.

Statutory liability. In the case of dwellinghouses, the landlord's repairing obligation has been extended by statute under the Housing (Scotland) Act 1987[2]. Also, as already noted, the repairing obligation we have been discussing refers only to urban leases. In the case of rural leases, where buildings are a subsidiary part of the subjects, there is no corresponding repairing obligation on the landlord at common law; however, in subjects where the Agricultural Holding (Scotland) Act 1991 applies, certain repairing obligations are imposed on both parties by statute[3].

If the leased premises are rendered dangerous by the landlord's failure in his repairing obligation, he may be liable in damages to anyone who is injured or whose property is damaged as a result. This liability extends, not only to the tenant, but also to anyone else who comes on to the property, possibly even a trespasser[4]. This responsibility for dangerous premises normally falls upon an occupier, but extends to a landlord where his failure in his duty to repair has caused the problem.

Contracting out. The landlord's common law repairing obligation is one which is very often contracted out of, particularly in commercial and industrial leases where the FRI lease (tenant's full repairing and insuring lease) is so common. From the landlord's point of view, therefore, the moral is quite obvious: if the parties have negotiated a full repairing lease, it is essential that the lease document makes the tenant's obligation clear. Otherwise, the common law may fill in the gap and make the landlord partially responsible for repairs. That is something he may not have intended, and something he may not thank his legal advisers for landing him with.

---

1 (1881) 8 R 459, 18 SLR 280.
2 Housing (Scotland) Act 1987, s 113 and Sch 10 (as amended by the Housing (Scotland) Act 1988, Sch 8); see ch 14, pt 2 below.
3 See ch 12, pt 2 below.
4 Occupiers' Liability (Scotland) Act 1960, s 3.

4 Legal Remedies of the Parties

In any kind of contract, where one party is in breach of his obligations, the other party will want some kind of legal redress either by forcing compliance or, in extreme cases, by backing out of the contract altogether. In either case he may also seek some kind of monetary compensation for any loss he has incurred as a result of the breach. This is true of all contracts, including leases, and there are standard breach of contract remedies designed to achieve the above ends; these remedies, and the extent to which they are relevant to the relationship of landlord and tenant, we will consider first. However, a landlord has certain additional powers, especially for the collection of rent arrears; these special remedies, which include the most powerful legal weapons at the landlord's disposal, we will afterwards consider separately.

1. STANDARD BREACH OF CONTRACT REMEDIES[1]

The standard breach of contract remedies are: (1) specific implement and interdict; (2) court action for debt; (3) rescission; (4) damages, and (5) defensive measures (lien and retention). Some of these have already been mentioned in chapter 3, and we will refer back there from time to time by way of illustration.

(1) Specific implement and interdict[2]

Nature of remedy. A party suffering from a breach of contract can seek a court decree that will force the other party to comply with his

---

1 See Gloag *The Law of Contract* (2nd edn, 1929) Part IV; Walker *The Law of Contracts and Related Obligations in Scotland* (3rd edn, 1995) ch 33; McBryde *The Law of Contract in Scotland* (1987) chs 14, 20, 21; Woolman *An Introduction to the Scots Law of Contract* (2nd edn, 1994) ch 8.
2 *Gloag* ch 36; *Walker* paras 33.20–33.22; *McBryde* ch 21; *Woolman* pp 143–144.

legal obligation. There are two types of court decree that will achieve this, a positive one (specific implement) and a negative one (interdict). The first applies where the offending party has failed in some positive obligation under the contract, eg to carry out repairs. This could therefore be available either to the landlord or the tenant, depending on who was responsible for repairs. Specific implement is enforced by a decree *ad factum praestandum* (for the performance of an act). Interdict applies where a party is carrying out some action prohibited under the contract. In chapter 3 examples were given of instances when the landlord used the remedy of interdict to stop the tenant from inverting the possession, ie using the property for a purpose other than that for which it was let.

If a party fails to obey either of these types of court order, he is guilty of contempt of court and liable to a fine or imprisonment. This is the only practical way of enforcing such a decree, but it means that specific implement and interdict are rather roundabout and clumsy remedies, and in many cases there are better alternatives. For example, many leases give the landlord the power, if a tenant fails in a repairing obligation, to do the repairs himself and charge them to the tenant; this is particularly useful at the end of a lease, allowing the landlord, after the tenant has vacated the property, to carry out all necessary dilapidations and then forward the bill to the tenant. Note, however, that this right is *not* implied by law, but must be expressly reserved in the lease contract. A tenant will also normally have a better remedy than specific implement. If his landlord fails to execute repairs, or carry out any other obligation for which he is liable, there is no need for the tenant to go to the trouble and expense of raising a court action; it is far easier for him simply to retain his rent (see below).

Where inappropriate. There are certain situations where specific implement cannot be used, notably for recovery of a liquid debt. It is *not* therefore possible for a landlord to seek a decree *ad factum praestandum* to recover his rent. The reason for this is quite simply that there is little point in threatening someone with jail for not paying his rent when, as we will see below, it is much quicker and easier to legally seize his assets.

Another situation is where an order of *ad factum praestandum* would relate to an act that is insufficiently clear and specific, so that the person subject to it might be unclear about exactly what act was to be performed and when.

Recent case law. This last point, and the general nature of specific implement and interdict in a landlord and tenant context, have been examined by the courts in several cases over the last few years. All of these cases related to lease provisions which, broadly speaking, reinforced the tenant's common law obligation to continue to occupy and use the subjects[1]. In all of them the tenants (no doubt because of the recession, and presumably being unable to find an assignee or persuade their landlord to accept a renunciation of the lease) had decided to cut their losses by vacating the premises. As we have already observed, this is something landlords are liable to be unhappy about[1]. The general lesson from these cases is that both of the above remedies have considerable limitations in this situation.

Firstly, an obligation of the tenant to remain in occupation of and to use the leased subjects, although of a positive nature, may be too general in nature to be enforced by an order *ad factum praestandum*. This was explained by Lord Kincraig in *Grosvenor Developments (Scotland) plc v Argyll Stores Ltd*[2].

'The obligation is to occupy and use the supermarket premises for the purpose of the retail sale of foodstuffs and all hardware, electrical goods and non-foods, commonly sold in supermarkets and discount stores and partly as an off licence until the year 2016. To occupy and use premises and carrying on a business therein involves continuous acts of management in which multifarious actions are required as, for example, engaging and dismissing staff, ordering, taking delivery of and paying for goods etc. An order to use the premises for the purpose of retail sale of inter alia "non-foods, commonly sold in supermarkets" for a period of 42 years requires for its obedience under pain of penalty a determination by the defenders as to what at any one time is commonly sold in supermarkets. This is far too general an obligation in my opinion to be enforced by specific implement. It is one which the defenders would have difficulty in deciding at any one time whether they were acting in breach of it or not. . . . An order from the court must be precise and specific so that the defenders know throughout the period when the order is in force exactly what they are required to do and what they are prohibited from doing.'

Although this principle was expressed *obiter* in the *Grosvenor* case, it was followed in *Postel Properties v Miller and Santhouse plc*[3],

1 See ch 3, pt 1 above.
2 1987 SLT 738 at 741.
3 1993 SLT 353.

in which an action *ad factum praestandum* was declared incompetent to enforce an obligation 'to keep and use the leased premises solely as retail premises'. It was emphasised that such an obligation was not necessarily invalid, but only that it could not be enforced by specific implement.

The main issue in the *Grosvenor* case concerned interdict, which the landlords sought against the tenants 'from ceasing to continue to occupy and use the supermarket premises . . . for the purposes of' trading as a supermarket. It was held that an interdict was incompetent because the obligation which the landlords wanted to enforce was a positive one, ie the obligation to occupy the shop and trade as a supermarket, and it could not be made the subject of an interdict by framing the decree in the form of a double negative. The *Grosvenor* case was recently approved in the Inner House of the Court of Session by a court of five judges in *Church Commissioners for England v Abbey National plc*[1]. It was emphasised that interdict is a preventive remedy, whose essential characteristic 'is that it orders the cessation of some specified act or proceeding which is taking place or about to take place[2]'. It is therefore not competetent to enforce an obligation which in substance is a positive one, even if it has been framed in a negative fashion.

However, in *Church Commissioners for England v Nationwide Anglia Building Society*[3] an interim interdict *was* held to be competent to prohibit tenants from vacating the premises when they were unwise enough to announce their intention to the landlords in advance. This was distinguished from the *Grosvenor* case because the order had not been sought in the form of a double negative, and was itself later distinguished in *Church Commissioners for England v Abbey National plc*, where the tenants had already vacated the premises at the time the action was raised.

It was pointed out in the last case that the landlords, had they asked for it, might have had an alternative remedy. Under ss 46 and 47 of the Court of Session Act 1988, in a situation where a person has done something that might have been prevented by interdict (in the above circumstances vacating the leased premises), that person may be ordered to perform an act that would reverse the situation and restore the status quo (eg re-occupy the vacated premises).

1 1994 SLT 959.
2 1994 SLT 959 at 968.
3 1994 SLT 898.

It may be in some cases that the landlord's only recourse will be to seek an alternative breach of contract remedy (eg damages)[1].

This is an issue that seems to be arising with increasing frequency (no doubt due to the property recession) and new cases continue to appear[2].

It is worth noting in passing that interdict is more than just a breach of contract remedy. It can be used under the civil law to force a person to refrain from any unlawful act, whether or not the unlawfulness results from breach of a contractual obligation. For example, interdict is commonly used under the law of delict (in England, tort) in cases of nuisance or trespass. The English equivalent of an interdict is an injunction.

(2) Court action for debt[3]

A court action for debt is appropriate for a contractual obligation to pay a liquid sum of money and it is the standard remedy open to any creditor. It is much easier to enforce than a specific implement action: instead of the clumsy method of threatening the debtor with contempt of court unless he pays, a court decree for debt is enforced by diligence. By this means a creditor may legally seize the property of his debtor. The two most common forms of diligence are **poinding** and **arrestment**. Poinding is the attachment of the debtor's moveable property, which may be followed by a warrant sale if he still fails to pay. Arrestment is the attachment of property belonging to the debtor (usually money) which is held by a third party, eg funds held by a bank in the debtor's bank account. A special form of arrestment (known as earnings arrestment) may be used to acquire earnings due to a debtor by his employer[4]. Another type of diligence is **sequestration for rent**, a form exclusively available to a landlord to enforce his right of hypothec; this, however, requires a special kind of court action[5].

In a landlord and tenant situation, the most obvious relevance of a court action for debt is for recovery of rent. However, if the arrears amount to a substantial sum (as they may well do in the case of a

1 See below.
2 See eg *Highland and Universal Properties Ltd v Safeway Properties Ltd* 1995 GWD 23-1261; *Retail Parks Investments v the Royal Bank of Scotland* The Scotsman, April 26 1995, Current Law Monthly Digest (May 1995 No 613).
3 *Walker* paras 33.15–33.19; *Woolman* p 143.
4 Debtors (Scotland) Act 1987, Pt III; see also Kelbie *Small Claims Procedure in the Sheriff Court* (1994) paras 11.14 et seq.
5 See pt 2 below.

commercial or industrial lease) a court action for debt is not usually the best method available to a landlord: he would be competing with other creditors on an equal footing, instead of enjoying the advantages conferred by the landlord's hypothec or by using summary diligence. These remedies will be considered in detail later in the chapter. However, there could be cases where court action is the only appropriate method: hypothec only covers the current year's rent, and so the right to enforce it may be lost if there is any substantial backlog of arrears; and summary diligence can be used only if a clause consenting to its use has been included in the lease document.

The above remarks are particularly relevant to commercial and industrial tenancies. However, it should be noted that the landlord's hypothec is not available in agricultural leases[1]. Also, where the amount involved is relatively small (as may be the case with a residential tenancy) it may be cheaper and generally more appropriate to use the simplified court action for debt available under the small claims procedure in the sheriff court[2]. The monetary limit for the small claims procedure is presently £750[3].

There can of course be debts other than rent which a tenant may owe to a landlord, or a landlord to a tenant, and for these a court action for debt would in all cases be the appropriate remedy. An example would be the one mentioned above where the lease document allows the landlord to do repairs and charge them to the tenant. It might also be the appropriate way of recovering service charges, if they appear in the lease as a separate item from the rent; only if they are included as part of the rent will the landlord's hypothec be available[4].

Court actions for debt are generally raised in the sheriff court, and have to be raised there in respect of sums up to £1,500[5].

(3) Rescission[6]

Rescission is the right of a party to back out of a contract altogether, and is available only if the other party's action is sufficiently

---

1 Hypothec Abolition (Scotland) Act 1880, s 1; see also pt 2 below.
2 Law Reform (Miscellaneous Provisions) (Scotland) Act 1985, s 18 (amending the Sheriff Courts (Scotland) Act 1971, ss 35–38).
3 Small Claims (Scotland) Order 1988, SI 1988/1999.
4 See ch 11 below.
5 Sheriff Courts (Scotland) Act 1971; Privative Jurisdiction and Summary Cause Order 1988, SI 1988/1993.
6 *Gloag* p 602 et seq; *Walker* paras 33.42–33.46; *McBryde* paras 14.49–14.84; *Woolman* pp 138–140.

serious to constitute a **material breach** of the contract. What amounts to a material breach justifying rescission is a matter of degree and it will be for the court to decide in any particular case. However, there are precedents concerning certain types of breach. In chapter 3, we have already seen examples of material breaches in a landlord and tenant situation, eg the right of a landlord to rescind if the tenant does not occupy the property, or the right of a tenant to rescind if the landlord does not provide premises reasonably fit for the purpose of the let. Either party could probably rescind for breach of a repairing obligation, if the breach was serious and had gone on long enough. In *Couper v M'Guiness*[1] it was held that a tenant's failure to observe lease conditions obliging him to keep the garden ground of the property in a clean and cultivated condition and to maintain a boundary fence were not material breaches entitling the landlord to rescind.

Under the Law Reform (Miscellaneous Provisions) (Scotland) Act 1985[2], a landlord may only rescind from a lease in cases where the court is satisfied that a fair and reasonable landlord would do so.

In the ease of a landlord, irritancy (where applicable) would usually be preferable to rescission, since its outcome is more certain[3].

(4) Damages[4]

Damages is a monetary payment that may be claimed in a court action as compensation for any loss resulting from a breach of contract. The measure of damages is the amount of the loss, so far as that can be quantified in money terms. Damages can be claimed in addition to any other breach of contract remedy, provided a loss has occurred as a result of the breach.

There are obviously cases where either a landlord or a tenant would be entitled to claim damages, some of which we saw in chapter 3; for example, where a tenant's neglect caused the landlord to suffer a loss in the value of his property (*Mickel v M'Coard*)[5], or where a landlord failed in his repairing obligation and the tenant suffered the effects of water penetration (*Gunn v National Coal Board*)[6].

---

1 (1948) 64 Sh Ct Rep 249.
2 s 5; see also section on 'Irritancy' in pt 2 below.
3 See pt 2 below.
4 *Gloag* ch 38; *Walker* paras 33.23–33.40; *McBryde* ch 20; *Woolman* pp 144–155.
5 1913 SC 896, 1913 1 SLT 463.
6 1982 SLT 526.

(5) Defensive measures[1]

Lien and retention. Defensive measures are extra-judicial measures which a party suffering from a breach of contract may take to protect his position. The first of these is lien, which is the right to hold in security some piece of property belonging to the other party, eg the right of a tradesman to hold on to goods he has been repairing until his bill is paid. There is no obvious application of the right of lien within the landlord and tenant situation, though no doubt circumstances could arise where it was appropriate.

Much more relevant in the present context is the other defensive measure, that of retention. This is the right of the party suffering from the breach to withhold money which he owes the other party. Retention is not always available, but only in certain specific circumstances, one of them being where the debt arises under the same contract as the broken obligation.

Retention of rent. It follows, therefore, that a tenant will be entitled to retain his rent if the landlord is in breach of any of his obligations under the lease contract. Retention of rent is, in fact, a long established tenant's remedy and is an extremely useful one[2]. Instead of going to the trouble and expense of raising a court action, the tenant need only do nothing and wait for the landlord to respond. If the landlord takes him to court for the rent, then the tenant can lodge a valid defence based on the landlord's breach of contract[3].

It is important to note that, like lien, retention is merely a right in security. It does not extinguish the rental debt, but only entitles the tenant to postpone payment until the landlord's breach has been remedied, after which he will have to pay the arrears in full.

This common law right of a tenant to retain his rent may be contracted out of by an express stipulation in the lease[4]. A tenant may also, by his actions, bar himself from the right to retain his rent; for example, in a case where a tenant endured the landlord's breach and continued to pay the rent over a period of time without

---

1 *Gloag* ch 25; *Walker* paras 33.4–33.8; *McBryde* paras 14.33–14.48; *Woolman* p 142.
2 Rankine *Leases* (3rd edn, 1916) pp 326–335; Paton & Cameron *Landlord and Tenant* (1967) pp 141–142.
3 *M'Donald v Kydd* (1901) 3 F 923, (1901) 9 SLT 114; *John Haig & Co Ltd v Boswall-Preston* 1915 SC 339, 1915 1 SLT 26; *Fingland & Mitchell v Howie* 1926 SC 319, 1926 SLT 283.
4 *Skene v Cameron* 1942 SC 393, 1942 SLT 210.

complaint, it was held that he had lost the right to retain his rent for that particular breach[1].

Abatement of rent[2]. This may be an exception to the rule, noted above, that the rent retained must be paid in full when the landlord remedies his breach. If a tenant has not received what he contracted for (eg if the property is partially or totally uninhabitable), he may be entitled to an abatement of rent. If the landlord sues the tenant for rent arrears, a successful counterclaim of abatement may establish that the rent retained was only partially due, or not due at all; if so, some of the retained rent, or even all of it, may not have to be paid over to the landlord (or, if already paid, may have to be refunded).

Damages. If the tenant has suffered loss as a result of the landlord's breach, he may of course, in addition to the right to retain his rent, be entitled to damages. Where rent has been retained, a claim of damages may (as with abatement) be lodged as a defence to an action for rent arrears by the landlord, or it may be the subject of a separate action. If a tenant is awarded damages, that exhausts his monetary remedy in respect of the breach concerned, and he will lose his right to retention unless a new breach occurs[3].

Residential tenancies[4]. For the tenant of a dwellinghouse, rent retention can be a useful remedy, but should be approached with some caution. As we will see in due course, a residential tenant often enjoys a statutory right to security of tenure beyond the contractual period specified in his lease. This applies (in the private sector) to regulated tenants, assured tenants and short assured tenants[5] and (in the public sector) to secure tenants[6].

It has been pointed out that retention of rent by a residential tenant may be problematical for several reasons[7]:

---

1 *British Railways Board v Roccio* 1970 SLT (Sh Ct) 11.
2 See *Renfrew District Council v Gray* 1987 SLT 70 and the prior case authority reviewed there; but see also *Pacitti v Manganiello* 1995 SCLR 557.
3 *Christie v Wilson* 1915 SC 645, 1915 1 SLT 265.
4 For very useful and comprehensive advice about rent retention to residential tenants (and their advisers) see 'Withholding Rent: a Shelter Scotland Guide to the Law' by Derek O'Carroll (Shelter Housing Action Note, December 1993); a summary of this paper can be found in SCOLAG Journal, December 1993.
5 See ch 13 below.
6 See ch 14 below.
7 See Shelter paper, supra, pp 4 and 5.

(1) It is not entirely certain that the common law right of retention applies to the statutory extension of a residential tenancy under the security of tenure provisions[1]. If this is so (and the matter is not entirely settled) the right of retention will only apply during the term of the lease stated in the lease contract and any extension of that term by tacit relocation[2]. When the landlord serves a notice to quit, that contractual tenancy is superseded by a statutory one[3].

(2) If the tenant has an assured tenancy or a short assured tenancy from a private landlord, three months rent arrears is a *mandatory* ground of eviction[4]. This means that if the rent retained amounts to three months or more, the sheriff will have no option but to grant the landlord possession if he raises an action to evict the tenant; there would be no opportunity for the tenant to lodge a counterclaim that he was entitled to retain the rent.

(3) If the tenant has a short assured tenancy from a private landlord[5], the tenant will have no security of tenure beyond the contractual period of his lease, which can be as little as six months. If he has caused trouble by retaining his rent, this may influence the landlord's decision about whether to renew the tenancy.

2. LANDLORD'S ADDITIONAL REMEDIES

Having examined those breach of contract remedies which apply to all contracts, we will now look at certain additional remedies which exist by virtue of the special nature of the lease contract. These are available to landlords, but *not* to tenants. They are: (1) irritancy; (2) hypothec; and (3) summary diligence.

It is not strictly correct to say that these arise only in landlord and tenant situations: irritancy and hypothec have their counterparts in feudal contracts as remedies available to superiors, and summary diligence is available under other deeds which contain acknowledgments of a liquid debt, eg standard securities. However, it *is* true to say that they are not generally available to all creditors, or other parties suffering from a breach of contract.

---

1 *Stobbs & Sons v Hislop* 1948 SC 216, 1948 SLT 248.
2 See ch 7, pt 2 below.
3 See sections on 'Security of tenure' in chs 13 and 14 below.
4 See ch 13, pt 3 below.
5 See ch 13, pt 5 below.

(1) Irritancy[1]

Irritancy means forfeiture and refers to a landlord's right to terminate a lease prematurely because of the tenant's breach of contract. There are two types of irritancy: (a) legal irritancy and (b) conventional irritancy.

(a) Legal irritancy

A legal irritancy is one which is implied by law, and is therefore available to any landlord, whether or not there is any mention of irritancy in the lease document. There is only one ground of legal irritancy, ie non-payment of rent for two years. If a legal irritancy has been incurred and the landlord has begun legal proceedings to evict the tenant, the latter has the right to *purge* the irritancy. The tenant may do this at any time before the landlord's irritancy action has been concluded and the landlord has obtained an extract decree from the court. This means that, at any time before the landlord has reached the stage where he is legally entitled to instruct an eviction, the tenant may pay off all the rent arrears; if he does so, the landlord will be forced to accept the money and his irritancy proceedings will be nullified[2].

Common law legal irritancies are rarely encountered nowadays as very few landlords will be willing to allow rent arrears to accumulate for as long as two years, when there are so many other legal steps that could be taken at a much earlier date.

There is another legal irritancy, imposed by statute, which allows agricultural tenants to be removed for six months rent arrears[3].

(b) Conventional irritancy

Nature of remedy. Conventional irritancies are much more common and have been the subject of controversy in recent years.

A conventional irritancy is so called because it exists by convention, or agreement. In other words, unlike a legal irritancy, it is not implied under the common law, but only exists if specifically provided for in the lease document. The grounds of conventional irritancy are unlimited, and in each case they will consist of those

1 *Rankine* p 532 et seq, *Paton & Cameron* ch 15.
2 *Rankine* pp 538–539, *Paton & Cameron* p 230.
3 Agricultural Holdings (Scotland) Act 1991, s 20; see also ch 12, pt 2 below.

which have been written into the lease in question; bankruptcy or liquidation of the tenant are common grounds of conventional irritancy and so are unauthorised assignation or subletting. Most importantly of all, rent arrears is also a standard ground of conventional irritancy, though usually for a much shorter period of arrears than the two years implied by law, eg one month or even 21 or 14 days. It is also common for irritancy clauses, after giving a list of specific breaches, to finish with a general statement that any other breach of the lease will also be a ground of irritancy.

Irritancy clauses have for many years been virtually standard in commercial, industrial and agricultural leases. They also often appear in residential leases, but in such cases their effect will generally be nullified as an attempt to contract out of statutory security of tenure provisions and will be superseded by statutory grounds of removal[1].

It should be emphasised that irritancy is always a *landlord's* option. If a landlord is in breach of contract, the tenant has only the normal remedies (eg rescission for a material breach), and he cannot use irritancy as a pretext for ending a lease because of his own breach[2].

Payment of rent after irritancy. After an irritancy has been incurred, if the tenant stays on in the property pending the outcome of the court action to remove him, the landlord is entitled to be paid a reasonable rent for the period of occupation[3]. However, the landlord should be clear about the basis on which the rent is being paid, because if he continues to accept rent without qualification or acts in any other way that is inconsistent with the lease being terminated, he may be held to have waived his right to enforce the irritancy. Whether the facts amount to waiver in any particular case will depend on the individual circumstances. In *HMV Fields Properties Ltd v Bracken Self Selection Fabrics Ltd*[4], after a notice of irritancy had been given, several rental payments were made by the tenant by credit transfer into the landlord's bank account. Most of these were returned promptly, with the exception of one payment, made on 24 June 1985, which was not returned until December of the same year. It was held that, although this was

---

1 See chs 13 and 14 below.
2 *Bidoulac v Sinclair's Tr* (1889) 17 R 144, 27 SLR 93.
3 *HMV Fields Properties v Skirt 'n' Slack Centre of London Ltd* 1987 SLT 2; see also section on 'Occupancy without title' in ch 1, pt 3 above.
4 1991 SLT 31.

prima facie evidence of waiver, the surrounding circumstances were enough to establish that the landlord had not intended to give up his right to proceed with the irritancy. This was inferred from the history and mechanism of rental payments and the fact that the parties had gone to arbitration over the question of irritancy prior to the offending payment being made.

Change of landlord. If ownership of a property changes after an irritancy has been incurred and a notice of irritancy has been given, the new owner may not proceed with the irritancy unless his predecessor has expressly assigned the notice to him[1].

Purging of irritancies: pre-1985 position. The most controversial aspect of conventional irritancies was that, prior to 1985, the tenant had no right to purge the irritancy unless the landlord agreed to let him do so[2]. In this way they differed from legal irritancies. Once the ground of irritancy had been incurred, the tenant might seek to remedy the breach, but the landlord was entitled to reject his offer and proceed with eviction.

The only exception to this strict rule was that a conventional irritancy could be purged if its terms merely echoed the common law position in respect of legal irritancies, ie if the termination ground was two years rent arrears[3]. This is still the position[4], but is of little practical importance, as few if any modern leases will contain such a generous irritancy provision.

The above had been the law for a very long time, but it is doubtful whether many tenants, when signing their leases, used to understand what draconian powers they were handing to their landlords. However, in 1975, they (or at least their agents) were given a sharp reminder. In *Dorchester Studios (Glasgow) Ltd v Stone*[5] the tenants under a sublease incurred an irritancy by neglecting to pay their rent within the 21-day period stated in the lease's irritancy clause. Eleven days after the expiry of this period, the landlords informed the tenants of their intention to evict them. The tenants immediately offered payment of the rent, but the landlords refused to accept it and raised an action in the sheriff

---

1 *Life Association of Scotland Ltd v Blacks Leisure Group* 1989 SLT 674.
2 *Rankine* pp 547–548; *Paton & Cameron* p 232; *McDouall's Trs v MacLeod* 1949 SC 593, 1949 SLT 449; *Lucas's Exors v Demarco* 1968 SLT 89.
3 *Rankine* p 547; *Paton & Cameron* p 232.
4 *British Rail Pension Trustee Co v Wilson* 1989 SLT 340.
5 1975 SC (HL) 56, 1975 SLT 153.

court to enforce the irritancy. The court decided in the landlords' favour and the tenants appealed all the way to the House of Lords, who upheld the original decision, rejecting the tenants' defence that the irritancy had been used oppressively[1].

After a pause for the implications of *Dorchester Studios* to sink in, a small outbreak of irritancy cases hit the casebooks, probably indicative of a much larger epidemic that did not reach the courts, or went unreported. All of them followed the decision in *Dorchester Studios*[2].

Oppressive use of irritancy. A tenant's only traditional defence to an action of irritancy (which still applies, in theory at any rate) was that the landlord was misusing his powers of irritancy, ie using it oppressively. However, any cases in which this defence has succeeded were in the last century[3], and the more recent trend, in *Dorchester Studios* and other modern cases, is for the courts to be very reluctant to accept it. In *HMV Fields Properties v Skirt 'n' Slack Centre of London Ltd*[4] an irritancy clause was invoked by landlords who had only recently bought the property in question, a shop in Hamilton, subject to the sitting tenancy. Moreover, according to the tenants, the new landlords' directors were all directors of another company which was not only a trade competitor of the tenants throughout Scotland, but which also had a shop in Hamilton directly opposite the one leased to the tenants. The tenants also alleged that the first notice they had been given of the change of landlords was two days before the rent was due, when an invoice was sent unobtrusively to the Hamilton shop in a plain brown envelope. By the time it had been forwarded to the tenants' head office in London and been paid, nearly a month had passed and the landlords proceeded to raise an action of irritancy because the rent had been paid outwith the 21-day period stated in the lease. All this led the tenants to suspect that the irritancy action, rather than being merely an exercise in efficient estate management, might just have been prompted by an ulterior motive. However, the court held that a defence of oppression will only succeed where there has been a clear abuse of rights or impropriety of conduct by the landlord. Here the landlords' motive, or alleged motive, fell short of

---

1 See below.
2 *HMV Fields Properties v Skirt 'n' Slack Centre of London Ltd* 1982 SLT 477; *HMV Fields Properties v Tandem Shoes Ltd* 1983 SLT 114; *What Every Woman Wants (1971) Ltd v Wholesale Paint & Wallpaper Co Ltd* 1984 SLT 133.
3 See *Rankine* p 548.
4 1982 SLT 477.

such impropriety, and so the tenants' averments with regard to motive were held to be irrelevant. In other words the landlord has to *do* something oppressive, not just be suspected, with however much justification, of having an ulterior motive.

1985 Act. It was clear from the *Dorchester Studios* case alone that the law was in need of reform. After ten years of discussion and controversy, the situation was somewhat remedied by the Law Reform (Miscellaneous Provisions) (Scotland) Act 1985. This provides that, in the case of monetary irritancies, the landlord must, after the irritancy has been incurred, give the tenant at least 14 days written notice to pay the arrears; only on the lapse of that further period without payment may he proceed to enforce the irritancy[1]. The landlord's notice has to be sent by recorded delivery. It should be noted that s 4 of the 1985 Act applies not just to irritancies for non-payment of rent, but also to other monetary breaches, eg failure to pay a service charge or other sum owed by the tenant.

In the case of non-monetary breaches (eg insolvency, unauthorised assignation or other ground stated in the irritancy clause), the court may only enforce the irritancy in cases where it feels that *in all the circumstances* (author's italics) a fair and reasonable landlord would do so[2]. Where the breach is one that could be remedied within a reasonable time (eg a tenant's failure to carry out repairs), the court is to take into account, when exercising its discretion, whether the tenant has been offered a reasonable opportunity to remedy the breach.

An interesting point to note is that these provisions apply, not just to conventional irritancies, but to circumstances where a landlord is attempting to rescind from a lease on the ground of a material breach of contract[3]. Presumably this is to prevent a landlord from switching his tactics from irritancy to rescission as a means of getting round the 1985 Act.

It would render this statutory reform fairly useless if the terms of a lease could contract out of the 1985 Act's effect, and so this is expressly forbidden[4]. Also the Act applies equally to leases that were entered into before and after it came into force, and even

---

1 Law Reform (Miscellaneous Provisions) (Scotland) Act 1985, s 4.
2 Ibid s 5; see also *Blythswood Investments (Scotland) Ltd v Clydesdale Electrical Stores Ltd (in receivership)* 1995 SLT 150 (discussed below).
3 Law Reform (Miscellaneous Provisions) (Scotland) Act 1985, ss 4(1)(b), 5(1)(b).
4 Ibid s 6(1).

expressly applies in cases where the actual breach occurred before the Act, provided the landlord had not already sent the tenant a written notice exercising his powers. Finally, the Act applies only to commercial and industrial leases; residential leases, agricultural leases and leases of crofts and small landholdings are specifically excluded, presumably because the existing statutory protection in these cases is thought to be sufficient[1].

Recent case law. Unfortunately, the most recent court decisions suggest that the 1985 Act has only been partially successful in remedying the problems it sought to address. In *CIN Properties Ltd v Dollar Land (Cumbernauld) Ltd*[2], the problems of conventional irritancies once more reached the House of Lords, in circumstances even more spectacular than in the *Dorchester Studios* case. The pursuers were the head tenants under a 99-year lease of 6.73 acres, which comprised a substantial portion of Cumbernauld town centre. The defenders were in the unusual situation of being both the owners of the property and the subtenants, ie they were simultaneously the landlords *and* the tenants of the pursuers in respect of the same property. (This rather strange setup was a legacy of the way the town centre development had originally been financed by Cumbernauld Development Corporation.) As well as their continuing obligation to pay rent, the defenders had paid the development corporation (the original subtenants) a capital sum of £2.2 million. On the other hand, the rent which they received from CIN Properties (the pursuers) was only a nominal rent of £1 a year.

Dollar Land (the subtenants) were late and erratic in their quarterly rental payments to CIN Properties during 1988 and failed to pay the rent due at 11 November 1988. On 15 December, in compliance with the 1985 Act, CIN Properties sent them a notice threatening irritancy if the rent was not paid by 4 January. The tenants failed to pay and on 5 January the landlords began irritancy proceedings that eventually reached the House of Lords.

With considerable reluctance, their lordships enforced the irritancy. While recognising that in cases like the present one the penalty suffered by the tenant (loss of a substantial investment) was out of proportion to the lapse which had engendered it, they nevertheless felt powerless to do anything about it. Parliament, in the 1985 Act, had already addressed the problem and enacted their own solution.

---

1 Ibid s 7.
2 1992 SLT 669.

The inappropriateness of the traditional law to the modern long investment lease had already been recognised in the *Dorchester Studios* case:

'The distinction between the feu contract and the lease has become unsubstantial since the former took to its death-bed. Moreover, the old view that the lease, unlike the feu contract, does not convey a right of property, wears today an air of unreality[1].'

This view was further elaborated in the *CIN Properties* case:

'The basis of the distinction between a conventional irritancy in a feu contract, which is purgeable, and one in a lease, which is not purgeable, is said to be that a feu confers a right of property while a lease is merely a personal contract. But feus are in most instances granted with a view to a dwelling-house or some other building being erected on the land, and it must be of some materiality that irritancy after that had been done would result in the value of the building being lost to the feuar. For practical purposes it is not possible to see a distinction of any real significance between a feu and a building lease for 99 or 125 years. While the rule excluding the opportunity of purgation may be entirely fair in cases where the payment of rent is the bare counterpart of the right of occupancy of, say, a farm, it is clearly capable of operating with extreme harshness in the case of a long building lease. In the *Dorchester Studios* case Lord Fraser of Tullybelton . . . observed that if a tenant had agreed to a lease containing an irritancy it was not in principle unfair to hold him to his bargain. However, the tenant may not himself have negotiated the lease but may be an assignee, as in this case[2].'

Lord Keith went on to point out that, in the event of the tenant going bankrupt or into liquidation, the law could operate to the prejudice of his creditors; they would forfeit the capital value of the tenant's asset, which would instead accrue as an undeserved windfall to the landlord.

We have only recently received judicial interpretation of the

---

1 *Dorchester Studios (Glasgow) Ltd v Stone* 1975 SC (HL) 56 at 67 per Lord Kilbrandon.
2 *CIN Properties Ltd v Dollar Land (Cumbernauld) Ltd* 1992 SLT 669 at 672 per Lord Keith of Kinkel.

1985 Act's provisions regarding non-monetary breaches and the standard of reasonableness, and it takes us in a rather unexpected direction. In *Blythswood Investments (Scotland) Ltd v Clydesdale Electrical Stores Ltd (in receivership)*[1] landlords sought to irritate two leases on the ground that the tenants had gone into receivership. The tenants based their defence on the provision of the 1985 Act that 'in all the circumstances of the case a fair and reasonable landlord would not' irritate on this ground. It was held that the phrase 'all the circumstances of the case' had the effect of making the provision much wider in its application than had probably been intended. The criterion was not whether enforcement of the irritancy would operate in a penal fashion or what the court would regard as fair and reasonable. It was how a fair and reasonable landlord would act in all the circumstances of the case, circumstances which could include not only the interests of the tenant but also the interests of other tenants in the area and *the fact that proceeding with the irritancy would confer considerable advantages on the landlord*! In other words it might be considered reasonable for a landlord to let consideration of his own potential gain outweigh any loss to the tenant!

Conclusion. In the *CIN Properties* case the House of Lords made it quite clear that it felt the present law could have the effect of inhibiting commercial development in Scotland and that further legislation was necessary. One suggested solution was to give the court power to attach conditions to a decree of irritancy, which could include an award of compensation to the tenant in respect of improvements carried out by him (eg by the erection of buildings)[2]. In relation to monetary irritancies, another possibility would be to extend the period of notice beyond 14 days, or even to put conventional irritancies in leases on the same footing as those in feu charters, ie allow them to be purged at any time before completion of the court action. If parliamentary time is found for this, it might be a good idea (in the light of the *Blythswood* case) for it also to reconsider what it meant by the 'fair and reasonable landlord' criterion. Meanwhile, when negotiating the terms of new leases, tenants' agents should continue to be vigilant regarding irritancy provisions and attempt, if possible, to have them modified in their clients' favour.

---

1 1995 SLT 150.
2 *CIN Properties Ltd v Dollar Land (Cumbernauld) Ltd* 1992 SLT 669 at 672 per Lord Keith of Kinkel.

(2) Landlord's hypothec[1]

Nature of hypothec. The landlord's right of hypothec is probably his most effective remedy for ensuring the payment of rent. Hypothec is a right of security enjoyed by a landlord over any moveable items which his tenant keeps on the leased premises. It is a 'tacit' or 'legal' right, ie, like a legal irritancy, it is implied by law and does not need to be specifically provided for in the lease contract. If the tenant is in arrears with his rent, the landlord may, after applying to the court (in an action known as a sequestration for rent), sell off enough of the tenant's moveables to pay the rent. The landlord has the right to insist upon the tenant keeping moveables on the premises of sufficient value to cover the current rent; in other words, the tenant has a duty to plenish the property[2]. If the tenant fails in this obligation, the landlord can apply to the court for a plenishing order, requiring the tenant to restock the premises. This can be done even if the reason for the lack of moveables is that the landlord has just carried out a sale to enforce his right of hypothec[3].

Items covered by hypothec[4]. The items covered by the landlord's right of hypothec are known as the *invecta et illata* ('things brought in and carried in'). This generally includes all moveable items on the leased premises, eg furniture in the case of a house let, stock-in-trade in the case of a shop lease, or machinery where the lease is of a factory. Certain items are specifically excluded, eg money, or the tenant's clothes.

With a few exceptions, hypothec also covers goods on the premises that do not belong to the tenant. In particular, items which the tenant has merely hired or is acquiring by hire purchase can be sold as if they were the tenant's own property. The owner of such an item is presumed to know about the landlord's right of hypothec, and to have consented to his property being included under it when he allowed the tenant to keep the item on the leased premises. For example, in the case of *Dundee Corpn v Marr*[5], landlords were held entitled to sell a jukebox that had been hired to the tenants by a third party. In *Ryan v Little*[6] the premises of a furniture dealer were the subject of a sequestration for rent action to enforce

---

1 *Rankine* pp 366–411; *Paton & Cameron* ch 13.
2 See above ch 3, pt 1.
3 *Macdonald v Mackessack* (1888) 16 R 168, 26 SLR 124.
4 *Rankine* pp 373–383; *Paton & Cameron* pp 202–206.
5 1971 SC 96, also reported as *Ditchburn Organisation (Sales) Ltd v Dundee Corpn* 1971 SLT 218.
6 1910 SC 219, *sub nom Little v M'Connell* 1909 2 SLT 476.

his landlord's hypothec. The landlord included in his sequestration articles of furniture which had been sold to a customer and paid for, but had not yet left the dealer's possession. It was held that these were covered by the right of hypothec. The property of a sub-tenant can be sold to cover his own arrears to the principal tenant and, where the landlord has not consented to the sublet, to pay off the principal tenant's rent arrears also, even when his own rent is up to date[1]. An article on loan to the tenant may also be included, provided that it was in the tenant's possession in the ordinary course of his business[2].

However, goods belonging to a lodger or to a member of the tenant's family (eg a piano belonging to the tenant's daughter) are not subject to hypothec[3]. Also, the right of hypothec has traditionally not been thought to cover goods belonging to third parties which are only on the premises temporarily, such as items that have been handed in for repair or for exhibition[4]. Some doubt must be cast on this principle, however, after the case of *Scottish & Newcastle Breweries Ltd v City of Edinburgh District Council*[5] where the rented premises were a pub and the landlords were held entitled to sell empty beer kegs awaiting collection by the brewers, whose property they were. This case suggests that the goods of third parties would have to be on the premises *very* temporarily not to be subject to the landlord's hypothec.

Because of this rule about the property of third parties, it has become common for the hirers of expensive moveables (such as factory machinery) not to hire to a tenant unless the landlord agrees to waive his right of hypothec with regard to their property. A reasonable landlord will probably agree to this, provided that the remaining moveables in the premises are sufficient to cover his rent. Since his refusal would probably cause the hire company to back off, he has nothing to gain by it, and there is no point in throwing obstacles in the way of his good tenants in order to take excessive measures against a few potential defaulters. In any case, prior intimation to the landlord by the owner of the item, at least in the case of single items where the whole of the landlord's security is not affected, is probably enough to exclude it from hypothec, as this would rebut the presumption that the owner consented to its inclusion[6]. However, if the landlord has already begun to enforce

1 *Steuart v Stables* (1878) 5 R 1024, 15 SLR 689.
2 *DH Industries Ltd v RE Spence & Co Ltd* 1973 SLT (Sh Ct) 26.
3 *Bell v Andrews* (1885) 12 R 961, 22 SLR 640.
4 *Pulsometer Engineering Co Ltd v Gracie* (1887) 14 R 316, 24 SLR 239.
5 1979 SLT (Notes) 11.
6 *Dundee Corpn v Marr* 1971 SC 96 at 101–102 per Lord President Clyde.

his right of hypothec by raising an action of sequestration for rent, the third party's only remedy is to approach the court with the request that his property be left to the last, and only sold if the tenant's own goods are insufficient to cover the rent[1].

Finally, it must be acknowledged that the law is not absolutely clear on the subject of which items are included in hypothec. Much of it depends on very old authorities, not all of which are entirely consistent. The most recent case law seemed to be pointing towards the view that the landlord is entitled to step in and grab virtually anything that happens to be on the leased premises, with few exceptions. However, the most recent case, on the surface at least, seems to go against this trend. In *Rossleigh Ltd v Leader Cars Ltd*[2], the tenants of garage premises transferred their business to an associate company and later went into voluntary liquidation, owing the landlords rent. In a reparation action by the landlords against the new occupants of the premises, the question arose as to whether the stock on the premises was covered by the landlord's hypothec. It was held that it was not because, although it was on the leased premises, it was in the possession, not of the tenants, but of a third party, ie the tenants' associate company. It did not matter that the associate company, rather than the tenants, were the ones in occupation of the premises. The court acknowledged that the stock might have been included in the landlord's hypothec if the status of the associate company had been that of subtenant, but that was not the case.

Where does this leave us with regard to the goods of third parties? In a slightly grey area perhaps, but the above case must be seen in perspective. Its rather unusual circumstances make it seem more exceptional than it really is. The *ratio* is that goods on the premises, not in the tenant's possession, are not included in hypothec. In most cases this would apply where the tenant himself is still in the premises, but the items are in the possession of another occupant, other than a subtenant. Examples of this would be the property of the tenant's lodger or a member of his family; and, as we saw above, these have long been recognised as excluded cases.

It might be thought that the *Rossleigh* case opens the door to limited companies evading their landlord's right of hypothec by a little judicious company re-organisation. However, it should be pointed out that the reparation claim in that case (against the tenants' associate company for inducing breach of contract) failed because the

1 *M'Intosh v Potts* (1905) 7 F 765, 13 SLT 108.
2 1987 SLT 355.

defenders had acted in good faith, without any intention of defrauding the landlords and unaware that their actions were causing the tenant to be in breach of the lease contract.

Rent covered by hypothec[1]. The landlord's hypothec secures only the current year's rent and not prior arrears. The current rental year in any lease runs from the anniversary of the date of entry. An action to enforce the right of hypothec, for any part of the year's rent, must be raised within three months of the last payment term of the year, or the right will be lost in respect of that year's rent. The traditional quarterly terms (to which new dates have recently been assigned)[2] are Candlemas (28 February), Whitsunday (28 May), Lammas (28 August) and Martinmas (28 November). A landlord can therefore, depending at what stage of the rental year the tenant goes into arrears, have as long as a year or as little as three months to enforce his right of hypothec before the right is lost. If a landlord fails to raise his action in time, this does not mean that he has lost all right to such prior rent, but only to the right of security conferred by hypothec: other remedies will still be open to him, such as summary diligence or a court action for debt.

Enforcement of hypothec[3]. The court action which a landlord must raise to enforce his right of hypothec is called an action of **sequestration for rent** (not to be confused with sequestration in bankruptcy). The landlord applies to the sheriff court for a warrant to sequestrate, which the sheriff usually grants automatically. Then, instead of serving the court summons on the tenant by post in the usual manner, he gives the warrant to the sheriff officer who goes to the leased premises and serves the summons personally, at the same time making an inventory of sufficient items to cover the rent that is owing. After that the sequestrated items are said to be *in manibus curiae* ('in the hands of the court'), ie they cannot be removed from the premises until after the judicial process has been completed. If the tenant removes them he will be in contempt of court and will be penalised (possibly even by imprisonment) if he does not restore them. If anyone else takes items away (eg another creditor, or someone who has purchased the items from the tenant), that person will have to pay the landlord the value of the goods taken. If they have been taken in bad faith (ie in the knowledge that the goods are the

---

1 *Rankine* p 384; *Paton & Cameron* pp 206–208.
2 Term and Quarter Days (Scotland) Act 1990; see also ch 1, pt 4 above.
3 *Rankine* p 401 et seq; *Paton & Cameron* p 215 et seq; MacPhail *Sheriff Court Practice* (1988) paras 23.13–23.23 and 25.166–25.171.

subject of a sequestration action), the person taking them may be held liable for the whole rent owing. After the court process has been completed, the landlord can instruct the sheriff officer to hold an auction of the sequestrated items, unless the tenant has since paid the rent plus all legal expenses incurred.

Leases subject to hypothec. The right of landlord's hypothec used to apply to all types of lease, but since the Hypothec Abolition (Scotland) Act 1880, it does not apply to ground let for agriculture or pasture exceeding two acres[1]. This effectively means that most agricultural leases are not subject to hypothec. There was formerly also an exception in respect of certain small dwellinghouses, but this exclusion no longer applies[2]. In cases where hypothec no longer applies the landlord (apart from his right in some cases to summary diligence – see below) has no real advantage over other creditors, or preference in the tenant's bankruptcy[3]. Hypothec applies to all other kinds of lease, but since sequestration for rent is a rather expensive action, involving the sheriff officer from a very early stage, it is not widely used for leases of low value, such as residential lets; where the small claims procedure in the sheriff court would normally be more appropriate.[4] In the case of commercial and industrial leases, however, hypothec is a very useful remedy.

Advantages of hypothec. The landlord's hypothec has several important advantages over other remedies of the landlord for collection of rent arrears. First of all, it can be enforced very quickly. If a landlord sues a tenant in an ordinary debt action, he may eventually be able to sell off the tenant's moveables, but only after the completion of the court process. By this time, if the tenant is in financial trouble, he may have removed the moveables from the premises, or other creditors may have already seized them. A sequestration action can be served at a few days' notice, after which the moveables are reserved for the landlord and cannot be removed by the tenant or anyone else.

Another important feature of hypothec is that it confers an advantage in the tenant's bankruptcy. As mentioned earlier, the two main forms of diligence available to ordinary creditors are poinding and arrestment. However, if a tenant (or any other type of debtor) is sequestrated for bankruptcy (or is wound up, in the case

---

1 Hypothec Abolition (Scotland) Act 1880, s 1.
2 Houseletting and Rating Act 1911 (now repealed).
3 *M'Gavin v Sturrock's Tr* (1891) 18 R 576, 28 SLR 414.
4 See section on 'Court action for debt' in pt 1 above.

of a limited company), any arrestments or poindings carried out within sixty days previously will cease to have effect[1]. This is called 'equalisation of diligences', and is to prevent creditors who are quick off the mark gaining an unfair advantage over the others. However, the landlord's sequestration for rent action to enforce his hypothec is not included in these provisions. And so, provided that the landlord has raised his sequestration action, his right of hypothec will not be affected by the tenant's bankruptcy or liquidation. This means that he will have a preferred claim for his rent up to the value of the moveables sequestrated, ie he will be paid his rent in full out of whatever assets the tenant has on the premises before the ordinary creditors get anything at all. Furthermore, there is recent authority for the proposition that, even where an action of sequestration for rent has not been raised to enforce the right of hypothec, the mere existence of the right amounts to a real right in security which gives the landlord a preferred claim[2]. In particular, where the tenant is a limited company, this means that the landlord's hypothec will have priority over the rights of floating charge holders[3].

The right of hypothec is also particularly useful in its ability to raise more money than other remedies. In a poinding, only items which are owned by the debtor can be attached. In many cases such items may well be in the minority, so the landlord's right to take property belonging to third parties can be extremely valuable.

Finally, hypothec is a useful deterrent. If a tenant is not in financial difficulty, but is the type who is habitually reluctant to part with his rent at the correct time, an unexpected visit from the sheriff officer can be very persuasive in bringing about future punctuality. The traumatic effect of such a visit, combined with the high legal expenses, makes sequestration for rent an experience most tenants will not be anxious to repeat in a hurry. However, in the case of tenants who are thought to be financially secure, it is probably in the interests of a good landlord/tenant relationship to keep such a tactic in reserve as a last resort.

Disadvantages of hypothec. Lest the case in favour of the landlord's hypothec seems too overwhelming, some words of qualification are required. We have already noted that hypothec only covers the current year's rent and that sequestration for rent is a relatively

---

1 Companies Act 1985, s 623; Bankruptcy (Scotland) Act 1985, s 37.
2 *Grampian Regional Council v Drill Stem (Inspection Services) Ltd* 1994 SCLR 36 (see further below).
3 Companies Act 1985, s 464(2).

expensive action. There is evidence, however, that landlords may have been discouraged from using their right of hypothec in recent years because of two more considerable stumbling blocks.

Firstly, a sheriff court decision in 1983 cast doubt upon whether the landlord's hypothec was a fixed security that took preference over the rights of floating charge holders[1]. However, the recent case of *Grampian Regional Council v Drill Stem (Inspection Services) Ltd*[2] took a contrary view, and although that was only another sheriff court decision, it is backed up by a considerable weight of academic authority[3].

Until comparatively recently, certain other prior rights presented a more formidable obstacle. When a sequestration for rent action had been carried out, the landlord was obliged, from the proceeds, to reimburse the Inland Revenue and the local rating authority in respect of up to one year's arrears of tax or rates. Moreover in respect of tax (though not rates) the landlord could be held liable for the full amount owed, even if that exceeded the amount raised by the sequestration. However, the right of the rating authorities has been abolished[4], and the Inland Revenue's right, which formerly extended to all tax owed by the tenant (including income tax and corporation tax) is now restricted to sums due to be paid by the tenant in respect of PAYE deductions and deductions from subcontractors in the construction industry[5]. Nevertheless, it still remains possible, if less likely, for a landlord to be held liable for more than was raised by the sequestration.

In the light of the changes mentioned above (and remembering hypothec's considerable virtues) its usefulness as a remedy may be due for re-appraisal.

(3) Summary diligence[6]

We saw earlier in the present chapter that diligence is the process by which a court decree is legally enforced; in particular, it provides

---

1 *Cumbernauld Development Corporation v Mustone* 1983 SLT (Sh Ct) 55.
2 1994 SCLR 36.
3 See eg 'A Legal Black Hole' by William G Simmons 1983 JLSS 352; 'Receivership and Sequestration for Rent' by George L Gretton 1983 SLT (News) 277.
4 Debtors (Scotland) Act 1987, s 74 (repealing the Local Government (Scotland) Act 1947, s 248).
5 Taxes Management Act 1970 (amended *inter alia* by the Finance Act 1989, s 155).
6 *Rankine* pp 357–60; *Paton & Cameron* p 145; Halliday *Conveyancing Law and Practice*, Vol I, para 4.61.

a way by which a creditor may legally seize the property of his debtor, two of the more common forms of diligence being poinding (attachment of the debtor's personal moveables) and arrestment (attachment of property in the hands of a third party). It is not usually possible to carry out these forms of diligence until the debt has been proved in court, as it would not quite be in accordance with justice to allow a creditor to seize another's property merely on the strength of his own word that he is owed the money. When a sheriff officer carries out an arrestment or a poinding, therefore, he will usually require to have an extract of a court decree as his legal authorisation.

However, there is one situation where the court process can be bypassed and a creditor can go ahead with a poinding or an arrestment without first having to prove his debt. This is by a procedure known as summary diligence. The theory behind this rather surprising power is that, where it applies, the party concerned has consented in advance to the possibility of summary diligence being carried out against him. This is because he has signed a legal deed (in the present context, a lease) which contains an acknowledgment of an obligation (in this case the undertaking to pay a specific amount of rent at certain intervals). The deed must also contain the party's consent to its being registered for execution, and this (whether he knows it or not) means that he has given his consent to summary diligence.

Before we go any further, some explanation is perhaps required of the phrase 'registration for execution'. The Keeper of the Registers of Scotland has under his charge a number of public registers. The best known of these are the Register of Sasines and the Land Register for Scotland, in which title deeds of heritable property have to be recorded before they become effective. Another important register is the Books of Council and Session. This has two functions, preservation and execution.

The function of execution is the one we are concerned with here, but it will be better understood if we explain the function of preservation first. Any valuable legal document – it may be a title deed, or a lease, or a will – may be sent to the Books of Council and Session as a precaution against its being lost. This does not need to be done immediately after the deed has been signed, but can be done at any time thereafter. For a fee, the Keeper will keep the document in the safety of his vaults and issue in its place an official photocopy (called an 'extract'). This extract is legally equivalent to the original deed and can be used in court or for any other legal purpose as if it were the original. Also, provided the requisite fee is paid, any number of extracts may be obtained, which can often be very useful.

Preservation of documents is the principal function of the Books of Council and Session. However, if the document contains a consent to registration for execution, this process can be carried out at the same time as registration for preservation. The Keeper keeps the document in the usual way and issues an extract, but in this case he adds to the extract a warrant for all necessary action to enforce payment of any sums payable in terms of the deed, ie to proceed with diligence. Such an extract for execution has the force and effect of a decree of the Court of Session, which is why a court action is rendered unnecessary.

In respect of certain types of deed (including leases) registration for preservation and execution is also competent in the books of the appropriate sheriff court[19].

Summary diligence, therefore, can greatly speed up the debt collection process. Obtaining a court decree takes time, at the very least a few weeks. If the debtor lodges a defence to the action, a court hearing will have to be fixed and it may take months. If it is a simple case of rent arrears, the tenant will probably not have a valid defence; however, by the time this can be established in court, he may well have bought himself enough time to disappear from the scene. But where a lease contains a consent to registration for execution, the landlord need only take the relatively short time necessary to obtain an extract from the Books of Council and Session, and then pass it to the sheriff officer to proceed with a charge followed by a poinding or an arrestment. The procedure will be the same as if a court decree had first been obtained. However, instead of an extract court decree, the sheriff officer will use as his authorisation the extract lease with the Keeper's warrant.

Summary diligence is therefore a better remedy than court action, because it is much quicker, and may help a landlord to jump a few places in a queue of creditors. It is not as good as hypothec, because it does not have the bankruptcy preference and other advantages mentioned above: whether or not it proceeds from a court decree or an extract lease, an arrestment or poinding has the disadvantages mentioned in the last section (equalisation of diligences, being restricted to property in the debtor's ownership). Summary diligence may be useful, however, for collecting arrears that are outwith the current rental year and for which the right of hypothec has been lost.

1 *Halliday* Vol 1, para 4.61.

5 Assignation and Subletting; Interposed Leases

1. ASSIGNATION AND SUBLETTING[1]

General

An assignation is where a tenant transfers his interest in a lease to another person (called the assignee), who thereafter takes his place as tenant under the original contract. The assignee becomes directly liable to the landlord for the rent and other obligations of the lease, and the original tenant (usually called the 'cedent') is relieved of all such liability for the future, his involvement with the lease having entirely ended. This is in marked contrast to the situation in England where, after an assignation (there called an assignment), the original tenant remains potentially liable and may be called upon to underwrite the obligations of his assignee or any other future tenants under the same lease[2]. This English principle is known as 'privity of contract' and has been the subject of much controversy south of the Border[3].

In the case of a sublease, the tenant creates a second lease between him and the subtenant, but his relationship with the landlord is unchanged and he remains directly liable to him for payment of the rent and performance of all other obligations under the original lease. There is no legal relationship between the landlord and the subtenant; the subtenant's landlord is the original tenant, usually in this context described as the principal (or head) tenant.

It may be wondered why a tenant would want to sublet, thereby leaving himself involved with a property he no longer occupies when, by assigning, he could be rid of it entirely. The reason is that

---

1 Rankine *Leases* (3rd edn, 1916) ch 9; Paton & Cameron *Landlord & Tenant* (1967) ch 10.
2 *Halsbury's Laws of England* (4th edn, 1981) vol 27, para 389.
3 However, under the Landlord and Tenant (Covenants) Act 1995, the English system will be identified as from 1 January 1996.

subletting could be to his advantage in certain situations. He may be making a profit by charging the subtenant a higher rent than he is paying to his landlord. If the lease is a fairly long one, it may suit him to sublet for a temporary period, while retaining the right to resume occupation at some future date before the term of the principal lease has expired. Or he may only want to sublet part of the property, remaining in occupation of the remainder; this could be useful if he is forced to contract his business temporarily, but hopes to expand it again in the future.

Need for landlord's consent

A point we have yet to consider is the role of the landlord in all of this. Does he have to be involved in an assignation or subletting?

Under lease terms. In the great majority of cases in fact he does, for the very simple reason that there is a standard clause in virtually all leases (often called the 'alienation clause') requiring the landlord's consent to any assignations or sublets[1]. It has been held that such a clause is effective[2]. However, if it were to be omitted, the common law would determine the position, and here the situation is much less clear cut.

Common law position. In order to understand the position at common law we have to look at the general law of contract, at the principles governing the assignation of contracts generally.

First of all it depends upon whether the contract in question is classified as an 'executed' contract (ie one where all that remains is for one party to transfer property or pay money), or an 'executory' contract (where there is a continuing obligation or obligations requiring performance). Clearly a lease falls into the latter category. Any executory contract may be assigned by one party without the other's consent *except* where there is an element of *delectus personae* ('choice of person'), ie where the party wishing to assign was chosen for the contract because of some personal quality or professional skill[3]. Partnerships and employment contracts are obvious

1 See ch 9 below.
2 *Marquis of Breadalbane v Whitehead & Sons* (1893) 21 R 138, (1893) 1 SLT 320.
3 See Gloag *The Law of Contract* (2nd edn, 1929) pp 416 et seq; Walker *The Law of Contracts and Related Obligations in Scotland* (3rd edn, 1995) para 29.19 et seq, esp para 29.26; McBryde *The Law of Contract in Scotland* (1987) paras 17.36–17.54; Woolman *An Introduction to the Scots Law of Contract* (2nd edn, 1994) pp 158–160.

examples of contracts with this element present: a person will naturally want to have control over the choice of his partner or employee.

The common law position with regard to leases, therefore, is that a lease can be assigned without the landlord's consent only when there is no element of *delectus personae*. The same principle applies to sublets. In another type of contract, this would be determined by examining the circumstances of the particular case, to see if the person wishing to assign his interest had been chosen for his personal qualities or skills. This may at one time have also been the appropriate approach for leases, but is no longer so. Over a long period of time it has been established in the courts that the nature of certain types of lease creates a presumption of *delectus personae*, whereas with some other kinds of lease it is presumed to be absent. Whether or not a lease can be assigned without the landlord's consent, therefore, depends, not on the circumstances of the individual case, but on the type of lease involved. In some of these cases the original reasoning is still relevant, though in others the reasons are largely historical. The following rules cover most common categories of lease[1]:

(1) *Delectus personae* is presumed to be present in agricultural leases of ordinary duration. The landlord, in other words, is presumed to have an interest in the skill of the person who farms his land. This means that here the landlord's consent *is* required for an assignation. There is no hard and fast rule regarding what constitutes an agricultural lease of ordinary duration and what amounts to one of unusual duration. Twenty-one years has been held to be usual and thirty-eight years unusual; if the period of let falls somewhere in between, there is no case law to guide us[2].

(2) It is also presumed in furnished house lets, and so they too will require the landlord's permission. Again, there is some logic to this, as a landlord may well want to control the choice of person who will use his furniture, especially if he intends to return to the house himself at some future date.

(3) *Delectus personae* is *not* presumed in agricultural leases of unusual duration, and so the landlord's consent is not required at common law. Presumably the reasoning is that the landlord's personal choice of tenant would require unusual longevity to survive a lease term of (say) 99 years.

---

1 *Rankine* pp 173–176; *Paton & Cameron* pp 149–151.
2 See *Rankine* p 173 and cases cited there.

(4) It is *not* presumed in unfurnished lets of urban subjects, which therefore do *not* require the landlord's consent. This is undoubtedly the most important rule of all, because this category includes a wide variety of leases, including all commercial and industrial leases and unfurnished house lets.

It will be seen that the common law position is somewhat unsatisfactory. While it may be interesting to speculate about the historical reasons for the above rules, the fact of the matter is that in *all* kinds of leases – not least in commercial and industrial lets – the landlord has an interest in retaining some control over the choice of tenant. This is a basic principle of sound estate management. Not only does the landlord want to make sure that he has a tenant who will look after his property, but he also needs someone who is financially secure and able to pay the rent. Particularly in commercial and industrial leases, the landlord will generally make financial and other inquiries about a tenant before agreeing to take him on; the point of this would be somewhat lost if the tenant could then transfer the tenancy, without consent, to someone who had not been vetted in this way.

In all cases therefore it is in the landlord's interest to contract out of the common law situation by including in the lease the standard provision requiring his consent to any assignation or sublet. Since such a clause *is* standard, the above rules are, in practical terms, of secondary importance; however, it is important to be aware of the common law position, if only in order to appreciate the need to clearly contract out of it.

Residential tenancies. In addition to the common law, leases of dwellinghouses, both in the private and public sector, are affected by statutory provisions regarding assignation and subletting, which will be considered at a later stage[1].

Form of assignation

Like the lease itself, an assignation should be in writing, whether signed before or after 1 August 1995[2]. There is an exception if the lease is for a year or less. However, although an oral agreement to assign a lease for more than a year may not be enforceable, it could

---

1 See ch 13, pts 4 and 7 and ch 14, pt 2 below.
2 Requirements of Writing (Scotland) Act 1995, s 1(2); see also ch 2, pt 1 above.

in the past form the basis of an enforceable agreement if followed by homologation or *rei interventus*, and this may still be the case under the statutory replacement of these principles introduced by the Requirements of Writing (Scotland) Act 1995[1]. An assignation would normally take the form of a formal deed signed by the tenant.

Where the landlord's consent is required, the easiest way to achieve this is to have him sign the deed as well. Where his consent is not required, the assignation, to be effective, must be intimated to the landlord by the tenant who is assigning; it is also of course in the latter's interest to do this, as he will not want the rent notices to continue to be sent to him. It has been held that, provided intimation has been given to the landlord, there is no need for the deed of assignation to have been delivered to the assignee for the assignation to take effect[2].

Transfer of tenancy of matrimonial home

It will be convenient to consider here a situation which is a kind of assignation, though not of the type considered above. It is not a voluntary assignation, but a compulsory one, which can be imposed by the court without the consent of either the landlord or the existing tenant. The Matrimonial Homes (Family Protection) (Scotland) Act 1981 was passed to protect the interest of a spouse (usually the wife) who might have no legal title to the matrimonial home either as joint owner or tenant. The Act gives the 'non-entitled' spouse (the one who is not the owner or tenant) occupancy rights to the home and also provides for the 'entitled spouse' to be excluded from the home in certain circumstances, eg where there is a history of domestic violence. In the case of leased property the court also has the power, in appropriate circumstances, to transfer the tenancy from the entitled to the non-entitled spouse[2]. The new tenant takes on all the liabilities of the tenancy, apart from any existing rent arrears, which remain the responsibility of the spouse who was the original tenant. If there is a joint tenancy, the court has the power to vest the tenancy in one party only. The landlord must be notified and be given an opportunity to object. Certain categories of lease are excluded from the provision, eg houses attached

---

1 Section 1(3) and (4); see also ch 2, pt 1 above and *Ahmed's Tr v Ahmed* 1992 GWD 36–2086.

2 *Smith v Place D'Or 101 Ltd* 1988 SLT (Sh Ct) 5.

3 Matrimonial Homes (Family Protection) (Scotland) Act 1981, s 13.

to agricultural holdings or houses let in connection with the tenant's employment.

Transfer of landlord's interest

We have seen that a tenant is generally not permitted to assign or sublet his interest without his landlord's consent. But what of the opposite situation? Does a tenant have a corresponding right to object to a change of landlord? The answer is no. He can have a new landlord imposed on him without having any say in the matter. The landlord is the owner of the property, any leases are incidents of ownership and so, if he sells the property, the new owner will automatically become the new landlord. This assumes that the conditions of the Leases Act 1449 have been fulfilled, conferring on the tenant a real right valid against the original landlord's singular successors[1]. If not, the tenant will be in an even worse position: the new owner will not be bound to recognise his lease at all.

2. INTERPOSED LEASES

The 1974 Act

Sale of the property by the landlord is the most obvious way by which a new landlord can be imposed upon a tenant, but it is not the only way. If a landlord creates an interposed lease, the tenant will end up with a new landlord, even though the original landlord has not sold the property. This is a back door method of creating a subtenancy. It occurs where a landlord under an existing lease grants a lease of his interest (the 'reversion') to a new tenant, the result being to interpose the new tenant between him and the original tenant. The latter is thereby degraded to the status of a subtenant without his consent. Interposed leases have always been valid in England; however, until 1974, they were thought to be illegal in Scotland[2]. The law of the two countries was brought into line by the Land Tenure Reform (Scotland) Act 1974, which made interposed leases legal, and extended this validity retrospectively to any interposed leases that had been created prior to the Act[3].

---

1 See ch 2, pt 4 above.
2 For a consideration of the law prior to 1974, *see Paton & Cameron* pp 170–171.
3 Land Tenure Reform (Scotland) Act 1974, s 17.

Relation to sale and leaseback transactions

There was a good reason for this change in the law, which otherwise might have seemed a little odd, if not a retrograde step. To understand why, we must first realise that an interposed lease situation can arise in circumstances other than those described above. It can arise accidentally, as an unintended by-product of a transaction designed to achieve some quite different purpose. In particular, an interposed lease or leases can come into being as a result of a sale and leaseback transaction.

Sale and leaseback is a method of raising capital by which an owner sells his property to an investor and then takes a lease of it back from the investor. The sale price will provide him with the lump sum he requires as capital, and, as with a conventional loan, he will thereafter pay a periodical sum to the person or institution who financed him; however, instead of instalments of interest, or of capital and interest, the payments will be rent under the new lease. In times of high interest rates, this can be a better method of raising capital than a conventional loan, as the rent payable by the former owner might well work out lower than the loan repayments would have been. It is also advantageous to the investor, as he gains a capital asset that he would not otherwise have had.

What has this to do with interposed leases? It may be that, prior to the sale and leaseback, part of the property has already been leased. The effect of the sale and leaseback will be to demote these existing tenants to subtenants. A hypothetical example may make this easier to follow.

A company, Freshfood Stores Ltd, owns a supermarket and three office suites on the upper floors of the same building. Freshfood occupy the supermarket themselves, but have leased the offices to three tenants. Freshfood want to raise money for their business, so they sell the property to Loanshark Investments and then lease it back from Loanshark. This happens in two stages: (a) the sale, after which the landlord of the three office tenants ceases to be Freshfood and becomes Loanshark and (b) the leaseback, whereby Freshfood is interposed between Loanshark and the office tenants. The nature of the transaction is such that the office tenants end up with Freshfood as their immediate landlord once more. However, their status has nevertheless been changed to that of subtenant without their consent. In any case, the second stage of the transaction (the leaseback) definitely creates an interposed lease, which would probably have been illegal in Scotland prior to 1974.

It was felt that this incidental and quite unintentional illegality was perhaps discouraging the use in Scotland of a useful commercial practice. Moreover, those transactions which had already taken place were tainted with the suspicion of illegality if they involved the creation of an interposed lease. The effect of the 1974 Act, by making interposed leases legal both for the future and retrospectively, was to facilitate sale and leaseback transactions by removing any possibility of illegality, even where the transaction took place prior to 1974.

Other advantages

In any case, quite apart from sale and leaseback situations, the practice of interposing leases can be justified in its own right. With commercial and industrial property it is commercially convenient and very common to have subtenancies, eg a landowner may lease land to a developer, who builds (say) an office block and then sublets the individual offices. There can also be situations where it will be convenient to create a subtenancy by interposing a lease. A development company which has completed a project (either on land which they own or hold on lease) may, after leasing out the various units, want to retain the development as an investment without having the trouble of day to day management. They could achieve this by interposing a lease to a management company between them and the tenants of the individual units. The legalising of interposed leases, therefore, adds flexibility to lease practice, giving Scottish commercial and industrial leases even more scope to be influenced by their English counterparts.

6 Long Leases

1. GENERAL

There is no prescribed length of time that determines whether or not a lease should be regarded as a 'long lease'. As we saw in the last chapter, the common law is rather vague about the dividing line between leases of 'ordinary' and 'unusual' duration. The statutory provisions considered below mainly apply to leases of more than twenty years. However, much longer leases are very common, ground leases in particular often extending to 99 years or more, in some cases even to 999 years. Perhaps the main point to note is that, the longer its term, the less a lease continues to resemble the basic concept of a contract conferring a temporary right of occupancy. We noted in chapter 1 that a lease of (say) 99 years confers upon the tenant something that is much more like a right of ownership[1]. The rent may be relatively low, particularly in ground leases where the tenant has built or paid for the buildings himself. Also, a lease with a long unexpired term has a market value, and a tenant wanting to sell his interest would normally be able to receive a capital sum (or 'grassum') in return for granting an assignation. If the unexpired term of the lease is long enough, the amount he receives may be comparable to the market price in an outright sale.

Long leases of commercial and industrial subjects are in fact much more common than outright sales of such property. This is partly due to the influence of the English business lease on its Scottish counterpart: as we saw in chapter 1, leasehold tenure has always been more prevalent south of the Border. This trend was reinforced by the provisions of the Land Tenure Reform (Scotland) Act 1974, which continued the process of reforming feudal tenure in Scotland by setting up the machinery to abolish

---

1 See ch 1, pt 1 above; see also judicial opinions in *Dorchester Studios v Stone* 1975 SC (HL) 56 and *CIN Properties v Dollar Land (Cumbernauld) Ltd* 1992 SLT 669, quoted in section on 'Irritancy' in ch 4, pt 2 above.

feuduties. As a result, while it is still possible for a landowner to dispose of land feudally, reserving to himself a right of superiority in the process, it is no longer possible to create new feuduties[1]. This means that, when disposing of land for commercial or industrial development, there is much more incentive for the landowner to grant a long lease which (in addition to any capital sum which the parties agree to) will give him a periodic return in the form of rent. As we will see below, this is no longer possible with residential property.

There are a number of statutory provisions relating to long leases, which will be our main concern in this chapter.

2. RECORDED LEASES

We saw in chapter 1 that, although writing is normally required for the creation of leases, they can be relatively informal, and any defects can often be cured by the actings of the parties. However, it is desirable for longer leases that have a capital value to be completed with greater formality. If a tenancy is a marketable asset, it is all the more important for the tenant to have a proper document of title. This is particularly so if he wants to borrow money on the security of his interest as a tenant; the creditor requires something of legal substance to which he can attach his right of security. This is the reason why, under the Registration of Leases (Scotland) Act 1857, it became possible to record a lease in the Register of Sasines.

The Register of Sasines is a public register in which title deeds have to be recorded in order to become effective. As well as long leases, it records, among other things, the deeds that create and transfer feudal rights of ownership and those that create rights in security over heritable property. It has no exact equivalent in England. Under the Land Registration (Scotland) Act 1979, the Register of Sasines is gradually being replaced by the Land Register of Scotland, the purpose being to introduce a system of registration of title. This is a modern, computer-based system which identifies individual properties with reference to a series of Ordnance Survey plans and is backed by a government guarantee of title. In time this will greatly simplify the conveyancing system in Scotland. However, the change is necessarily a slow one, involving a separate transfer between the registers for each individual property, usually

1 Land Tenure Reform (Scotland) Act 1974, s 1.

carried out when the property changes hands. The registration process is therefore being introduced in a piecemeal fashion, and to date the operational counties are Renfrew, Dunbarton, Lanark, Glasgow, Clackmannan, Stirling, West Lothian and (from 1 April 1995) Fife. In those areas, therefore, and eventually throughout Scotland, a lease can no longer be recorded in the Register of Sasines, but may, subject to the same conditions, be registered in the Land Register instead.

A lease may be recorded in the Register of Sasines if (a) it is self-proving; and (b) its duration exceeds 20 years[1]. The same conditions basically apply for registration in the Land Register, though strictly speaking it is at the discretion of the Keeper what form of document is acceptable[2]. In order to be self-proving in terms of the Requirements of Writing (Scotland) Act 1995, the signature of each party to a lease will normally have to be witnessed by one witness or (if that has not been done at the time of signing) have a certificate endorsed on the lease by the court, to the effect that they are satisfied as to the authenticity of the signatures[3]. Without this, a lease may be valid, but it cannot be recorded or registered in the appropriate register[4].

The recording of a lease in the Register of Sasines is equivalent to possession of the property by the tenant, and also renders unnecessary the other conditions of the Leases Act 1449[5]. One of the effects of recording, therefore, is to create a real right valid against the landlord's singular successors.

In the case of long leases registrable in the Land Register, this principle has been taken a stage further: the 1449 Act has been superseded and registration is now the *only* way of obtaining such a real right[6]. This should have the effect of making the registration of long leases virtually standard under the new system. In the past, leases of more than twenty years that were not recorded in the Register of Sasines would still have been protected by the 1449 Act. However, in those areas where the 1979 Act has come into operation, the tenant will have to register a long lease in the Land

---

1 Registration of Leases (Scotland) Act 1857, s 1 (as amended by the Land Tenure Reform (Scotland) Act 1974, Sch 6, para 1); Requirements of Writing (Scotland) Act 1995, s 6.
2 Land Registration (Scotland) Act 1979, s 4(1).
3 Requirements of Writing (Scotland) Act 1995, ss 3 and 4.
4 See ch 2, pt 1 above.
5 Registration of Leases (Scotland) Act 1857, s 1 16(1) (as amended by the Land Tenure Reform (Scotland) Act 1974, Sch 6, para 3); see also ch 2, pt 4 above.
6 Land Registration (Scotland) Act 1979, s 3(3); see also ch 2, pt 4 above.

Register, or he will not obtain a real right valid against the land-lord's singular successors.

Recording (or registering) a lease helps to make it a marketable commodity, which may be used as security for a loan. Prior to 1970, the method of achieving such a security was for the tenant to assign the lease to his creditor. This meant that the creditor would nominally be the tenant, but that the original tenant remained in possession; thus the condition of possession required by the Leases Act 1449 would not be fulfilled, and the creditor would not be given a real right valid against the landlord's singular successors. The effect of this would have been to nullify the creditor's security if the ownership of the property changed. By making the recording of a lease equivalent to possession, the creditor was given a means of avoiding this pitfall.

Since 1970, the reason for recording leases is slightly different. The Conveyancing and Feudal Reform (Scotland) Act 1970 created a new form of heritable security called the standard security[1]. This deed is now the only valid method of creating rights in security over interests in heritable property, whether they be feudal interests (ie perpetual ownership rights) or leasehold interests. To be effective, a standard security must be recorded in the Register of Sasines or registered in the Land Register. It is therefore necessary that the legal interest over which the security is granted should already appear in the relevant register. A standard security, therefore, can only be granted over a leasehold interest if the lease itself has been recorded or registered.

A lease can be recorded or registered at any time after the date of entry.

3. CREATION AND VARIATION OF LEASE OBLIGATIONS

We saw in chapter 2 that the effect of the Leases Act 1449 was to create a real right valid against the landlord's singular successors, and we have just seen above that a similar result is obtained by recording a lease in the Register of Sasines or registering it in the Land Register. A further consequence is that the lease obligations, so far as they are not of a personal nature, can be enforced against the tenant by the landlord's singular successor. Furthermore, when the tenant's interest in a lease is assigned, the new tenant

1 Conveyancing and Feudal Reform (Scotland) Act 1970, s 9.

automatically takes over all the original tenant's obligations under the lease. This effectively means that the obligations in a lease run with the land, ie they are effective not only against the original parties to the contract, but also to the successors in title of both landlord and tenant. When we also consider the fact that there are many leases with very long terms, and that long leases can be recorded in the Register of Sasines or registered in the Land Register, then lease conditions begin to acquire very similar characteristics to the real burdens and conditions that appear in feudal titles.

Creation of obligations

A recent statutory provision has made the parallel with feudal titles even more marked. When a feudal interest is being disposed of, it has always been possible to create real burdens and conditions, not only in a feu charter or feu contract granted by a superior, but also in a disposition (the deed granted by a vassal when he is disposing of a property outright to a new owner)[1]. This is very useful when the property is being subdivided; for example, with housing estates or blocks of flats, one way of imposing common repairs provisions, or other mutual obligations, is to include them in the dispositions to individual proprietors. The same can be done with industrial estates, office blocks or shopping centres. An alternative method is to include the obligations in a deed of conditions, applicable to the whole area and incorporated by reference into the individual dispositions, thus avoiding the need for the repetition of much similar material[2].

However, in the past, there was no parallel facility for leases. At common law, there was no authority to suggest that it was competent for a tenant to grant an assignation incorporating new conditions that would be valid not only against the assignee but also against the assignee's singular successors. Moreover, it was extremely doubtful whether a tenant, even under a recorded lease, was entitled to grant a deed of conditions[2].

One way round this was to sublet, imposing new conditions in the sublease. However, as we will see below, leases (and subleases) of residential property for a period of more than twenty years have been prohibited since 1974; this exclusion also prohibits subleases, granted after 1974, of leases which were granted before that date.

---

1 Halliday *Conveyancing Law and Practice* (1985), Vol II, para 19.13 et seq.
2 Conveyancing (Scotland) Act 1874, s 32.

Section 3 of the Law Reform (Miscellaneous Provisions) (Scotland) Act 1985 has made it possible for the assignor of a recorded lease to impose conditions which, when the assignation is recorded in the Register of Sasines or registered in the Land Register, will be effectual against the assignee's singular successors[1]. The obligation cannot be a monetary one, unless it is (a) rent or an apportionment of rent; (b) a continuing expense (eg a service charge), or (c) is imposed under a heritable security. The 1985 Act also made it possible to grant a deed of conditions in relation to leasehold property and for its terms to be incorporated by reference into an assignation.

The main difficulty that s 3 was designed to resolve related to residential property. This makes it, to some extent, of minor importance, as long residential leases are now fairly rare, for reasons explained more fully below. However, it adds a new flexibility into lease practice which will be useful in other areas. For example, it can be employed in commercial and industrial leases as an alternative to subletting, if a proliferation of subleases is thought undesirable. In such cases, of course, subletting is used, not just to impose new obligations on the various subtenants, but also to earn a profit by subletting at a higher total rent than that paid by the principal tenant to his landlord. The wording of the 1985 Act suggests that this might now be possible with an assignation[2].

Variation or discharge of lease obligations

Another important stage in the reform of Scottish land tenure came with the provision in the Conveyancing and Feudal Reform (Scotland) Act 1970 for the variation or discharge of land obligations by the Lands Tribunal for Scotland. The main reason for this was that conditions in feudal titles were often very old and, as a result, not only irrelevant but often very restrictive regarding the uses to which an owner could put his property; for example, a large town house which was feued towards the end of the last century solely as a dwellinghouse, might today enjoy a market only for commercial uses. Prior to 1970, the only way to get round this was to apply to the superior for a minute of waiver, for which he would usually charge a sizeable sum of money, if he were willing to grant a waiver at all. If a lease is of considerable length, a similar situation

---

1 Registration of Leases (Scotland) Act 1857, s 3(2)–(5) (added by Law Reform (Miscellaneous Provisions) (Scotland) Act 1985, s 3).
2 Law Reform (Miscellaneous Provisions) (Scotland) Act 1985, s 3(3)(a).

could easily arise in relation to the landlord in respect of lease obligations, and so the 1970 Act included land obligations under a recorded lease among those which could be varied or discharged by the Lands Tribunal[1].

The Lands Tribunal's powers do not extend to all obligations in a recorded lease, only to those that are 'land obligations' within the meaning of the 1970 Act. In *George T Fraser Ltd v Aberdeen Harbour Board*[2], it was held that the Tribunal had no power to qualify the alienation clause (ie the prohibition of assignation and subletting). The reason was that the obligation related to the tenant rather than to the land itself: it created a continuing *delectus personae*.

The Lands Tribunal may either vary or completely discharge a land obligation. Its criteria are: (1) by reason of changes in the character of the land or the neighbourhood the obligation has become unreasonable or inappropriate; (2) the obligation is unduly burdensome compared with any benefit resulting from its performance; or (3) the existence of the obligation impedes some reasonable use of the land[3]. The Tribunal has power to award compensation to persons who would have benefited from the continuance of the obligation (benefited proprietors), eg if the obligation is designed to protect the amenity of the area. In the case of a lease, a benefited proprietor would be either the landlord, or neighbouring landowners. Such an award is at the Lands Tribunal's discretion, and they have the power to decide who are benefited proprietors entitled to compensation[4]. No application can be made for the variation or discharge of a land obligation within two years of its creation; in the present context that would mean within two years of the granting of the lease that contained the obligation.

4. LONG RESIDENTIAL LEASES

The 1974 Act

As has already been mentioned, long leases of residential property are a special case. The Land Tenure Reform (Scotland) Act 1974

---

1 Conveyancing and Feudal Reform (Scotland) Act 1970, s 1(2) and s 2(6); Land Registration (Scotland) Act 1979, s 29(2); see also *McQuiban v Eagle Star Insurance Co* 1972 SLT (Lands Tr) 39.
2 1985 SLT 384.
3 Conveyancing and Feudal Reform (Scotland) Act 1970, s 1(3).
4 *Smith v Taylor* 1972 SLT (Lands Tr) 34.

prohibits the creation of long leases of dwellinghouses for a period in excess of twenty years[1]. This is in marked contrast to the situation in England, where long leases of residential property are a common alternative to freehold ownership.

The reason for this Scottish provision is historical and requires some explanation. Traditionally in Scotland most heritable property, including dwellinghouses, was held on feudal titles. Long leases of residential property were possible, but relatively uncommon. This was largely because, under the feudal system, it was possible to create an annual feuduty, which was to be paid in perpetuity by the owner (or vassal) to the feudal superior. When land was being disposed of for development, therefore, there was no need for the owner to grant a long lease if he wanted to receive a periodic payment in addition to a capital sum; he could dispose of the property feudally and collect an annual feuduty instead of a rent.

In modern times, the imposition of feuduties was considered unfair and was much resented by property owners, particularly householders. The main purpose of the 1974 Act, therefore, was to prohibit the creation of new feuduties and set up machinery for the redemption of existing ones. It was feared, however, that this might cause a massive switch to leasehold tenure by developers, thus perpetuating the system in another form by imposing rents instead of feuduties. As we have already seen, such long leases are already common for commercial and industrial properties. The purpose of this provision in the 1974 Act was to plug this potential loophole in relation to dwellinghouses. Because a lease has to be for over twenty years to be recorded in the Register of Sasines or registered in the Land Register, this effectively means that there cannot be any new recorded leases of residential property.

If a property, or part of it, subject to a lease of over twenty years, is used as a dwellinghouse without the landlord's consent, the landlord may give the tenant twenty-eight days' notice to stop the residential use, failing which he may have the lease terminated.[2] If it is proved that the residential use has the landlord's knowledge and consent, the tenant may not be removed, but the remaining duration of his lease will be restricted to twenty years[3]. Normally, of course, a landlord will know what kind of use a building is designed for; however, conversions or other adaptations could be made by

---

1 Land Tenure Reform (Scotland) Act 1974, s 8.
2 Ibid s 9.
3 Ibid s 9(4).

tenants, or a landlord might have granted a ground lease, unaware of what type of building the tenant intended to erect.

There still exist some long residential leases that were created prior to 1974, and their validity is not affected by the 1974 Act. Some of these may contain an obligation on the landlord, at the lease's expiry, to grant a renewal for a period in excess of twenty years. It was initially uncertain whether such renewals could still be granted in the light of the 1974 Act. The Law Reform (Miscellaneous Provisions) (Scotland) Act 1985 has made it clear that they can[1].

Conversion of leases into feus

For the historical reasons mentioned above, such long residential leases were always comparatively rare. They were made even rarer by the provisions of the Long Leases (Scotland) Act 1954[2]. This allowed long leases of dwellinghouses, granted prior to 10 August 1914 for a period of not less than fifty years, to be converted into feus by the tenant serving notice upon the landlord. The notice had to be served within five years of the 1954 Act coming into force, ie before 1 September 1959. This means, of course, that the provision is no longer effective; however, while it was in force, the number of tenants taking up this option to acquire ownership had the effect of making long residential leases even less common than they were before. Nevertheless, there are still a few of them around.

5. RENEWAL OF LONG LEASES[3]

A long lease (either of residential or any other kind of property) sometimes contains an obligation upon the landlord to grant a renewal of the lease at its expiry. As we saw above, the 1985 Act made it clear that such a renewal was valid in respect of residential leases. However, the situation may arise, for any kind of property, where the landlord fails to grant a renewal. In the case of very long leases, the identity of the current landlord may be unknown. Accordingly, the 1985 Act made it possible for a tenant in such a situation to apply to the sheriff, who has power to grant a renewal

---

1 Law Reform (Miscellaneous Provisions) (Scotland) Act 1985, s 1.
2 Long Leases (Scotland) Act 1954, Part I.
3 Land Registration (Scotland) Act 1979, s 22A (added by the Law Reform (Miscellaneous Provisions) (Scotland) Act 1985, s 2).

of the lease as if he were the landlord. Where the landlord's identity is known, he must have been given three months' notice of the tenant's desire for a renewal before an application to the sheriff can be made.

For the purpose of this section, a long lease is defined as a probative one for more than twenty years[1].

1 Land Registration (Scotland) Act 1979, s 28(1); but see ch 2, pt 1 above.

7 Termination of Leases

1. PREMATURE TERMINATION

There are a number of ways in which a lease may come to an end. As well as termination at the contracted expiry date (the ish) there are many situations where it may end prematurely, ie at some point prior to the contracted date of expiry. In some cases the termination occurs in accordance with the lease terms, in others it comes about quite independently of them.

The following are the main types of premature termination: (1) break; (2) renunciation; (3) irritancy; (4) rescission; (5) frustration; (6) bankruptcy of tenant; and (7) death of tenant.

(1) Break

A break can occur when there is an appropriate break clause in the lease. There are three types of break clause: (a) 'landlord only' breaks; (b) 'tenant only' breaks; and (c) mutual breaks. A 'landlord only' break is where the lease allows the landlord, by notice to the tenant, to terminate the lease at some intermediate point prior to its expiry date, but where there is no corresponding right given to the tenant. A 'tenant only' break is where only the tenant has an option to break and a mutual break is where either party may exercise such an option. The lease may state one or more dates for the occurrence of a break, eg halfway through its duration, or every five years. Where there is a mutual break at (say) year ten of a twenty year lease, this is really no different from a ten year lease with an option to renew it for a further ten year period.

(2) Renunciation

Since the purpose of all contracts, including leases, is to legally bind the parties, neither party to a lease may renounce it unilaterally, unless of course there is some legal ground of termination.

83

In *Salaried Staff London Loan Co Ltd v Swears and Wells Ltd*[1], where a tenant repudiated a lease without the landlords' consent, it was held that the landlords were not limited to a claim of damages for the breach of contract; they were entitled to enforce all of the tenants' obligations, including the continued payment of the rent.

However, there is no reason why both parties, if they want, cannot agree to a premature termination. Sometimes a tenant may want to renounce for reasons that suit the landlord, eg if he wants to lease larger premises from him. Even where the landlord does not have such a motive, he may not want to hold to a lease a tenant in financial difficulty, if there is a more sound tenant in the offing who could take his place.

(3) Irritancy

Irritancy has been considered fully in chapter 4 and need not further concern us here.

(4) Rescission

We have already seen, in chapter 4 and elsewhere, that either party may rescind a lease contract if the other is guilty of a material breach of contract[2]. Where there is an irritancy clause in the lease, a landlord would probably be better to rely upon it as the surer method though, since the modification to the common law by the Law Reform (Miscellaneous Provisions) (Scotland) Act 1985, the outcome of an irritancy action is now less certain. However, as we saw in chapter 4, the provisions of the 1985 Act apply, not only to irritancy, but also to rescission on the ground of a material breach of contract. This means that an irritancy action will still have the comparative advantage, because a landlord will not have to establish in court that the tenant has committed a material breach of contract. Nevertheless, he has still to satisfy the court, in the case of a non-monetary irritancy, that the situation is one where a fair and reasonable landlord would insist on termination.

---

1 1985 SLT 326.
2 See ch 4, pt 1 above.

(5) Frustration

Any contract of a continuing nature may end prematurely if its purpose is frustrated[1]. One of the ways this can happen is by supervening impossibility, ie where the contract becomes impossible to perform because of something that occurs after it has been entered into. There are two types of supervening impossibility which can particularly apply in the case of leases: (a) *rei interitus*, or total destruction of the contract's subject matter, and (b) constructive total destruction, which is damage falling short of total destruction, but nevertheless so severe as to render the subject matter no longer fit for the purpose of the contract. Provided that the cause of the damage is accidental and not the fault of one of the parties, the effect is to terminate the contract without liability of either party. Thus a lease may be terminated prior to its expiry date if the leased property is accidentally destroyed or severely damaged (most commonly as a result of fire)[2].

Frustration can also occur in circumstances where there is no actual physical damage to the property but something else happens that makes it impossible for the lease to continue. In *Mackeson v Boyd*[3], a nineteen year tenancy of a furnished mansion house was interrupted during the 1939–45 war, when the property was requisitioned by the military authorities and the tenant was ejected. The court held that it had become impossible for the tenancy to continue and that the tenant was entitled to abandon the lease.

The doctrine of frustration is common to the law of contract in both Scotland and England. In theory, therefore, it should be possible for an English lease to be terminated by frustration; however, the English courts have not applied the doctrine to leases in the way that the Scottish courts have done, and the circumstances where an English lease may be terminated by frustration are extremely rare[4].

---

1 Gloag *The Law of Contract* (2nd edn, 1929) ch 19, esp pp 347–349; Walker *The Law of Contracts and Related Obligations in Scotland* (3rd edn, 1995) paras 31.49–31.57; McBryde *The Law of Contract in Scotland* (1987) ch 15; Woolman *An Introduction to the Scots Law of Contract* (2nd edn, 1994) pp 194–202.

2 *Duff v Fleming* (1870) 8 M 769, 7 SLR 480; *Cantors Properties (Scotland) Ltd v Swears & Wells Ltd* 1978 SC 310, 1980 SLT 165, affirming 1977 SLT (Notes) 30.

3 1942 SC 56, 1942 SLT 106; see also *Tay Salmon Fisheries Co Ltd v Speedie* 1929 SC 593, 1929 SLT 484.

4 *National Carriers Ltd v Panalpina (Northern) Ltd* [1981] AC 675, [1981] 1 All ER 161.

It is common for commercial and industrial leases to contain a provision contracting out of the operation of frustration[1].

(6) Bankruptcy of tenant[2]

At common law the bankruptcy of the tenant does not automatically bring a lease to an end. Instead the tenancy passes to the tenant's trustee in bankruptcy, who is the person appointed to ingather the tenant's estate and distribute it among his creditors.

However, there is a standard provision in many leases prohibiting the transmission of a lease to a trustee in bankruptcy. Also, most conventional irritancy clauses list bankruptcy as a ground of irritancy.

Even if a lease does not contain such provisions (and it usually will), a trustee will become a tenant only if he agrees to adopt the lease; since this would make him liable for all future rent and past rent arrears, there is not much incentive for him to do so.

And so, although in theory it is possible for a lease to continue after a tenant's bankruptcy, in practice it will usually come to an end. A reasonable landlord will probably allow the trustee a temporary period of occupation to sort out the tenant's affairs, provided of course that the rent is secure.

If the tenant is a limited company, the lease will automatically come to an end when the company is wound up, as the tenant will then no longer be in existence. However, the lease will probably prohibit the transmission of the tenancy to a liquidator or receiver, and receivership or liquidation are standard grounds of conventional irritancy. The lease will probably therefore be terminable by the landlord at an earlier stage.

If the lease is to a partnership, the bankruptcy of one of the partners will dissolve the partnership, unless the partnership agreement provides otherwise[3]. If the partnership does end, this will naturally terminate the lease.

Alternatively, the lease may continue if the trustee (or liquidator or receiver) finds a new tenant for the premises and the landlord gives his consent to an assignation.

---

1   See section on 'Insurance' in ch 9 below.
2   Rankine *Leases* (3rd edn, 1916) p 693 et seq; Paton & Cameron *Landlord and Tenant* (1967) ch 12.
3   Partnership Act 1890, s 33(1).

(7) Death of tenant[1]

If a tenant dies, the lease passes to his executor[2]. The executor then has the power to transfer the tenancy to the person, or one of the persons, due to inherit the deceased's estate. However, this can be done only with the landlord's consent, so in practice the result may be that the lease comes to an end.

The above assumes that the deceased tenant has either not left a will (ie died intestate), or that his will makes no provision for the disposal of the lease. However, a tenant may actually bequeath his tenancy, and here the landlord's consent will not be required unless the lease contains an express prohibition against assignation or against a bequest of the lease.

Usually, of course, a lease will at the very least contain a prohibition against assignation without the landlord's consent. And so, in practice, the death of the tenant will also usually bring the lease to an end. This also illustrates the need for a landlord to make sure he inserts the appropriate clause in the lease; it is as much in his interest to keep control over bequests as it is with assignations.

A lease to a partnership will end on the death of one of the partners, unless the partnership agreement provides otherwise. However, if the partnership agreement makes it clear that the death of a partner will *not* dissolve the partnership, the lease will continue[3].

The above mainly applies in the case of commercial and industrial leases. In agricultural and residential lets, there is sometimes a statutory right of transmission on the death of a tenant[4].

2. TERMINATION AT ISH

Tacit relocation[5]

Having considered the various ways in which a lease may end prematurely, we must now look at the procedure for bringing it to an end at the contracted termination date.

1 *Paton & Cameron* ch 11.
2 Succession (Scotland) Act 1964, s 16.
3 Partnership Act 1890, s 33(1); *Gordon & Co v Thomson Partnership* 1985 SLT 122.
4 See ch 12, pt 6, ch 13 and ch 14 below.
5 See *Rankine* ch 22; *Paton & Cameron* ch 14.

One could be forgiven for thinking that the answer was obvious: if both parties have signed a contract providing that the lease is to last for a stated period, surely it will come to an end when that period expires?

Unfortunately, it is not as simple as that. Even though the specified termination date may have arrived, the lease does not automatically come to an end at that time. This only happens if either the landlord or the tenant intimates that he wishes the lease to end by sending the other a notice to quit. If neither sends such a notice, the law presumes that both want the lease to continue and it is automatically extended for a further period by a principle known as tacit relocation (silent renewal). If the original lease duration was less than a year, the extension will be for the same period, eg a six month lease will be extended for a further six months, a three month lease for another three months etc. If the original lease duration was a year or more, the period of extension will be one year. If either party wants to end the lease at the expiry of the extended period, he will require to send a notice to quit, or else a further extension of the same length will take place. Furthermore, until such time as either party takes the necessary steps to end it at the current termination date, the lease will continue to be extended indefinitely.

For example, suppose A leases a property to B for a period of five years, the period of notice required being forty days. If the lease is to end at the stated period, either the landlord or the tenant must send to the other a notice to quit at least forty days before the end of year five. Otherwise the lease will continue by tacit relocation for another year, and the earliest date it can be terminated will be the end of year six. If neither party sends to the other a notice to quit at least forty days prior to the end of year six, it will not be terminable before the end of year seven, and so on *ad infinitum*.

A lease on tacit relocation continues on exactly the same terms and conditions as the original lease contract. It is because of this factor that the principle of tacit relocation is of such practical importance, particularly for landlords, as we will see below. The only exception to this rule is the duration: as we saw above, a lease for more than a year will be extended for one year only. Nor will the extended lease incorporate any terms that are inconsistent with a lease from year to year. In *Commercial Union Assurance Co*[1], the leases in question contained options to renew on the same terms, but the expiry date passed without the tenant exercising the

---

1 *Commercial Union Assurance Co* 1964 SC 84, 1964 SLT 62.

options, or either party taking steps to terminate the leases. It was held that the leases had continued for a year on tacit relocation, but that the option rights were no longer enforceable.

It is important to note that the effect of tacit relocation is to continue or extend the existing lease for a further period. It is therefore not strictly correct (despite the literal meaning of the term) to talk of a lease being renewed by tacit relocation, as this might suggest that a new lease had been created.

Period of notice. The period of notice to quit is most often 40 days, but may vary according to the type or length of lease or the terms of the lease contract. This complex area is discussed in more detail below.

Contracting out. In theory, as the principle of tacit relocation is based on the implied consent of the parties, it should be possible for the parties expressly to agree something different in the lease contract[1], though until recently there was little or no authority for this. However, in *Macdougall v Guidi*[2] the lease of a shop contained a provision that the lease 'shall not be capable of renewal or continuation by tacit relocation'. It was held that this provision was effective in terminating the lease at the ish and that the landlord was entitled to remove the tenant, even though less than 40 days notice had been given.

In the case of agricultural holdings, contracting out of tacit relocation is expressly forbidden by statute and any lease term purporting to do so will be ineffective[3]. It would now appear that contracting out is possible with other types of lease.

Even where it has not been contracted out of (and a timeous notice to quit has not been sent) tacit relocation may be excluded by circumstances that are inconsistent with a continuation of the existing lease by implied consent, eg where a new lease has been agreed by the parties[4].

Practical importance of tacit relocation. We saw above that when a lease continues by tacit relocation, it does so on the same terms and conditions as the original lease. One of these conditions will be the amount of rent payable, and this is why it is so important for landlords or their agents to be aware of the law here. When a tenant's

---

1 13 *Stair Memorial Encyclopaedia* para 453.
2 1992 SCLR 167.
3 Agricultural Holdings (Scotland) Act 1991, s 3; see also ch 12, pt 3 below.
4 13 *Stair Memorial Encyclopaedia* para 460; *Paton & Cameron* p 226.

lease is due to end, the landlord will probably not want to evict him, but he will certainly want to put up the rent. He can achieve this only by terminating the existing lease and negotiating a new one at a revised rent. If he fails to send a notice to quit, or sends it late, the tenant will be able to insist that the lease continues for a further year at the old rent, and since this might by now be several years behind the current market rental, the landlord's negligence on this point could lose him quite a lot of money, particularly at the rent levels charged for commercial and industrial property.

Because of this danger, it is a common practice for landlords to arrange for all their leases to expire at particular times in the year, eg at Whitsunday or Martinmas. In this way it becomes a fairly simple twice-yearly administrative exercise to check which leases are due to expire, send out notices to quit at the required time and then negotiate renewals. However, it is not usually convenient for the date of entry to be at one of these terms: tenants are generally anxious to commence business as soon as possible and would not take kindly to a suggestion that, for administrative convenience, they should wait a few months until the next term of Whitsunday or Martinmas; landlords, in any case, will be equally anxious to start collecting their rent. As a result of this, many leases are not for a round period, such as exactly three years, five years, twenty years etc. Instead there will be an irregular period from the date of entry until the first term of Whitsunday or Martinmas, and the five years, or whatever is the agreed duration, will run from then.

Notice to quit

As we have observed before, it is not unusual for the provisions of the common law to be unclear and uncertain in their application. In respect of notices to quit (and the related topic of removings) not only is this true, but the effect of statutory intervention (particularly the Sheriff Courts (Scotland) Act 1907) has been to increase the muddle, with the result that the law here is both unnecessarily complex and extremely confusing. This has been recognised by the Scottish Law Commission which has commissioned research on the matter and followed it with recommendations for simplifying the law[1]. However, no legislation has yet resulted.

---

1 Scottish Law Commission: 'Research Paper on Actions of Ejection and Removing' by A G M Duncan (January 1984); 'Report on Recovery of Possession of Heritable Property' (HMSO 1989).

Period of notice. Under a combination of common law and statute (and subject to a number of qualifications that will be made below) the required periods of notice are as follows:

(1) In the case of all agricultural holdings, the period of notice must be not less than one year and not more than two years prior to the date of expiry[1]. If a lease of land exceeding two acres is *not* an agricultural holding, the period of notice is the same, except in the case of leases for less than three years, for which the minimum period of notice is six months.

(2) For all other leases of more than four months, the period is 40 days.

(3) For all other leases of four months or less, the period of notice is one-third of the duration of the let. In the case of dwelling-houses, this is subject to a statutory minimum of four weeks[2].

Except where otherwise noted, the above provisions derive from the Sheriff Courts (Scotland) Act 1907, ss 34 to 38.

The statutory provisions relating to periods of notice assume that the lease in question will expire either at Whitsunday or Martinmas (now redefined as 28 May and 28 November respectively)[3]. However, in cases where the lease provides for a termination date other than one of those terms, it is generally assumed that the period of notice will be calculated in relation to that other date[4]; for example, if a lease in category (2) above expires on 31 March, 40 days notice should be given prior to that date.

If the lease does not specify an ish, it will be assumed to fall on the anniversary of the date of entry or (in the case of leases for less than a year) on the same day of the month as entry[5].

In calculating the period of notice, it is not entirely clear whether the specified period should include or exclude the date of service and/or the termination date[6]. It is therefore safest to exclude both of these days from the calculation.

Requirement of writing. In the case of urban leases[7] there is no requirement at common law for written notice and an oral intimation by

1 Agricultural Holdings (Scotland) Act 1991, s 21; see also ch 12, pt 3 below.
2 Rent (Scotland) Act 1984, s 112.
3 Term and Quarter Days (Scotland) Act 1990; see also ch 1, pt 4 above.
4 *Rankine* p 573; *Paton & Cameron* p 270.
5 13 *Stair Memorial Encyclopaedia* para 475.
6 13 *Stair Memorial Encyclopaedia* para 480; see also 'Termination Date in a Notice to Quit' by DC Coull 1989 SLT (News) 431.
7 See ch 1, pt 3 above.

either party is thought to be sufficient[1]. Needless to say, this is *not* advisable. In the case of agricultural holdings, a written notice *is* required[2]. Finally, ss 34 to 37 of the Sheriff Courts (Scotland) Act 1907 (as well as specifying the periods of notice noted above) require such notices to be in writing, and forms of notice are also prescribed by the Act. However, for long there has been some doubt whether these provisions are applicable generally, and the weight of authority strongly favours the interpretation that they only apply where the removing procedures introduced by the 1907 Act are to be used[3].

1886 Act. Under the Removal Terms (Scotland) Act 1886, where a lease is due to end at Whitsunday or Martinmas and 40 days notice is required, the notice to quit must be given at least 40 days prior to 15 May or 11 November respectively; however, if the tenant is to be removed, unless the lease expressly stipulates otherwise, he need not do so until noon on the twenty-eighth day of the month concerned[4]. Although the 1886 Act, on the face of it, applies only to houses, a house is defined very widely as a 'dwelling-house, shop or other building and their appurtenances', as well as houses let with agricultural land[5]. At least some commercial leases, therefore, would appear to fall within its scope.

The provisions of this Act sit rather uneasily with those of the Term and Quarter Days (Scotland) Act 1990, which has redefined Whitsunday and Martinmas as 28 May and 28 November respectively[6]. For the time being, however, the 1886 Act remains in force.

Contracting out. In the case of agricultural holdings, the statutory minimum period of notice of 1 year cannot be contracted out of and any provision in the lease document for a shorter period will not be effective[7]. In relation to other types of lease, there is some uncertainty about whether the lease document may substitute shorter periods of notice[8], and it would be safest not to rely on such a provision when serving notice. However, it would normally be

---

1 *Paton & Cameron* pp 272-273; 13 *Stair Memorial Encyclopaedia* para 482.
2 Agricultural Holdings (Scotland) Act 1991, s 21(3).
3 *Paton & Cameron* p 273; 13 *Stair Memorial Encyclopaedia* para 478.
4 Removal Terms (Scotland) Act 1886, s 4.
5 Ibid s 3.
6 See ch 1, pt 4 above.
7 See ch 12, pt 3 below.
8 See *Duguid v Muirhead* 1926 SC 1078 at 1082-1083 per Lord Constable and *Viscountess Cowdray v Ferries* 1918 SC 210 at 219 per Lord Johnston.

competent for the parties to agree in the lease for a longer period of notice to be given.

Practical considerations. It will be seen that the state of the law in this area is quite unsatisfactory. The only safe advice to give practitioners is to play it safe at every stage. In particular, the following points should be noted:

(1) Despite the uncertainties about its application, the provisions of the Sheriff Courts (Scotland) Act 1907 should be adhered to. This means that notices should be in writing, should observe the periods of notice laid down, and should use the forms contained in the Act. In addition, in the cases of agricultural holdings and residential tenancies, the respective provisions of s 21 of the Agricultural Holdings (Scotland) Act 1991 and s 112 of the Rent (Scotland) Act 1984 should be complied with.

(2) If the lease is one to which the Removal Terms (Scotland) Act 1886 applies, 40 days notice should be given prior to 15 May or 11 November. This is against the spirit of the Term and Quarter Days (Scotland) Act 1990, but the relationship of the two Acts to each other does not seem to have been thought through, and the above seems the only safe course. However, as well as only applying to houses and some commercial lets, the 1886 Act only applies in cases where the lease states the ish to be either Whitsunday or Martinmas and requires that 40 days notice should be given. Such provisions are more likely to appear in commercial than residential leases.

(3) Any provision in a lease substituting a shorter period for any of the statutory periods of notice should not be relied upon.

3. REMOVINGS

We saw above that, if a lease is terminated at the expiry date by a notice to quit, the parties often agree to a new lease, usually at a higher rent. However, this of course need not be the case. The parties may not be able to agree the terms of a renewal, or the landlord may simply want the tenant out. But what happens if the landlord gives notice, for the proper period and in the proper form, but the tenant does not move out when the expiry date arrives?

The first and most important point to note is that the landlord cannot take the law into his own hands. He has to abide by the due process of law by raising a court action to have the tenant removed.

This will give the tenant the opportunity to lodge a defence, and only if the court eventually grants a decree of removing will the landlord be in a position to instruct the sheriff officer to proceed with an eviction. In the case of lets of dwellinghouses, this principle is reinforced by statute[1]; however, the necessity for court action to remove a tenant at the end of his lease is also a common law principle and applies to all leases[2].

If a landlord attempts to remove a tenant without raising a court action, he may, at common law, be liable to the tenant in damages[3]. Furthermore, in the case of residential accommodation, the common law has been considerably reinforced by statute: any coercion or harassment of a residential occupier by his landlord, or anyone else, may make the person who is responsible for the coercion or harassment not only liable in damages, but also subject to criminal proceedings[4].

Form of action

Actions for the recovery of heritable property must normally be taken in the sheriff court in the form of a summary cause[5]. There are some exceptions to this, eg where, along with the removing, there is an additional or alternative claim for a sum of money exceeding £1,500[5], or where there is some other substantive claim, such as a declarator of irritancy which is being sought as a prerequisite of the removing; in such cases several types of action are still competent[6].

Violent profits[7]

At common law a payment known as violent profits may be due to an owner of heritable property from anyone (not just a former tenant) who occupies his property illegally. Violent profits are a form

---

1 See ch 13, pt 9 below.
2 *Fairbairn v Miller (Cockburn's Tr)* (1878) 15 SLR 705.
3 *Rankine* p 592; *Paton & Cameron* p 249.
4 See ch 13 below.
5 Sheriff Courts (Scotland) Act 1971, s 35(1) (c) (as amended by the Sheriff Courts (Scotland) Act 1971 (Privative Jurisdiction and Summary Cause) Order 1988, SI 1988/1993.
6 13 *Stair Memorial Encyclopaedia* para 474.
7 *Rankine* pp 580–586; *Paton & Cameron* pp 279–283.

of penal damages designed to act as a deterrent against illegal occupancy and to compensate the owner for being deprived of the benefits of possession. They may therefore be payable by a tenant who continues to occupy a property after his lease has been legally terminated[1]. However, they may not be payable by a tenant who remains on in the property with the landlord's consent while negotiating a new lease, even if the negotiations fall through[2], though a sum in lieu of rent may be payable on a different legal basis[3].

The measure of violent profits derives from very old authority and custom, and varies according to the area concerned. In burghs it is estimated at double the rent. Elsewhere, it is based on the greatest profit that the landlord could have made, either by possessing the property himself or by letting it to others, together with compensation for any damage caused to it by the illegal possessor.

If a tenant lodges a defence to an action of removing, the sheriff has discretion to demand caution (ie security) from him for violent profits[4]. This does not mean that the tenant will necessarily end up having to pay violent profits; that will depend on the outcome of the action. In an extraordinary removing, such as irritancy, caution for violent profits may be refused on the ground that the tenant cannot be branded as a violent possessor until the irritancy or other termination ground has been proved[5]. The position is similar if the owner is seeking to eject the occupant as a squatter, but he claims to be a tenant[6].

4. TENANT'S FIXTURES AND IMPROVEMENTS

It may be that, during the currency of the lease, the tenant will make some additions to the property at his own expense. These may have the effect of improving the property and increasing its value. But what happens when the lease comes to an end? Can the tenant take away any items he has added or will he have to leave

---

1 *Jute Industries Ltd v Wilson & Graham Ltd* 1955 SLT (Sh Ct) 46; (1955) 71 Sh Ct Rep 158.
2 *Hyams v Brechin* 1979 SLT (Sh Ct) 47.
3 See ch 1, pt 3 above.
4 Ordinary Cause Rules 1993, r 34.5 (also applicable to summary causes under the Act of Sederunt (Summary Cause Rules, Sheriff Court) 1976, rule 3 (as amended)).
5 *Simpson v Goswami* 1976 SLT (Sh Ct) 94; but see 13 *Stair Memorial Encyclopaedia* para 507 and *Imperial Hotel (Glasgow) Ltd v Brown* 1990 SCLR 86.
6 *Middleton v Booth* 1986 SLT 450.

them on the property? If the latter is the case, can he claim any compensation from the landlord?

We will see in chapter 12 that the tenant of an agricultural holding is entitled to compensation for any improvements he has made to the holding[1]. Alternatively, he may remove fixtures at the end of the lease, after first giving the landlord an opportunity to purchase them[2]. In a dwellinghouse leased by a public sector landlord, a tenant may be reimbursed at the end of his lease for improvements he has made with the landlord's consent[3]. In other leases, the position regarding additions by the tenant will often be regulated by the lease document[4]. Here we will consider the position at common law.

If an item added to a property is sufficiently attached to it, eg a building or something attached to a building, it will become part of the property. In other words, it will be a heritable fixture[5]. Since the heritable property that is being leased belongs to the landlord this means that, in theory, any fixture added to that property will also belong to him, even though the fixture might have been added or paid for by the tenant.

However, there are two exceptions to this rule which have long been recognised at common law. **Trade fixtures** added by the tenant may be removed by him provided they can be removed without any substantial damage to the property. A trade fixture is something that has been attached to the property for the purpose of the tenant's trade or business, eg heavy factory machinery that may be bolted to the floor. In *Syme v Harvey*[6], the tenants of a nursery garden were held entitled, at the end of their lease, to remove greenhouses, forcing pits and hotbed frames added by them for the purpose of their trade. Although it is normally at the end of a lease that questions relating to trade fixtures arise, the right of the tenant to remove trade fixtures is an incident of the landlord and tenant relationship which can be exercised during the currency of the lease also[7].

A similar rule applies to **ornamental fixtures**, which are things

---

1 Ch 12, pt 4 below.
2 Ch 12, pt 2 below.
3 See ch 14, pt 2 below.
4 See ch 9 below.
5 For a brief discussion of the law of fixtures, see Gloag & Henderson *Introduction to the Law of Scotland* (10th edn, 1995) para 36.5; see also McAllister & Guthrie *Scottish Property Law* (1992) ch 6.
6 *Syme v Harvey* (1861) 24 D 202, 34 Sol Jo 98.
7 *Lloyds Bowmaker Ltd v William Cook Engineering (Evanton) Ltd* 1988 SCLR 676.

that have been attached for the better enjoyment of the articles themselves, rather than with the purpose of improving the property. In the English case of *Spyer v Phillipson*[1], the tenant of a flat installed valuable antique panelling, ornamental chimney pieces and 'period' fireplaces, the last two requiring a small amount of structural alteration. After the tenant's death, his executor was held entitled to remove the additions: they had been installed, not in order to benefit the property, but for the enjoyment of the articles themselves, and they could be removed without irreparable damage to the property.

1 *Spyer v Phillipson* [1931] 2 Ch 183, [1930] All ER 457, CA.

8 Tenancy of Shops

We saw in chapter 1 that a major difference between the law of Scotland and England was the lack of statutory control of commercial and industrial leases in Scotland. There is, however, a minor exception to this in the form of the Tenancy of Shops (Scotland) Act 1949 which gives limited rights of security of tenure to shop tenants[1]. The 1949 Act was originally passed as a temporary measure to protect the rights of shopkeepers, but after a number of yearly extensions was made permanent in 1964.

Definition of shop

A shop is defined for the purposes of the Act as, 'Any premises where any retail trade or business is carried on'. Retail trade or business is stated to include the business of a barber or hairdresser, the sale of refreshments or intoxicating liquors, the business of lending books or periodicals when carried on for purposes of gain, and retail sales by auction. It does not include the sale of programmes and catalogues and other similar sales at theatres and places of amusement[2]. The Act would therefore appear to apply to hairdressers shops, cafes, pubs, profit-making libraries and auction salerooms, but not to theatres or other places of activity where retail sales are incidental.

The above definition has been further clarified by a number of court decisions. The principle emerging seems to be that premises which are not exclusively retail may still come within the definition of a shop as long as the retail element is substantial. Properties held to come within the definition include a sub post office[3], opticians'

---

1 Tenancy of Shops (Scotland) Act 1949 (as amended by the Tenancy of Shops (Scotland) Act 1964 and the Sheriff Courts (Scotland) Act 1971).
2 Shops Act 1950, s 74(1).
3 *King v Cross Fisher Properties Ltd* 1956 SLT (Sh Ct) 79, (1956) 72 Sh Ct Rep 203.

premises[1], premises used for the repair of boots and shoes where a minor but substantial part of the tenant's income came from articles for sale[2], and garage premises where the tenant's profits derived equally from retail activities and repair work, even though a larger area was used for repairs[3]. Among those properties excluded from the definition of a shop, and hence from the application of the Act, are a blacksmith's premises[4], a travel agent's[5] and a dry cleaner's[6]. Also held to be excluded from the definition was a builder's yard because not only was the retail element subsidiary, but the property was mainly open space which was not, in the court's opinion, the type of property the Act was intended to protect[7].

Application for renewal

The Act can be invoked when a shop lease is due to expire and the landlord has sent the tenant a notice to quit. If the tenant is unable to obtain a renewal on satisfactory terms, he may, within twenty-one days, apply to the Sheriff Court for a renewal of the lease. The sheriff has the power to renew the lease for a period not exceeding one year on such conditions as he thinks reasonable. The parties will thereafter be considered to have entered a new lease for that period. If the landlord wants to remove the tenant at the end of the extended period, he will require to send a fresh notice to quit[8]. A further application may be made by the tenant at the end of the renewed term, and at the end of any future periods of renewal which may be granted. Each application should be regarded on its own merits, without the court being influenced by any arguments that might have been put forward at earlier applications[9].

It has been held that the effect of the sheriff granting a renewal is to create a new statutory tenancy, and so it does not matter if the

---

1 *Craig v Saunders & Connor Ltd* 1962 SLT (Sh Ct) 85, (1962) 78 Sh Ct Rep 154.
2 *Oakes v Knowles* 1966 SLT (Sh Ct) 33.
3 *Thom v British Transport Commission* 1954 SLT (Sh Ct) 21; see also *Grosvenor Garages (Glasgow) Ltd v St Mungo Property Co Ltd* (1955) 71 Sh Ct Rep 155.
4 *Golder v Thomas Johnston's (Bakers) Ltd* 1950 SLT (Sh Ct) 50.
5 *Wright v St Mungo Property Co Ltd* (1955) 71 Sh Ct Rep 152.
6 *Boyd v Bell & Sons Ltd* 1970 JC 1, 1969 SLT 156.
7 *Green v M'Glughan* 1949 SLT (Sh Ct) 59, (1949) 65 Sh Ct Rep 155.
8 *White v Paton* (1953) 69 Sh Ct Rep 176; *Scottish Gas Board v Kerr's Trs* 1956 SLT (Sh Ct) 69, (1956) 72 Sh Ct Rep 139.
9 *Wallace v Bute Gift Co Ltd* 1954 SLT (Sh Ct) 55.

original lease has already expired at the time of the sheriff's decision[1].

It has also been held that the Act does not extend to an application by a subtenant for a renewal of a sublease from the principal tenant[2].

Grounds for refusal

The Act lays down the following grounds upon which the sheriff may refuse a renewal:

(1) That the tenant is in breach of a material tenancy condition. Where the use clause in a lease provided that the shop should be used exclusively as a newsagent's and stationer's, the tenant was held to be in material breach of a tenancy provision for selling cigarettes and tobacco[3].

(2) That the tenant is bankrupt.

(3) That the landlord has offered to sell the tenant the premises at a price, failing agreement, to be fixed by arbitration[4].

(4) That the landlord has offered the tenant suitable alternative premises on reasonable terms[5]. Premises where the tenant would have suffered a loss in passing trade have been held unsuitable[6].

(5) That the tenant has given the landlord notice to quit and the landlord has contracted to sell or let the premises, or has committed himself in some other way, as a result of receiving the notice.

(6) That greater hardship would be caused by renewing the lease than by refusing the application. There have been a number of cases on this ground. An example is the case of *Skelton v Paterson*[7], where a tenant who had invested his savings in the shop was granted a renewal as the landlord was considered to be suffering less hardship from being denied the opportunity to expand his business. On the other hand, in *Anderson v National Bank of*

---

1 *McMahon v Associated Rentals Ltd* 1987 SLT (Sh Ct) 94.
2 *Ashley Wallpaper Co Ltd v Morrisons Associated Companies Ltd* 1952 SLT (Sh Ct) 25, (1952) 68 Sh Ct Rep 94.
3 *McCallum v Glasgow Corpn* (1955) 71 Sh Ct Rep 178.
4 *J Bartholomew & Son v Robertson* (1960) 76 Sh Ct Rep 64.
5 See *Robertson v Bass Holdings* 1993 SLT (Sh Ct) 55.
6 *Hurry v M'Lauchlan* (1953) 69 Sh Ct Rep 305.
7 (1954) 70 Sh Ct Rep 287.

Scotland Ltd[1], it was held that a bank which was the landlord of a shop and, to the tenant's knowledge, had for some years desired possession of the shop in order to rebuild its premises would suffer greater hardship than the tenant, and accordingly a renewal of the tenancy was refused. The rather strange concept of a bank suffering hardship suggests that the application of this criterion does not always lead to an obvious outcome; it also confirms that the party suffering the hardship need not be a natural person provided that (as in the case of a limited company) it has legal personality[2]. It has been suggested in more than one case, though none seem to have been decided directly on this point, that the imposition of several successive yearly renewals on him could eventually amount to greater hardship for the landlord[3].

The unsuccessful party has the appeal rights available in a summary cause[4].

It will be seen, therefore, that these measures fall very far short of the comprehensive provisions which apply to business leases in England under the Landlord and Tenant Act 1954. In any case, unlike the Landlord and Tenant Act 1954, the Tenancy of Shops Act applies only to shops and not to factories or office premises, which remain virtually free of statutory control in Scotland.

---

1 (1957) 73 Sh Ct Rep 10.
2 See also *Jalota v Salvation Army Trustee Co* 1994 GWD 12–770.
3 *Wallace v Bute Gift Co Ltd* 1954 SLT (Sh Ct) 55; *White v Paisley Co-operative Manufacturing Society Ltd* 1956 SLT (Sh Ct) 95, (1956) 72 Sh Ct Rep 289.
4 Tenancy of Shops (Scotland) Act 1949, s 1(7) (substituted by the Sheriff Courts (Scotland) Act 1971, Sch 1); see also *McMahon v Associated Rentals Ltd* 1987 SLT (Sh Ct) 94; *Jalota v Salvation Army Trustee Co* 1994 GWD 12–770.

9 Common Lease Terms

We saw in chapter 1 that, at common law, the minimum requirements for a lease are a landlord, a tenant, subjects of let, a rent and
a duration. However, the sort of lease normally encountered nowadays usually goes far beyond these basics and can be a very lengthy,
complex and forbidding document. The purpose of this book is to
give a general introduction to the law of leases, and so it is outwith
our scope to provide styles of documents[1]. However, to adhere
rigidly to an exposition of the common law and statute law would
leave the reader with something missing from an overall picture of
leases. The common law in particular is so frequently contracted
out of that to look at it in isolation would give a misleading impression of what actually happens in practice.

The purpose of the present chapter, therefore, is to draw attention to some of the more important provisions that are commonly
found in a modern lease. Our main point of reference will be a
commercial or industrial lease, although many of the clauses can be
found in other types of lease as well. However, in leases of
dwellinghouses, and to a lesser extent in agricultural leases, the
lease terms take second place to the statutory framework, since the
frequent prohibition against contracting out nullifies anything
inconsistent with the statutory provisions. And so the realm of
commercial and industrial leases, where the lease terms reign
supreme, will be our main point of focus. These leases are also
likely to be the longest and most complicated; they are the ones
where there is often most money at stake, and where landlords and
tenants have the most to gain by going to great lengths to protect
themselves and/or bamboozle the other.

This brief survey is not intended to be comprehensive, but
merely to help the beginner to chart his way through the horrendous jungle of verbiage he is likely to encounter, and to enable him

---

1 For modern styles of the various types of leases see Halliday *Conveyancing Law
and Practice*, Vol III (1987), Part 1.

to establish some basic landmarks. Two of the more important clauses, those relating to rent reviews and service charges, will be dealt with in chapters 10 and 11, as each deserves a chapter on its own.

(1) Alienation

The alienation clause will include the standard provision prohibiting the tenant from assigning or subletting the lease without the landlord's permission. It will also have the effect of preventing the lease transmitting to one of the tenant's heirs after his death. It is common also to include a prohibition against creditors or managers of creditors, which will prevent the lease, without the landlord's consent, from transmitting to the tenant's liquidator or trustee in bankruptcy.

These provisions are important for the landlord if he wants to retain control over the choice of tenant who occupies his property. As we saw above, the omission of this clause would allow the tenant of a commercial or industrial lease to assign or sublet without the landlord's consent, that being the position at common law[1].

A tenant would normally want the clause modified by the addition of a qualification that the landlord's consent 'will not be unreasonably withheld'. Unfortunately, the addition of this phrase adds an element of ambiguity. Who decides what is reasonable and what is unreasonable? The landlord and tenant may well have different views, so the court (or possibly an arbiter) would have to decide, and the door has thus been opened to unwelcome litigation. However, it is a qualification that is difficult to escape from. It is in the tenant's interest to have some defence against the stranglehold of an unreasonable landlord and, as we will see in chapter 10, too tight a control by a landlord over assignations can limit the amount of rent he is able to charge at rent review.

In England, the landlord's reasonableness is imposed by statute[2]. The same statutory provision declares it to be unreasonable for a landlord to demand a money payment in exchange for his consent, and reasonable for him to refuse consent if the change of tenant would diminish the value of the property or neighbouring premises belonging to the landlord. These statutory provisions do not apply in Scotland, but it is likely that a court would find their principles

---

1 See ch 5 above.
2 Landlord and Tenant Act 1927, s 19.

persuasive when interpreting a similar provision in a Scottish lease. It has been held in England that the onus is on the tenant to establish that the landlord is being unreasonable[1].

In the Scottish case of *Renfrew District Council v AB Leisure (Renfrew) Ltd (In Liquidation)*[2], the clause in question provided that the landlord's consent to an assignation would not be unreasonably withheld, and in particular would not be withheld where the assignee's resources were adequate. As a condition of granting an assignation, the landlords wanted the arrears of rent to be paid, and the court agreed that this was reasonable. However, the landlords also wanted to make their consent to an assignation conditional upon an immediate rent review taking place, a full repairing and insuring clause being added to the lease and rent reviews being reduced from five yearly to three yearly intervals. The court held that the landlord was not entitled to impose these last three conditions, which effectively would have created a new lease in different terms. On the other hand, in *Lousada & Co v JE Lesser (Properties) Ltd*[3] it was held that landlords were not acting unreasonably in making their consent to an assignation conditional upon the conclusion of negotiations regarding an outstanding rent review for the property; they were not (as in the *Renfrew District Council* case) seeking to obtain a collateral benefit in return for their consent, but only to secure their rights under the existing lease.

Where an agreement appears to be a device intended to defeat the terms of the lease, the court will scrutinise such an arrangement closely. In *Brador Properties Ltd v British Telecommunications plc*[4] the tenants attempted to get round a prohibition against subletting by creating licences instead of subleases[5]. The provision was interpreted strictly and it was held that subleases had been created, in breach of the provision in the principal lease.

(2) Payment of rent

The dates when the rent is payable will depend upon what is stated in the lease. The commonest provision in commercial and industrial leases is for it to be paid quarterly in advance at the four

---

1 *Mills v Cannon Brewery Co* [1920] 2 Ch 38 at 46, 89, LJ Ch 354.
2 1988 SLT 635.
3 1990 SLT 823; see also *Continvest Ltd v Dean Property Partnership* 1993 GWD 40–2678.
4 1992 SLT 490.
5 See ch 1, pt 3 above.

Scottish quarter days, ie Candlemas (28 February), Whitsunday (28 May), Lammas (28 August) and Martinmas (28 November)[1]. There will usually also be a provision for interest to be paid to the landlord in the event of late payment of rent or of any other sum of money due under the lease. Since this provision could be invoked at any time over the period of the lease, during which time interest rates will fluctuate, it is probably better not to state a specific rate in the lease, but to relate it to a current bank rate, eg 3–4 per cent above the base rate of a specified bank. The landlord should be careful not to state a rate that is too high, otherwise a court might declare it to be a penalty (ie an attempt to punish the tenant rather than a reasonable pre-estimate of the landlord's loss); if this happened, the clause would be unenforceable[2].

(3) Use of premises

The clause dealing with the use of the premises is generally referred to as the 'use clause' (or in England the 'user clause'). It reinforces the common law provision that the tenant may only use the property for the purpose for which it was let, not only by stating the general purpose of the property (eg shop, office, factory or dwellinghouse) but also, in the case of commercial and industrial leases, laying down the type of business that has to be carried on. The latter is particularly important in shop leases, where the landlord may want to control the trade mix and ensure that there are not too many shops of the same type in one area; he may also be able to charge a shop tenant a higher rent, if he can assure him of a monopoly or partial monopoly in the locality.

However, as we will see in chapter 10, keeping this degree of control, while it may be to the landlord's advantage in terms of estate management, could rebound upon him financially, by limiting the amount of rent he is able to charge at a rent review[3]. It is therefore not in the landlord's interest to tie the tenant down too tightly to a particular use of the premises. He may allow a qualification that his consent to a change of use 'will not be unreasonably withheld'. In leases of offices or factories, he may want to consider

1 See ch 1, pt 4 above.
2 See Gloag *The Law of Contract* (2nd edn, 1929) pp 673–679; Walker *The Law of Contracts and Related Obligations in Scotland* (3rd edn, 1995) paras 20.23–20.36; McBryde *The Law of Contract in Scotland* paras 20.125–20.159; Woolman *An Introduction to the Scots Law of Contract* (2nd edn, 1994) pp 152–154.
3 See ch 10, pt 3 below.

whether it is necessary to limit the tenant to a specific type of business at all, as the considerations of trade mix that apply with retail premises are not really relevant with other types of property. Another solution is to limit the tenant to a use within a particular class of the Town and Country Planning (Use Classes) (Scotland) Order 1989[1]. This could have the effect of limiting a property to a general category of use, without specifically stating a particular kind of business; on the other hand, this could create practical problems if the order, or any other legislation referred to, is later amended or replaced during the currency of the lease[2].

It is common in use clauses for there also to be a prohibition against any uses of the property that would cause a nuisance to neighbouring tenants or otherwise affect the amenity of the area.

(4) Insurance

The most common type of commercial and industrial lease today is the tenant's full repairing and insuring lease (the FRI lease), in which the tenant is made entirely responsible for all repairs and for payment of insurance premiums. In the case of insurance, where the property is situated on its own (eg a factory on an isolated site) the lease may make it the tenant's responsibility to take out insurance for the full value of the property, and the landlord will safeguard his position by reserving the right to approve the choice of insurance company and the amount of the cover, as well as to inspect the insurance policy and the premium receipts. He will also want to have his insurable interest noted on the policy.

If the property is not an isolated one (eg if it is in a shopping centre, office block or industrial estate) the landlord will invariably prefer to effect the insurance himself and recover the cost of the premiums from the tenant by way of a service charge[3]. This not only has the advantage of administrative convenience, but the landlord will be making absolutely sure that his valuable property is insured to its full value. Also, by taking out a block insurance for a number of properties, he may be able to get better terms from the insurance company. In fact, so paramount is the landlord's interest in making sure that his property is adequately insured, that it is common for him also to take over the insurance arrangements in isolated properties, unless the tenant is eminently trustworthy and of good standing.

---

1 SI 1989/147.
2 See *Brewers' Company v Viewplan plc* [1989] 45 EG 153.
3 See ch 11 below; see also *Barras v Hamilton* 1994 SLT 949.

It is common in insurance clauses for the landlord to contract out of the common law doctrine of *rei interitus*. We saw in chapter 7 that a lease may be terminated prematurely by supervening impossibility if the premises are totally or almost totally destroyed by fire or otherwise[1]. If a landlord wants to ensure that he can hold a tenant for the full term of his lease (and a landlord who wants to maximise his investment generally will), he can provide in the lease that, in the event of such damage or destruction, the lease will not end but will carry on in full force and effect. The tenant, however, would normally be given the right to a rent abatement for the period during which the property was being rebuilt.

(5) Alterations and additions

It is normal for leases to provide that the tenant may not make any alterations or additions to the premises without the landlord's consent. Also, where alterations have been made, with or without consent, the landlord will hold the tenant bound, if he so requires it, to remove any alterations or additions at the end of the lease.

The landlord in this situation is not trying to prevent the tenant from making alterations, but trying only to keep control of the situation. He will want to ensure that any alterations are of a sufficiently high standard and are not damaging the property in any way. Also, he will not want the property changed too much to suit the tenant's specialist business, as this might reduce its market value in the event of a relet to another tenant.

(6) Repair and maintenance

We saw in chapter 3 that, at common law, the landlord is obliged to keep the property in a tenantable and habitable condition[2]. In FRI leases, therefore, it is necessary to contract out of this provision by specifically making the tenant responsible for all repairs. In order to best ensure that the value of his property is maintained, the landlord will usually also reserve the right, in the event of the tenant failing in his maintenance obligations, to carry out any necessary repairs himself and to charge them to the tenant. He will probably also reserve a right of access to the property to inspect its condition. In properties where there is multiple occupancy (eg

1 See ch 7, pt 1 above.
2 See ch 3, pt 2 above.

office blocks or shopping centres) the landlord will normally undertake any common repairs himself and recoup a proportion of the cost from each tenant by way of a service charge[1].

It is also common for a landlord to contract out of his obligation to provide subjects that are reasonably fit for the purpose of the let. This is done by inserting a condition that the tenant accepts the property as being in good condition and repair and fit for the purpose of the let.

The combined effect of these standard provisions goes to the heart of the concept of the FRI lease. The investment landlord wants a 'clear lease', ie one where the return on his investment is maximised by passing as many of his overheads as possible on to the tenant. This is fine for the landlord, but we must also look at things from the tenant's point of view, and it is clear that an over-enthusiastic application of this principle may not only involve the latter in additional expense, but also put him in some danger.

Inherent defects. The most obvious manifestation of the above is seen in the vexed question of inherent (or latent) defects. The meaning of the term 'inherent defect' will depend upon how it is defined in the lease in question. However, it usually arises in leases of new buildings in relation to some fault of construction or design that was not apparent at the beginning of the lease. At a future date the defect may emerge, requiring expensive repair work, or even substantial rebuilding. It seems unfair that this should be the responsibility of the tenant. The question arising here is this: do the normal terms of an FRI lease make it so?

In England it has been held that a fairly standard tenant's repairing obligation made him responsible for rectification caused by inherent defects, provided it fell short of having to reconstruct substantially the whole of the premises[2]. It is doubtful whether a simple repairing obligation could have that effect in Scotland, unless it also contracted out of the landlord's common law obligations to provide and maintain suitable premises. Also, in extreme cases, the defect may cause sufficient damage to amount to frustration by constructive total destruction, thus relieving the tenant of responsibility. However, as we have already seen, all of these common law provisions can be contracted out of. The difference between the two countries boils down in practice to one of lease wording:

---

1 See ch 11 below.
2 *Ravenseft Properties Ltd v Davstone (Holdings) Ltd* [1980] QB 12, [1979] 1 All ER 929.

provided that the lease provisions are sufficiently comprehensive in their scope, a Scottish tenant may also be made liable for damage caused by inherent defects[1].

It is accordingly in the tenant's interest to insist that his repairing obligation be modified to free him of such responsibility. A landlord will be inclined to resist this, of course, and the outcome will depend on the respective negotiating strengths of the parties, ie whether there is a greater shortage of tenants or of premises for let. It should be pointed out, however, that the landlord has other directions in which he may look for reimbursement. He may be able to insure against the defects, or he may have a claim against the contractor responsible, provided that the latter's errors have not been sufficiently prevalent to force him into bankruptcy[2].

Older buildings. It is not only in the case of new buildings that pitfalls await the unwary tenant. The standard provision (mentioned above) whereby the tenant accepts the property as being in good condition and repair could potentially make him liable for substantial renewal or rebuilding costs, resulting from wear and tear that occurred prior to the commencement of his tenancy[3]. Allied to this is the question of whether it is fair to make the tenant liable for *extraordinary* as well as ordinary repairs. Such a repair could arise, not just from the age of the building, but also in a new building with a latent defect of a major nature. It would appear to be possible for the lease terms to impose a liability for extraordinary repairs: in *House of Fraser plc v Prudential Assurance Co Ltd*[4] it was held that the lease wording was sufficiently comprehensive to make the tenants liable for the cost of such a repair, in that case to a defective retaining wall. (It was also alleged by the tenants, to no avail, that the defect in the retaining wall was an inherent one.)

A tenant should therefore try to ensure that the lease terms limit his liability for extraordinary repairs. One way is to agree only to keep the premises in the same condition as they were at the beginning of the lease, as evidenced by a schedule of condition agreed

---

1 *Thorn EMI Ltd v Taylor Woodrow Industrial Estates Ltd* (1982) C of S (Outer House), 29 October (unreported).
2 For a fuller discussion of the subject of inherent defects (as well as repairing obligations generally) see Ross & McKichan *Drafting and Negotiating Commercial Leases in Scotland* (2nd edn, 1993) ch 8.
3 See *Lord Advocate v Shipbreaking Industries Ltd (No 2)* 1993 SLT 995.
4 1994 SLT 416.

between the parties. Another way is to make an exception of 'fair wear and tear' from the tenant's repairing obligation[1].

It is also possible that a landlord may be the one to slip up when trying to frame a repairing obligation that is sufficiently comprehensive. In *Blackwell v Farmfoods (Aberdeen) Ltd*[2] the tenants bound themselves to accept the 'premises' (a unit within a building in multiple occupancy) in their existing condition; however, it was held that the lease wording did not make the tenants liable to pay for a repair to the common parts of the building, and so this liability reverted to the landlord.

Landlord's repairing obligations. Let us finally take a brief look at landlord's repairing obligations, which sometimes still occur. We saw earlier that the landlord's repairing obligation at common law is not a warranty, ie his obligation does not arise until the defect has been drawn to his attention. It has been held that, where the terms of the lease make the landlord responsible for repairs, this is not an absolute obligation unless the lease makes it clear; otherwise the landlord's duty is merely to take reasonable care in his maintenance obligation[3].

(7) Irritancy

Irritancy has already been fully dealt with in chapter 4[4]. Despite the modification in the law by legislation, a wise tenant will not accept an irritancy clause in unqualified form, but will want to reserve the right, within a reasonable period, to remedy any breach that might give rise to irritancy.

(8) Arbitration

It is common for leases to provide that any disputes between the parties should be referred to arbitration rather than decided by the court. It is arguable, however, whether this would effect any

1 See *Ross & McKichan* paras 8.14 and 8.15.
2 1991 GWD 4-219.
3 *John Menzies plc v Ravenseft Properties Ltd* 1987 SLT 64.
4 See ch 4, pt 2 above.

significant savings in time or money, and a case could be made for omitting such a clause[1]. An exception would be in the case of rent reviews, where a disputed rent should be fixed by an arbiter or expert (usually a surveyor) who is qualified to make valuations[2].

1 See *Ross & McKichan*, paras 12.11–12.16.
2 See ch 10, pt 4 below.

10 Rent Reviews

1. GENERAL

Historical background

Twenty years ago including a chapter on rent reviews in a book of this nature might have appeared a little odd. It might have seemed to be an undue concentration upon a routine aspect of lease drafts-manship in a work purporting to be an elementary treatise on the substantive law of landlord and tenant.

Yet today the subject of rent reviews is undoubtedly one of the most complex and important areas of modern lease law, as well as being the fastest growing[1]. And, though it does centre upon certain problems of conveyancing practice, the continuing deluge of case law on the subject makes it far more than that. Finally, even though the bulk of this unwelcome effusion originates in England, the Scottish lawyer does not have the option of taking refuge behind a barrier of national chauvinism: enough strands of the web have reached over the Border to secure him firmly in its grip!

So what has given rise to all this fuss? The answer, as we might have suspected, is money. We are here in the realm of commercial and industrial lets, ie leases of shops, offices and factories. Since the 1939–45 War financial institutions, such as banks, insurance companies or pension funds, have widely invested in this type of property. At the same time, there has been an increasing trend for companies and firms to rent the property they occupy rather than tie up their capital by buying it. And because the years since 1945 have also seen many periods of high inflation, particularly in the 1970s, it has become normal for rents to be periodically reviewed to keep up with rising rental values.

---

1 For a more detailed discussion of rent reviews from the Scottish viewpoint, see Ross & McKichan *Drafting and Negotiating Commercial Leases in Scotland* (2nd edn, 1993) ch 6.

112

The most common period for review nowadays is five years, although periods of three years have been known.

Need for a review clause

If we have a lease of comparatively short duration (say five years), reviewing the rent is not a problem. As we have already seen, the landlord will simply serve a notice to quit prior to the end of the term, preventing the onset of tacit relocation and entitling him to remove the tenant if necessary[1]. The landlord will then inform the tenant that he may stay on, provided that he enters into a new lease at a new rent. As long as the notice to quit is sent in time, the matter is comparatively simple.

However, there has been an increasing demand, from both land-lords and tenants, for leases of much longer duration. A financial institution will want its rental yield to be secure and not subject to periodic uncertainty by the need to find a new tenant: if the tenant wants out, the onus will be on him to find someone to assign to. Tenants, on the other hand, may want the legal right to stay on in the premises for a reasonably extended period. This is particularly true in Scotland, where there is no equivalent of the (English) Landlord and Tenant Act 1954, allowing tenants of business premises to apply for a renewal of their lease when it is due to end.

We thus have a situation where each party may want a binding contract for a lengthy period of time. However, the landlord will not agree to this unless there is some mechanism for changing one of the main contractual terms (ie the level of rent) at more frequent intervals. The answer is to include a rent review clause in the lease.

Drafting problems

This may seem straightforward enough, but if we gain nothing else from the rent review case law, we will learn the folly of such a naïve outlook, as we see past clauses, again and again, being minutely scrutinised by the courts and found wanting; as drafting pitfalls, which the most able lawyer could have been forgiven for overlook-ing, have proved fatally expensive for either landlord or tenant. Knowledge of the law in this area is therefore essential for the lawyer who wants to avoid such mistakes in future leases. But

1 See ch 7 pt 2 above.

unfortunately it does not end there. The long duration of many commercial and industrial leases means that we will be atoning for the unwitting sins of the past for many years to come. Today's and tomorrow's disputes will continue to be fought over clauses drafted in an earlier age of innocence. And so, if such disputes are to be kept to a minimum, it is necessary for landlords and tenants of existing leases to have advisers who are alert to the problems.

The Scottish dimension

As if all this were not enough, the Scottish lawyer is faced with additional difficulties. Almost all of the case law is English. So how much of it applies in Scotland? As we have already noted, there are considerable differences between Scottish and English lease law. On the other hand, the law of contract and principles of contractual interpretation, upon which many of the cases hinge, contain much common ground. The unhelpful answer is that some of the case law undoubtedly applies to Scotland, some does not, and the sparsity of Scottish authority can make it uncertain where the border between the two lies.

This lack of Scottish case law at first sight seems a little strange. In England there is an unending flow of rent review cases, whereas in Scotland the tap seems to be turned off, leaving us with the occasional drip. This is only partly explained by the difference in size of the two countries and the greater financial incentive for litigation provided by higher rental values in the south of England. The main reason is probably the difference between Scottish and English arbitration law. As we will see shortly, it is common for rent review disputes to be settled by arbitration. In England either party to a dispute has the right to appeal to the court against an arbitrator's decision on points of law[1], and such appeals are the source of much rent review case law from south of the Border. The parties may agree in advance to exclude the jurisdiction of the courts, but this right has existed only since 1979, and there has been a long tradition of judicial review of arbitration in England[2]. In Scotland, a limited right of appeal on points of law by stated case to the Court of Session was introduced for the first time in 1972. From the outset this right could be contracted out of, and in practice it often is[3]. In this way Scottish landlords and tenants are spared the distress of

1 Arbitration Act 1979, ss 1 and 2.
2 Ibid s 3.
3 Administration of Justice (Scotland) Act 1972, s 3; see also pt 4 below.

having their disputes unduly prolonged, but at the expense of an even greater than usual English influence in the development of the law.

Problems of generalisation

Another difficulty with rent review law is that the doctrine of judicial precedent cannot quite operate in the normal way to build up a body of principles. The reason for this is that the issues in a rent review case are normally matters of construction, ie interpreting the wording of a particular lease. And although similar provisions appear in different leases, there can be an infinite number of variations in the wording of individual documents. The result is that any attempt to build a structure of principle from the case law is liable to rest on a foundation of shifting sands. The nature of the problem has been recognised by the courts, notably by the Court of Appeal in 1992:

> 'However, if I may say so, to try to apply one authority given in relation to a different rent review clause in different circumstances to another situation is always a dangerous course to adopt, and in the normal event it is more appropriate for issues of this sort to be determined by looking at the facts of the particular case and applying those facts to the particular rent review clause which is under consideration[1].'

And more recently, Judge Colyer (in considering the validity of a rent review notice) has elaborated upon this theme:

> 'The task of the court is to construe a document – that is the lease – and then, in the light of that decision on the construction of the document, to conclude whether in the facts of a particular case the communication made by that particular tenant does or does not satisfy the requirements of the instrument which has just been construed. It is quite wrong, therefore, in my view, slavishly to take decided cases and to say: "Well, here was a letter written in identical terms in relation to an identical clause. Without more ado that is conclusive; the court must come to the same conclusion in this case as it came to in the other case." In this manner a seductive jurisprudence

---

1 Woolf LJ in *Patel v Earlspring Properties* [1991] 46 EG 153 at 154.

is being constructed about the phraseology of rent review clauses, and even that of letters given in response to them. I have to say that I think this is entirely misguided. We must bear in mind that unless they are landmark decisions which lay down principles of law . . . all such decisions will be either pure construction of documents or pure decisions on facts of particular cases, or a combination of both. So "precedent" is not wholly compelling or conclusive, although it may provide illustration or inspiration for arguments as to the instruction and effect of leases[1].'

Topics to be considered

Despite the above word of caution, rent review case law provides us with quite enough landmark decisions and other useful illustrations to be going on with, and recurring themes emerge which allow for a certain amount of generalisation. The main topics to be discussed are the mechanism for initiating a review, including the consequences of late notice, the basis on which the new rent will be calculated, and the methods of settling disputes, by an arbiter or expert. There remain innumerable decisions that turn upon unique points of interpretation, from which it is impossible to generalise, but we will look at one or two examples, to illustrate the sort of disaster that can result from careless draughtsmanship. Finally, we will briefly look at two alternative methods of calculating the rent level, by index linked or turnover rents.

2. THE REVIEW MECHANISM

Whether time is of the essence

Some of the most serious problems to have arisen concern the procedure when a rent review date arrives. These difficulties may best be understood by initially asking ourselves a number of hypothetical questions. What happens if a landlord lets a rent review date pass without asking for a review? Does he lose his right to review the rent until the next review date in the lease, which may be four or five years in the future? Or can he review late? If the latter is the

---

1 *Prudential Property Services Ltd v Capital Land Holdings Ltd* [1993] 15 EG 147 at 151.

case, can he charge the increase retrospectively to the missed review date, or only from the later date when he began proceedings? Many leases in the past have tried to clarify matters by laying down a strict timetable for initiating a review. For example, a lease may specify a minimum period (say six months) prior to the review date for the landlord to send the tenant a 'trigger' notice, stating the proposed new rent. The tenant may be given a fixed period (often as little as twenty-one days) within which to reject the landlord's proposal, failing which he will be deemed to have accepted the landlord's figure. There may also be a time limit for referring the matter to a third party in the event of a dispute. Such timetables may superficially seem to be a good idea, but it eventually became clear that they create more problems than they solve. What happens if a landlord is late in sending a trigger notice or referring a dispute to arbitration? Will he be stuck with charging the old rent for another five years? Or what if the tenant fails to send a counter-notice within the prescribed period? Will he have to pay the landlord's proposed new rent until the next review date? Bearing in mind that the figure in the landlord's trigger notice, being his first salvo in the negotiating battle, is likely to be unrealistically high, the consequences to the tenant of such a slip could be financially disastrous. On the other hand, if such dire consequences are not to follow a failure to observe the time limits, what is the point of having a timetable at all?

The United Scientific *principle*. The key to answering these questions is found in the leading cases of *United Scientific Holdings Ltd v Burnley Borough Council* and *Cheapside Land Development Co Ltd v Messels Service Co*[1]. These two cases, which raised basically the same principles, were heard together in the House of Lords. In each case there had been a failure on the part of the landlords to adhere to the rent review timetable and in each case the Court of Appeal upheld the tenants' view that the landlords had lost their right to review the rent until the next review date. However, the House of Lords reversed that judgment and found for the landlords in each case. The ratio of the decision is found in Lord Diplock's now famous dictum:

> 'So upon the question of principle which these two appeals were brought to settle, I would hold that in the absence of any contra-indications in the express words of the lease or in the

1 [1978] AC 904, [1977] 2 All ER 62.

inter-relation of the rent review clause itself and other clauses or in the surrounding circumstances the presumption is that the time-table specified in a rent review clause for completion of the various steps for determining the rent payable in respect of the period following the review date is not of the essence of the contract[1].'

In other words there is a presumption that time is not of the essence in relation to the review timetable. This means that, unless there are circumstances to rebut the presumption, a landlord will not lose his right to review the rent because of a late notice and a tenant will not be stuck with a landlord's proposed rent by failing to send his counter-notice in time. And where a landlord reviews late, he will be entitled to backdate the increase to the original review date. This last point had been decided in the earlier case of *CH Bailey Ltd v Memorial Enterprises Ltd*[2], and was quoted with approval by their lordships in the *United Scientific* and *Cheapside* cases.

The decision in these cases reversed what had been thought to be the position in English law. At the core of their lordships' reasoning was the point that delay in fixing a new rent does not cause any serious detriment to a tenant. Instead, it may be to his advantage, as he will have the use of the money representing the difference between the old and new rents for a longer period before having to pay it to his landlord. This contrasts with the considerable detriment to a landlord if he is unable to increase the rent until the next review period (ten years in the *United Scientific* case). Moreover, if the tenant wants to know what the new rent is going to be he can get a fair idea of the current market level by consulting his surveyor. Alternatively, if a landlord fails to send a trigger notice in time, it is open to the tenant to send a notice specifying a period within which the landlord is required to notify the tenant if the rent review is going ahead. Such a notice, if sent by the tenant, would make time of the essence in relation to the landlord's reply.

Application to Scotland

It is now established that the *United Scientific* principle applies in Scots law. This was first accepted in a series of Outer House decisions without the underlying theory being considered in any great

---

1 [1978] AC 904 at 930.
2 [1974] 1 All ER 1003, [1974] 1 WLR 728.

depth[1]. The principle was subjected to its first close scrutiny from the Scottish viewpoint in *Visionhire Ltd v Britel Fund Trustees Ltd*[2], in which the landlords, after initiating the review process, allowed the review date to pass without submitting the matter to arbitration. In such a situation the lease allowed the tenants to send the landlords a notice containing their own rental proposal, which would prevail if the landlords then failed to submit to arbitration within three months. The tenants sent a notice proposing the existing rent and the landlords failed to make their application within the three-month deadline. The landlords were therefore about to lose their right to review unless they could establish that time was not of the essence.

The Lord Ordinary decided that the presumption against time being of the essence was a purely English principle which did not apply in Scots law, and this caused some agitation among the legal and surveying professions in Scotland who saw themselves (unlike their English colleagues) being deprived of a safety net – albeit, as we will see soon, a net full of large holes. However, an appeal to the Inner House reversed this aspect of the Lord Ordinary's decision:

'It seems to me therefore that there is no essential difference between the positions adopted in the two countries and that the rules which according to English law are stated as presumptions are really to be seen as rules of construction which take their place along with various other rules in order to ascertain what the intention of the parties truly was in order that the contract which they have made should be enforced[3].'

Unfortunately for the landlords, in the particular circumstances of that case (ie the service of a notice by the tenants), the presumption was rebutted, time *was* of the essence and the landlords still lost their right to review. The affirmation of the general principle, however, confirms that the English authority is relevant and clears up some of the complications in the Scottish position; unfortunately, as we will see shortly, it does not clear up all of them[4].

---

1 *Scottish Development Agency v Morrisons Holdings Ltd* 1986 SLT 59; *Yates, Petitioner* 1987 SLT 86; *Leeds Permanent Pension Scheme Trustees Ltd v William Timpson Ltd* 1987 SCLR 571; *Legal and Commercial Properties Ltd v Lothian Regional Council* 1988 SLT 463.
2 1991 SLT 883.
3 1991 SLT 883 at 888 per Lord President Hope.
4 See section below on 'Waiver of right to review'.

Retrospective reviews

After the decisions in *United Scientific* and *Cheapside*, a number of landlords woke up to the idea that this apparent change in the law offered them the chance to put right past blunders that they had thought irreparable. Before long there began to appear a number of English cases in which the landlords were held entitled to review the rent retrospectively. In many of these the time that had elapsed since the review date was considerable, eg eighteen months[1], twenty-two months[2], twenty-four months[3], and even twenty-seven months[4]. In one case (*Telegraph Properties (Securities) Ltd v Courtaulds Ltd*)[5] six years was held to be an unreasonable delay, but that case was later overruled by the Court of Appeal in *Amherst v James Walker Goldsmith & Silversmith Ltd*[6].

It is perhaps worth looking at that last case a little more closely, as it represents the most extreme application to date of the *United Scientific* doctrine. In *Amherst* the landlords' notice, in terms of the lease, should have been served by 25 December 1974. They were a month late in serving it and the tenants refused to accept the notice as valid, their claim being upheld in court. However, in 1980, the landlords, encouraged by the *United Scientific* decision, served a fresh notice on the tenant. It was held that time was not of the essence and the landlords were entitled to review the rent retrospectively despite the fact that they had served their new notice five years after the review date. In the course of his judgment, Oliver LJ said:

> 'I know of no authority for the proposition that the effect of construing a time stipulation as not being of the essence is to substitute a fresh implied term that the contract shall be performed within a reasonable time . . . I would in fact go further and suggest that, despite what Lord Salmon said in the *United Scientific* case, even delay plus hardship to the tenant would not disentitle the landlord to exercise the right which he has, on the true construction of the contract, unless the combination amounted to an estoppel . . .

1 *H West & Son v Brecht* (1981) 261 EG 156.
2 *Printing House Properties Ltd v J Winston & Co Ltd* (1982) 263 EG 725.
3 *Vince v Alps Hotel Ltd* (1980) 258 EG 330.
4 *London and Manchester Assurance Co Ltd v GA Dunn & Co* (1983) 265 EG 39, CA.
5 (1980) 257 EG 1153.
6 [1983] Ch 305, [1983] 2 All ER 1067, CA.

'In particular, I cannot, speaking for myself, see how the right can be lost by "abandonment". So far as I am aware, this is not a term of art but I take it to mean the unilateral signification of an intention not to exercise the contractual right in question. If that is right I cannot see how it could bind the landlord save as a promise (promissory estoppel) or as a representation followed by reliance (equitable estoppel) or as a consensual variation of the agreement or as a repudiation accepted by the other party[1].'

Waiver of right to review. The above seems to make the position clear enough. Unfortunately, it only makes it clear in England, and in Scotland the position is a little more complex. In *Banks v Mecca Bookmakers (Scotland) Ltd*[2], the landlords had several leases with the tenants, whom they notified in April 1978 of their wish to review the rents. This was nearly a year after the rent review date in some of the leases, and nearly two years after it in the others. It was held that the acceptance by the landlords of rent at the old rate after the review dates, without qualification or any explanation, implied abandonment of the landlord's right to seek review until the next review dates. Pointing out that the concept of waiver was not raised in *CH Bailey Ltd v Memorial Enterprises Ltd*[3] or in the *United Scientific* and *Cheapside* cases, Lord Grieve went on to say:

'As I understand the law of Scotland the question of "waiver" is concerned with whether or not a right under a contract has been abandoned. It is a question of fact, and, as such, the question whether or not a person has abandoned a right cannot be affected one way or the other by prejudice suffered by the person who alleges that the right has been abandoned. Accordingly in cases such as this where the issue is concerned with the alleged abandonment of a right, prejudice need not be averred, and indeed would be irrelevant if it was[4].'

Neither the concept of waiver nor the *Banks* case were referred to in *Amherst*, even though it was heard a year after the Scottish case had been reported. It is clear that the two cases are incompatible, one rejecting and the other recognising the concept of

---

1 [1983] Ch 305 at 315–316.
2 1982 SC 7, 1982 SLT 150.
3 [1974] 1 All ER 1003, [1974] 1 WLR 728.
4 1982 SLT 150 at 153.

abandonment, one giving a landlord the right to backdate even where the tenant has suffered hardship, the other depriving him of the right to review even without hardship. What is not clear is whether the discrepancy reflects an underlying difference in the law of the two countries or merely a different interpretation of common principles. The principle of waiver is certainly not peculiar to Scots law, and it is not immediately obvious that the English doctrine is different from the Scottish one. *Halsbury's Laws of England*[1] defines waiver as 'the abandonment of a right in such a way that the other party is entitled to plead the abandonment by way of confession and avoidance if the right is thereafter asserted, and is either express or implied from conduct'. So far, this seems in line with the *Banks* decision, but Halsbury goes on to say that, not only must there be a promise or assurance (which may be express or implied) by the party alleged to have granted the waiver, but that the other party must have acted upon it and altered his position in some way. The Scottish version, as formulated by Professor Gloag, seems remarkably similar[2]. 'The party who alleges waiver must in some way have altered his position, or abstained from fulfilling the condition, in reliance on the words or conduct of the other. "The essence" of the plea of personal bar "is that owing to the action of one party the other party is put in a worse position than he would otherwise have been in".'

So now we have both Scotland and England apparently on the side of the English authority. Gloag apparently regards waiver as an aspect of personal bar, the Scottish equivalent of the English doctrine of estoppel, which was one of the possible exceptions to the rule acknowledged in *Amherst*. Also, the tenant having acted to his detriment, which was declared to be irrelevant in *Banks*, is considered an essential factor. But, unfortunately, the saga does not end there. The need for prejudice to exist in cases of waiver has been questioned as an unwarranted introduction of English principles into Scots law by Professor Gloag and his sources[3]. If that line of reasoning is followed, *Banks* must be regarded, not as a maverick decision, but as reflecting a genuine difference in the law north of the Border.

For a number of years *Banks* remained the sole Scottish authority on this point. However, in *Falkirk District Council v Falkirk*

---

1 16 *Halsbury's Laws of England* (4th edn) para 1471.
2 Gloag *The Law of Contract* (2nd edn, 1929), p 281.
3 McBryde *The Law of Contract in Scotland* (1987) paras 23.01–23.20; see also *Armia Ltd v Daejan Developments Ltd* 1979 SC (HL) 56, 1979 SLT (HL) 147.

Taverns Ltd[1] a plea of waiver was again attempted, this time unsuccessfully. Once again the landlords had accepted rent at the old rate after the review date but, unlike the situation in *Banks*, had initiated the review process in time and (according to the landlords' averments) had continued to assert in correspondence their intention to review the rent (the delay having been caused by a misunderstanding of the legal position). The Lord Ordinary did not criticise *Banks*, or even discuss its merits at all, but held that the above facts, alleged by the landlords, were grounds for distinguishing it. This falls somewhat short of an authoritative affirmation of *Banks*, but at least gives us a tentative indication that it should be accepted as a true statement of the Scottish position. An even clearer indication has recently been given in the sheriff court decision of *Waydale Ltd v MRM Engineering*[2] in which (in circumstances very similar to those of *Banks*) a plea of waiver was accepted and *Banks* was followed.

Summary of Scottish position

And so what conclusion can we draw from all of this? It may help if we distinguish between two separate types of case. The first is where the landlord has in fact initiated the rent review process prior to the review date, but either the landlord or the tenant has not strictly conformed to the review timetable laid down in the lease, eg where there has been late service of a landlord's trigger notice or of a tenant's counter-notice. Here it is clear that Scots and English law are in line and that the *United Scientific* principle applies in both countries: this is confirmed by the *Visionhire* case and the other Scottish authority. The second situation is where the landlord has let the review date pass entirely and has continued to accept rent at the old rate without qualification before deciding (or remembering) to ask for a review. It is plain that this makes no difference in England, from the number of late reviews that were allowed there after the decision in the *United Scientific* case[3]. But in Scotland, in the light of the *Banks* case, the landlord is likely to be held to have waived his right to a review, and will be prevented from increasing the rent until the next review date.

1 1993 SLT 1097.
2 1995 GWD 23-1263.
3 See above section on 'Application to Scotland'.

Rebuttal of presumption

Let us now return from this brief excursion into comparative law and pick up the main thread of the story. That does not mean, alas, that the difficulties have gone, but only that, for the time being, we are back to ones that straddle the Border. We have seen that there is a general presumption in relation to rent review timetables that time is not of the essence. However, there are a number of situations where it has been established that the presumption has been rebutted and time *is* considered to be of the essence:

(a) *Where the lease expressly states that time is of the essence in relation to the review timetable or any part of it.* As we will see below, this is probably the only situation where the position is relatively straightforward. Problems have mainly arisen where the lease is ambiguous about which provision or provisions are subject to the declaration that time is of the essence. It is therefore important for the lease draftsman to make this clear[1].

(b) *Where the tenant serves a notice on the landlord making time of the essence.* It is clear from Lord Diplock's judgment in *United Scientific* that the tenant has this option. However, it may only apply if the tenant has no other remedy available. In *Factory Holdings Group v Leboff International*[2], the tenant sent a notice to the landlord requiring the landlord to refer the dispute to arbitration within twenty-eight days and purporting to make time of the essence. In terms of the lease it was equally open to the landlord and the tenant to apply for the appointment of an arbitrator. It was held that the tenant was not entitled to serve a notice making time of the essence because, in the particular circumstances of the case, he did not need that remedy. In *Visionhire Ltd v Britel Fund Trustees Ltd*[3] a lease provision entitled the tenants, if the landlords had not referred the dispute to arbitration by the review date, to send a notice requiring them to do so within three months. It was held that sending such a notice made time of the essence, and that it was unnecessary for the tenants to serve a further notice in order to achieve this.

(c) *Where there is an inter-relationship between the rent review clause and a tenant's break provision.* This is the one contra-indication specifically mentioned in the *United Scientific* case as implying that time is of the essence and rebutting the presumption. The reason is

---

1 See *Ross & McKichan* para 6.9.
2 [1987] 1 EGLR 135, 282 EG 1005.
3 1991 SLT 883; see also above section on 'Application to Scotland'.

quite logical. If the tenant is given the option of terminating the lease prematurely, and he is required to give notice of his intention on or shortly after the landlord's last date for sending his rent review trigger notice, the presumption is that the purpose of the break provision is to allow the tenant to get out of the lease if he thinks the new rent is too high. Time is of the essence in relation to the tenant's notice exercising the break, because the landlord needs to know whether or not he will have to look for another tenant[1]. It would therefore be grossly unfair on the tenant if he let pass his opportunity to terminate the lease only to receive a late trigger notice from the landlord demanding an unacceptably high rent. Subsequent to the *United Scientific* decision, there have been a number of English cases where an inter-related rent review and break clause has been held to make time of the essence[2]. However, there have also been cases where the presence of a break clause has not had that effect. In *Edwin Woodhouse Trustee Co v Sheffield Brick Co*[3], the tenant had a right to break at the rent review date. The tenant had to give six months' notice of his intention to exercise the break, but there was no corresponding provision for a landlord's trigger notice. It was held that time could not be of the essence in relation to a date that was not specified in the lease. In *Metrolands Investments Ltd v JH Dewhurst Ltd*[4], the rent review and break timetables, on the surface, seemed closely integrated. However, one of the events in the landlord's timetable was the actual obtaining of the arbitrator's decision (as opposed to a referral to arbitration or applying for an arbitrator to be appointed). As this was outwith the landlord's control, it was held that time could not be of the essence in relation to the rent review timetable. The fact that the tenant would want to know the new rent before deciding whether or not to exercise his option to break was countered by the fact that, under the terms of the lease, he also had the right to begin the arbitration process if he felt there was likely to be any delay. 'For these reasons,' said Slade LJ, 'there can, in our judgment, be

---

1 *United Scientific Holdings Ltd v Burnley Borough Council, Cheapside Land Development Co Ltd v Messels Service Co* [1978] AC 904, [1977] 2 All ER 62 at 929 per Lord Diplock.

2 *Saloom v Shirley James Travel Service Ltd* (1981) 259 EG 420, CA; *Legal and General Assurance (Pension Management) Ltd v Cheshire County Council* (1984) 269 EG 40, CA; *Coventry City Council v J Hepworth & Sons Ltd* (1983) P & CR 170, 265 EG 608, CA; *William Hill (Southern) Ltd v Govier & Govier* (1984) 269 EG 1168.

3 (1984) 270 EG 548.

4 [1986] 3 All ER 659, CA.

no doubt that the potential detriment to which the lessor under this particular lease would have exposed itself by agreeing that time should be of the essence as regards the stipulated date for the obtaining of the arbitrator's decision would have far outweighed any potential detriment to which the lessee would have exposed itself by agreeing that it should not be[1]. This is fine as far as the landlord is concerned but it is not really satisfactory from the tenant's point of view. The tenant might very well have had the right to initiate arbitration proceedings, but he had no more control than the landlord over when the arbitrator would reach his decision, and no matter how diligent he was with his referral, he might still have lost the right to exercise his option to break by the time he found out what the new rent was going to be. It is difficult to see how that particular lease could have been interpreted in a way that was entirely fair to both parties.

These and other familiar arguments cropped up in the Scottish case of *Scottish Development Agency v Morrisons Holdings Ltd*[2]. There a tenant's break clause and the rent review clause were held not sufficiently inter-related to make time of the essence because (1) there was no provision for a landlord's trigger notice, whereas notice by the tenant was required to exercise his break (2) the lease required the rent to be assessed by the Valuation Department for Scotland, and the landlord had no control over the timing of that (it took two years!) (3) the lease required the valuation to be made as at the rent review date and the valuation could not be known for certain in advance of that date and (4) it was open to the tenant to make his own enquiries about the likely rent level. Presumably the same option was open to the tenant in the *Metrolands* case, though the point was not made in that case.

(d) *Where the lease contains other contra-indications making time of the essence.* In other words, although time is not made expressly of the essence, somewhere in the lease there is wording to indicate that this was the parties' intention. (The fact that it is more likely to reflect a drafting idiosyncrasy of their lawyers is not a relevant consideration!). Here we are once more thrust into the jungle of apparently conflicting decisions, both north and south of the Border. It is difficult to draw general principles here because so much has depended on the individual wording of particular leases, and considerable financial consequences to both landlords and tenants

1 *Metrolands Investments Ltd v J H Dewhurst Ltd* [1986] 3 All ER 659, CA at 670–671 per Slade LJ, (1986) 277 EG 1343.
2 1986 SLT 59.

have hung upon minor differences in what seem to be substantially similar clauses. 'It is highly undesirable that decisions of this type of dispute shall turn upon fine distinctions,' said Sir John Donaldson MR in one of the most problematic cases[1], and his words have been echoed by many judges, both north and south of the Border, when reaching decisions in this field. Unfortunately, this excellent sentiment is generally followed by yet another application of a finely-honed forensic scalpel, after which another legal hair has been parted lengthwise. In *Drebbond Ltd v Horsham District Council*[2], a notice by the landlord requiring arbitration had to be served within three months 'but not otherwise'. It was held that these last three words made time of the essence. In *Mammoth Greeting Cards Ltd v Agra Ltd*[3] the same was true in relation to the tenants' counter-notice, where failure to respond within two months meant that the rent 'shall be conclusively fixed at the amount stated in the lessor's notice'. On the other hand in *Touche Ross & Co v Secretary of State for the Environment*[4], a notice had to be given 'as soon as practicable and in any event not later than' a particular period. It was held that time was *not* of the essence. (Admittedly, that case also hinged on the fact that part of the timetable – the appointment of a surveyor by the President of the Royal Institution of Chartered Surveyors – was outwith the control of the parties, the same reason given in the 'break' cases.) In *Lewis v Barnett*[5], the penalty laid down in the lease for the landlord failing to apply in time for the appointment of a surveyor was that his trigger notice would 'be void and of no effect'. Time was held to be of the essence. A provision that timeous service of the landlord's trigger notice was to be a 'condition precedent' of the review taking place was held in one case[6] *not* to make time of the essence, whereas in another[7] it was held that it did. And in the most extreme case of all *Trustees of Henry Smith's Charity v AW ADA Trading and Promotion Services Ltd*[8], the lease contained an elaborate timetable, in which the consequences of failing to meet any of the various

---

1 *Trustees of Henry Smith's Charity v AW ADA Trading and Promotion Services Ltd* (1984) 47 P & CR 607, 269 EG 729, CA.
2 (1978) 37 P & CR 237, 246 EG 1013, DC.
3 [1990] 29 EG 45.
4 (1983) 46 P & CR 187, 265 EG 982, CA.
5 (1982) 264 EG 1079, CA.
6 *North Hertfordshire District Council v Hitchin Industrial Estate Ltd* [1992] 37 EG 133.
7 *Chelsea Building Society v R & A Millet (Shops) Ltd* [1994] 09 EG 182.
8 (1984) 47 P & CR 607, 269 EG 729, CA.

deadlines were clearly spelled out. The landlords served their trigger notice in time, but were late in referring the matter to arbitration. It was held that if the parties had agreed to confine their movements so tightly, they must be presumed to have meant it, and time was held to be of the essence. The landlords had wanted the rent raised to £29,000 per annum, but were held to the existing rent of £8,000 per annum for another five years. This means that, if the landlords' estimate bore any resemblance to the market rent, their failure to serve the notice in time cost them in the region of £100,000! This gives a fair idea of the amount of money at stake in some of these cases.

In *Taylor Woodrow Property Co Ltd v Lonrho Textiles Ltd*[1], the deputy judge was faced with the task of reconciling the *Henry Smith* case with the earlier case of *Mecca Leisure Ltd v Renown Investments (Holdings) Ltd*[2]. Both were Court of Appeal cases, making them both binding precedents in his court, and they appeared to contradict each other. He reached the conclusion that the distinction lay in whether the 'deeming' provisions in the timetable were one way or two way. In other words, if the tenant, by sending a counternotice late, was deemed to have accepted the figure in the landlord's trigger notice, but there was no scope for the landlord suffering a comparable sanction, time was not of the essence. The result would be the same if a tardy landlord was in danger of being held to the existing rent, without the tenant running the risk of any comparable penalty. However, if the clause was framed in such a way (as in the *Henry Smith* case) that *either* party's delay at a crucial moment might mean their financial ruin, then time *was* presumed to be of the essence and either party could be strictly held to the consequences of their mistake.

In the words of Dillon LJ in the *Touche Ross* case, 'there is no magical formula which alone achieves the result of making time of the essence of a contract'[3]. It depends upon the wording of the lease in the individual case and to some extent (one suspects) on how the judge in question wants to interpret it.

Scottish cases. Unfortunately, the Scottish authority, although more sparse, has decisively succeeded in extending the confusion northwards. In *Yates Petitioner*[4], Lord Davidson, following the dissenting opinion in the *Mecca* case, held that time was of the essence

---

1 (1986) 52 P & CR 28, (1985) 275 EG 632.
2 (1985) 49 P & CR 12, (1984) 271 EG 989, CA.
3 *Touche Ross & Co v Secretary of State for the Environment* (1983) 46 P & CR 187, 265 EG 982 at 190 per Dillon LJ.
4 1987 SLT 86.

for service of the tenant's counter-notice. Fortunately for the tenant in that case, the trigger notice served by the landlord was too informal to be valid. Furthermore, a new angle was added. Time was also of the essence in relation to the landlord's trigger notice, and his fault was not serving it too late but too early! The reason was that, if the tenant was given the landlord's proposed new rent too far away from the review date, it made it more difficult for him to judge whether the figure was a reasonable one, as the market could change in the interim. And so the landlord was required to give 'precisely, or in any event, substantially three months' notice prior to the relevant terms'. This was to apply even if it meant the landlord having the notice delivered by hand on a Sunday!

In *Leeds Permanent Pension Scheme Trustees Ltd v William Timpson Ltd*[1], the landlord was three weeks late in serving his trigger notice. It was held that time was not of the essence and he was allowed to review. In *Legal and Commercial Properties Ltd v Lothian Regional Council*[2], the lease contained an elaborate timetable and the tenant failed to serve a counter-notice within the required twenty-eight days. Lord Jauncey considered the *Henry Smith* and *Yates* cases, but was reluctant nevertheless to regard time as being of the essence. He held that it was not of the essence because (1) there was no time limit imposed on the landlord's application for the appointment of a surveyor and (2) the lease expressly gave the landlord the opportunity to review at a later date if he missed the review date. In other words, there was a 'one-way' deeming provision – only the tenant and not the landlord risked the supreme penalty for delay. This gives a pretext for not following the *Henry Smith* case, but the reasons for distinguishing *Yates* seem much more elusive. And so, in this particular area, we must reluctantly conclude that the case conflict has extended to Scotland.

Validity of notices

We have seen that, where time is of the essence, disaster can strike either landlord or tenant: a late trigger notice or reference to arbitration can cost a landlord his right to review, or a tenant serving a late counter-notice may be stuck with the landlord's optimistic first proposal. Unfortunately the dangers do not end there. Even if a landlord indicates his wish to review in time, or a tenant makes

1 1987 SCLR 571.
2 1988 SLT 463.

known his disagreement with the proposed rent within the required period, such a communication may be ineffective if it does not amount to a valid notice in terms of the lease. Where time is not of the essence this need not matter, as a replacement notice which does meet the necessary requirements can be sent late. But when time *is* of the essence, this luxury is not available, and a timeous notice worded with insufficient care may have the same unfortunate consequences as a late notice or no notice at all.

Once again it is difficult to generalise, as the requirements for a valid notice may vary according to the lease terms. However, the case law reveals a number of lessons that should be of help to the drafters of notices.

Wording of notice. If its wording is too informal, or contains extraneous material, a notice may be invalid. In *Yates, Petitioner*[1] this was the result when a trigger notice was couched in informal terms, included social pleasantries, and seemed more like an invitation to negotiate than a formal notice. Also, there have been many cases in England where tenants indicated in time that they were unhappy with the landlord's proposed new rent, but the wording of their communication rendered it ineffective as a counter-notice. Examples include: 'We would hardly need add that we do not accept your revised figure[2]', 'Our client contends . . . that the open market rental value . . . is at this time less than the present rental value[3]', 'We cannot agree with your rent increase[4]', 'Will you please accept this letter as counter-notice to the effect that we consider that the rent of £50,000 is excessive and will appreciate it if you will kindly forward to us the comparables on which you have based this figure[5]', and 'I am writing to inform you that the Board does not accept your proposed increase of £6,500[6]'.

More recently, the courts seem to have taken a slightly more liberal view and the following have been held to be valid counter-notices: 'Please accept this letter as formal objection and counter-notice. We would suggest an early meeting to discuss the

---

1 1987 SLT 86; see also *Dunedin Property Investment Co Ltd v Wesleyan & General Assurance Society* 1992 SCLR 159 as another Scottish example.
2 *Bellinger v South London Stationers Ltd* (1979) 252 EG 699.
3 *Oldschool v Johns* (1980) 256 EG 381.
4 *Amalgamated Estates Ltd v Joystretch Manufacturing Ltd* (1980) 257 EG 489.
5 *Edlingham Ltd v MFI Furniture Centres* (1981) 259 EG 421.
6 *Horserace Totalisator Board v Reliance Mutual Assurance Society* (1982) 266 EG 218.

matter in detail[1]', and 'I note that your assessment of rental is £190,000 per annum which I consider to be excessive[2]'. However, much will still depend upon the requirements of the particular lease.

Amount of rent. If a lease requires the landlord's trigger notice not only to intimate his intention to review, but also to state his proposed rent, then the omission of a rental figure may invalidate the notice[3]. Where a notice inadvertently stated one amount in words followed by another in figures, this was not held to be fatal[4]; needless to say, this is *not* recommended practice! It may not be necessary for the tenant to state a counter-proposal in his notice[5], but this again will depend on the lease provisions.

'Subject to contract' and 'without prejudice'. The attachment of either or both of these phrases to a piece of correspondence will normally reserve the legal position of the party using the phrase. Although they originate in other areas of law, they may have some function in rent reviews while the parties are merely in negotiation; on the other hand, their use may also allow one party to change his mind after agreement was thought to have been reached[6]. The main problems arise when one of these phrases is added, either by a landlord or a tenant, to a notice which the lease makes a formal requirement. If the sender is lucky the words 'subject to contract' or 'without prejudice' may in a particular context be considered merely to be 'meaningless estate agent's verbiage' and have no effect[7]; at the worst, an otherwise satisfactory notice may be rendered legally ineffective[8].

Notice by fax. Where a lease required notices to be sent in writing, a notice sent by facsimile transmission has been held to be sufficient[9]. It is of course always possible that the particular requirements of other leases might not be satisfied by this method.

---

1 *Glofield Properties Ltd v Morley* [1988] 02 EG 62.
2 *Barrett Estate Services Ltd v David Greig (Retail) Ltd* [1991] 36 EG 155; see also *Patel v Earlspring Properties* [1991] 46 EG 153.
3 *Commission for the New Towns v R Levy & Co Ltd* [1990] 28 EG 119.
4 *Durham City Estates Ltd v Felicetti* [1990] 03 EG 71.
5 *Patel v Earlspring Properties* [1991] 46 EG 153.
6 *Henderson Group plc v Superabbey Ltd* [1988] 39 EG 82.
7 *Royal Life Insurance v Phillips* [1990] 43 EG 70 (also useful for a review of the case law on this topic).
8 *Shirlcar Properties Ltd v Heinitz* (1983) 268 EG 362.
9 *EAE (RT) Ltd v EAE Property Ltd* 1994 SLT 627.

Purpose of notice. When considering the requirements of the lease in question, the purpose which the notice is designed to achieve should always be kept in mind. For example, if the purpose of a tenant's counter-notice is merely to challenge the figure in the landlord's trigger notice, then a clear written indication of disagreement may be enough[1]. However, there have been a number of rent-review clauses where the purpose of a counter-notice is also an election by the tenant to have the rent determined by a third party, and here more will be required. In *Prudential Property Services Ltd v Capital Land Holdings Ltd*[2], Colyer J (after a useful review of the earlier authority) confirmed that such a notice, to be valid, must make it clear that the tenant is exercising the relevant election either by (a) indicating that the letter is a counter-notice under the relevant clause or (b) spelling out the consequences which it is intended to achieve. The notice in that case was held to be valid despite containing a reference to the wrong clause of the lease; it would, in any case, have been rather unfair to penalise the tenant for this as he had repeated the wrong reference from the landlords' trigger notice!

It has been held in a recent Scottish decision that for an error to invalidate a notice there has to be something that might mislead the other party[3].

Practical considerations

Drafting of lease. The law regarding review machinery may not be a model of clarity, but the lessons to be learned from this horrendous muddle are easier to formulate:

(1) When drafting a rent review clause in a new lease, do not include a strict timetable. If the reader has gained nothing else from the above account (apart from a headache), he may just have got the impression that, for both landlords and tenants, timetables are not a good idea! After all, the tenant has signed a lease containing rent review dates and should not have to be reminded when they are due to arrive. The landlord will probably, as a matter of practice, write informally to the tenant well in advance of the date, proposing a new rent and starting off negotiations, but there is no need for a formal requirement to send a trigger notice. If the tenant is worried about the possibility of the review date being missed and

---

1 *Barrett Estate Services v David Greig (Retail)* [1991] 36 EG 155.
2 [1993] 15 EG 147.
3 *Prudential Assurance Co v Smiths Foods* 1995 SLT 369.

a retrospective increase being imposed on him perhaps years later, the solution is simple. A provision can be inserted allowing the landlord to review late, but at some later anniversary of the review date rather than retrospectively. On the other hand, landlords commonly want to include a provision expressly allowing them to review retrospectively and backdate the increase, and whichever prevails will probably depend on the relative negotiating strengths of the parties and the quality of their respective representation. In either case it is in the tenant's interest to make sure that the date of valuation is still the original review date. Otherwise the landlord might, at a time of rental stagnation, be tempted to deliberately postpone the review until rent levels have risen again.

(2) A landlord would be advised to include a disclaimer to the effect that accepting rent at the old level after the rent review date will not amount to a waiver of his right to review. Whether or not this would be effective in avoiding the disastrous outcome to the landlord in the *Banks* case has not been tested in court, but it is worth a try.

(3) In addition to the general inadvisability of having a strict timetable, the tenant in particular should resist inclusion of a provision deeming him to have agreed to the landlord's rental figure if he fails to send a timeous counter-notice. This is especially so if time is expressly declared to be of the essence for the counter-notice, as that would probably be upheld by the court. If the tenant loses the right to challenge the landlord's inevitably optimistic figure, the consequences could be financial disaster.

Review clauses in existing leases. So much for the lessons to be learned by future lease drafters. But what about the poor lawyers and surveyors who will have to live for years to come with the timetables in existing leases, drafted before the benefit of all this hindsight was available? How are we to advise them? There are a few practical considerations that may ease their burden:

(1) In order to minimise the possibility of missing a review date, the landlord's agent should have a proper administrative system for reminding him when the rents in the various leases under his care are due for review.

(2) The landlord's agent should check the rent review terms of *each individual lease* where a review is due, and make sure that all time limits are strictly observed, whether or not time is stated to be of the essence. No matter how standard the terms of his leases, an individual check is still necessary: when the lease was drafted,

many years before, the standard style might have been different, or the tenant's agent might have negotiated changes, now forgotten. Since the courts have shown how much can depend upon minor differences of wording, this is an essential precaution.

(3) The tenant's agent, for his part, should also check his lease and make sure that he observes all time limits incumbent upon him, particularly if he is required to send a counter-notice to the land-lord's trigger notice.

(4) As well as meeting all deadlines laid down, both landlord and tenant should observe any requirements of the lease regarding the form of the notices involved. If no requirements are laid down, the notice should be made as formal as possible, stating the sender's intentions clearly and unambiguously[1].

3. VALUATION INSTRUCTIONS

Surely, the reader will be thinking, as he moves thankfully on to the next topic, things must get easier from now on. To fix the rent level at review, surely all we need to do is simply put a provision in the lease that the parties should agree a market rent. If they can't agree, then the lease should lay down some mechanism for an arbiter or some other independent third party to tell them what the rent is. What could be simpler?

Unfortunately there is much more to it than that. We are not yet through the minefield. The following cautionary tale will illustrate the point.

In *Goh Eng Wah v Yap Phooi Yin*[2], an appeal to the Privy Council from the Federal Court of Malaysia, the tenants took a 30-year lease of a piece of land on which they erected a cinema at their own expense. At a subsequent rent review, it was held that the level of rent should be based on the value of both the land *and* the build-ing, even although they had paid for the latter themselves. Effectively, therefore, the tenants were paying for the cinema twice: once when they erected it, then again in the form of an inflated rent. '(If) the parties intended that the rent fixed by an arbitrator should ignore the buildings on the land,' said Lord Templeman, 'they should and would have given express instructions to the arbi-trator for that purpose[3]'. In other words, the job of an arbiter or

---

1 See section on 'Validity of notices' above.
2 [1988] 32 EG 55.
3 [1988] 32 EG 55 at 55.

other independent party is to value the property which he sees on the ground, subject to any instructions given to him in the lease. Unless the lease tells him otherwise, therefore, he must include in his valuation the effect of any additions or improvements provided by the tenant.

The hypothetical letting

We will return to this subject shortly when discussing the disregard of tenant's improvements. The above story, however, should be enough to illustrate that a rent review clause, to be fair to both parties, will have to contain valuation instructions a little more subtle than a simple request to fix a market rent. The way this is normally achieved is by means of a fiction called the hypothetical letting. After all, if it is a market rent that is to be fixed at the review date, we must ask ourselves how that is normally determined. The answer is that it is usually fixed in quite different circumstances from those a landlord and tenant are in at a rent review date. A market rent is what a tenant will be willing to pay and a landlord willing to accept for premises that are vacant and available for let. Usually there will be other premises which the tenant, should he so wish, could choose instead. Likewise, the landlord will possibly have other tenants to choose from. Neither party, therefore, is under any legal or other compulsion. Moreover, the premises are as provided by the landlord, not yet altered in any way by the tenant. Nor has the property acquired any value in the way of goodwill brought about by the tenant having occupied the property over a period of time.

This is in contrast to the real situation of the parties at a rent review date. The premises are not vacant, the property is not actually on the market. It is occupied by the tenant. Without the landlord's permission the tenant is not at liberty to go elsewhere, nor is the landlord free to take another tenant. They are both bound by the contract of lease. It may be that one of them wants out but is being held to the bargain by the other. Moreover, the tenant, by having occupied the property over a period of time, may be committed to it in other ways; he may, as we have seen, have made improvements, he may have established goodwill in that particular location and, even in the absence of these, it would probably be easier for him to stay where he is rather than to move. Unlike our fictional tenant on the lookout for suitable premises, he may well have a vested interest in staying put.

The hypothetical letting, therefore, is a simulation of a real market situation, created for the purpose of a rent review. It is a construction to be made by the valuer in accordance with the instructions in the rent review clause. The way this is usually achieved is by stating a number of factors that should be taken into account and others that should be left out when making the rental valuation, ie the normal assumptions and disregards.

The normal assumptions

It is, of course, up to the parties to decide what these should be when drawing up the lease, but common assumptions to be found are: (1) that there is a willing lessor and a willing lessee; (2) that the premises are vacant; (3) that no premium is payable by either party; (4) as to the length of the term of the lease yet to run; (5) that the tenant has fulfilled his obligations under the lease; and (6) that the hypothetical let is on the same terms as the actual lease. As we will see, numbers (1), (2), (5) and (6) of these may be implied without being expressly stated in the lease, but it is probably safer to include them. These are not all the assumptions that are sometimes made, but are some of the more common and important ones[1]. Let us look at these one at a time.

(1) *The assumption of a willing lessor and a willing lessee.* The best analysis of these fictional characters was made by Donaldson J in the case of *FR Evans (Leeds) Ltd v English Electric Co Ltd*[2]. Neither of them is the actual landlord or tenant but 'is a complete abstraction, and, like the mule, has neither pride of ancestry nor hope of posterity'.

> '(The willing lessor)is a hypothetical person with the right to dispose of the premises on an 18-year lease. As such, he is not afflicted by personal ills such as a cash-flow crisis or importunate mortgagees. Nor is he in the happy position of someone to whom it is largely a matter of indifference whether he lets in October 1976 or waits for the market to improve. He is, in short, a willing lessor. He wants to let the premises at a rent which is appropriate to all the factors which affect the marketability of these premises as industrial premises – for example, geographical location, the extent of the local labour

---

1 For a more detailed consideration of valuation assumptions, see *Ross & McKichan* paras 6.19–6.30.
2 (1977) 36 P & CR 185, 245 EG 657.

market, the level of local rates and the market rent of competitive premises, that is to say, premises which are directly comparable or which, if not directly comparable, would be considered as viable alternatives by a potential tenant.

'Similarly, in my judgment, the willing lessee is an abstraction – a hypothetical person actively seeking premises to fulfil needs which these premises could fulfil. He will take account of similar factors, but he too will be unaffected by liquidity problems, governmental or other pressures to boost or maintain employment in the area and so on[1].'

These parties may resemble the actual landlord and tenant, but they need not do. They are a necessary invention for our market simulation.

In *Dennis & Robinson v Kiossos Establishment*[2] the rent at review was to be a 'full yearly market rent', defined *inter alia* as being that 'at which the property might reasonably be expected to be let on the open market . . .' It was held that these words implied the assumptions of a willing lessor and lessee (as well as the fact that there would be a letting of the property and a market in which that letting was agreed), even though these assumptions were not expressly stated in the lease.

(2) *The assumption that the premises are vacant.* In the real world, as opposed to the hypothetical let, the tenant may have sublet the property and, if this was taken into account, it might affect the rental value at review. It could have the effect of either increasing or decreasing the rental value depending on the terms of the sublease and the amount of rent payable under it, and thus could either favour the landlord or the tenant. It is generally thought fairer to both parties to assume vacant possession so that any distortion by subletting will not be taken into account. The assumption of vacant possession will also mean that the tenant's fixtures and fittings, which might have added to the rental value, will also not be taken into consideration. If no assumption of vacant possession is made, the other terms of the lease may imply it[3] though not if actual sublets were in existence or contemplated at the beginning of the lease[4].

---

1 *FR Evans (Leeds) Ltd v English Electric Co Ltd* (1977) 36 P & CR 185 at 189–190, 191, 245 EG 657.
2 (1987) 282 EG 857, CA.
3 *Avon County Council v Alliance Property Co Ltd* (1981) 258 EG 1181.
4 *Forte & Co Ltd v General Accident Life Assurance Ltd* (1986) 279 EG 1227; *Laura Investment Co Ltd v Havering London Borough Council (No 2)* [1993] 08 EG 120.

If vacant possession is assumed, this could imply that the tenant had not yet carried out any preliminary works necessary to fit out the property for the purpose of his business, and he could claim he was due a reduction in rent to take account of the fact. But at the time of a rent review the property is already fitted out, and so such an assumption is not in accordance with reality. The assumption of vacant possession, therefore, is often qualified by a further assumption that the premises are fit for immediate occupation and use[1].

(3) *The assumption that no premium is payable by either party.* If a tenant pays a capital sum (or premium) at the beginning of the lease, then presumably the rent agreed may be at a lower level than it would have been without such an additional payment. Alternatively, in times of recession a *reverse* premium may be paid by the landlord (possibly in the form of a rent-free period) as an inducement to the tenant to agree to a rent that may be above the true market level[1]. In order to determine the true market rent at a rent review, therefore, it should be assumed that no such premium is payable by either party.

(4) *The term of the lease still to run.* There are at least two possible assumptions here, either that the full term of the lease should be taken into account, or only the unexpired residue. For example, let us suppose that we are at year twenty of a twenty-five year lease with five-yearly rent reviews. Depending on what assumptions are made, this can be valued either as a twenty-five year lease or a five-year lease. The rent will generally be higher for the former as a tenant will be willing to pay extra for a longer period of security of tenure. It is in the tenant's interest, therefore, that a lease for the unexpired residue should be assumed, as this reflects the reality of the situation. Landlords, however, may want an assumption that there is a lease for the full original term. This point is even more important in Scotland than in England. In England, the fact that a tenant may have a right to renew his lease under the Landlord and Tenant Act 1954 may mitigate the effect on the rental value towards the end of a lease[2]. In Scotland, there will be no such effect, and so the discrepancy may be greater. A tenant, therefore, should resist any attempt by a landlord to include an assumption that the full term of the lease has still to run.

---

1 See also section on 'Rent free periods and inducements' below.
2 *Pivot Properties Ltd v Secretary of State for the Environment* (1980) 41 P & CR 249, 256 EG 1176, CA.

A third possible assumption is that the valuer should take into account the full term of the lease, but dating from the beginning of the lease rather than the review date; however, it is doubtful whether this is effectively different from assuming a lease of the unexpired residue[1].

If the lease does not state which assumption should be made, the court will not normally imply that there is a lease for the full original term dating from the review date[2].

(5) *The assumption that the tenant has fulfilled his lease conditions.* If, for example, necessary repairs have not been carried out, this will probably have the effect of lowering the value of the property. If the lease is a full repairing one then the tenant could potentially benefit, by way of a lower rental, from having failed in a lease obligation. This would obviously be unfair to the landlord, and so an assumption in the above terms is usually made. If not included, it may be implied[3].

Another application of this principle (which may be stated as a separate assumption) is the assumption that any destruction of or damage to the property has either not occurred or has been reinstated. This will of course generally reflect the reality of the situation: even if the property is not yet reinstated at the date of the review, under the lease conditions it generally will be, from the insurance proceeds. The tenant may want a qualification that the reinstatement assumed should only cover works that fall within his repairing obligation or are covered by insurance; otherwise (for example) the reviewed rent might include the value of works which had not been carried out and which were the responsibility of the *landlord*.

(6) *The assumption that the hypothetical let is on the same terms as the original lease.* There are many terms in a lease that may affect the rental value of the property. For example, if a landlord undertakes to repair or to insure the property, he will be able to charge a higher rent than if these had been the tenant's responsibility. This

---

1 *Lynnthorpe Enterprises Ltd v Sidney Smith (Chelsea) Ltd* [1990] 40 EG 130 at 133 per Dillon LJ.

2 *Lynnthorpe supra; British Gas plc v Dollar Land Holdings plc* [1992] 12 EG 141; *Ritz Hotel (London) Ltd v Ritz Casino Ltd* [1989] 46 EG 95. See also *Prudential Assurance Co Ltd v Salisbury Handbags Ltd* [1992] 23 EG 117 and section on 'Excluding the effect of future reviews' below.

3 *Harmsworth Pension Fund Trustees v Charringtons Industrial Holdings* (1985) 49 P & CR 297.

assumption is therefore fair as it reflects the actual position of the parties. If the terms of the lease do not indicate otherwise, this is another assumption that will normally be implied, ie that the hypothetical lease is on the same terms as the actual lease (other than as to the amount of rent)[1]. However, so much can hang on minute differences of wording in individual leases, that once more it is best to include this assumption clearly and explicitly; we will see below that infelicitous wording of this assumption can sometimes have unexpected and unwanted consequences[2].

The usual disregards

Unlike the assumptions, these have a statutory origin and derive from s 34 of the Landlord and Tenant Act 1954 (which does not apply to Scotland). We have already noted that, under that Act, a tenant of business premises in England may apply for a renewal of his lease when it is due to come to an end. If he is granted a renewal, the rent is fixed subject to the disregards set out in s 34. Their statutory application is therefore when leases are due to end, rather than to rent reviews in mid-term, but the same disregards are generally incorporated into rent review clauses, both in Scotland and England. They are: (1) any effect on rent of the tenant being in occupation; (2) tenant's goodwill; (3) tenant's improvements; and (4) the effect of any licence. It is of course open to the parties to include disregards different from or additional to those in the 1954 Act, but the latter are the ones most commonly encountered.

(1) *Effect of the tenant being in occupation.* As we have already seen, the hypothetical tenant, who is willing to pay the market rent for the property he wants, is a free agent. He is not yet in occupation of the property he needs and is not committed to any one property. Any attempt to charge him more than the market rent is liable to make him go elsewhere. The actual tenant at rent review is less fortunate. He is in all probability committed to one property, the one he is occupying, because of goodwill he has built up there, because he has gone to the bother of making improvements to it, or simply because he does not want to go to the trouble and expense of moving. In the real world he might be prepared to pay over the odds to

---

1 *Basingstoke and Deane Borough Council v Host Group Ltd* (1987) 284 EG 1587, CA.
2 See section on 'Excluding the effect of future reviews' below.

stay where he is. It is generally felt that this is not a factor that the landlord should be entitled to take account of, hence the present disregard. Incidentally, at the end of a lease, as opposed to a mid-term rent review, there seems to be nothing to prevent a Scottish landlord from charging extra to let the tenant stay on. As we have seen, he is likely to be prevented from doing so in England by the operation of the 1954 Act.

(2) *Effect of the tenant's goodwill.* If a tenant has been in business for a period of time, and has been operating well, he is likely to have enhanced the value of that business by the build-up of goodwill, ie the probability that clients and customers will return to him. This value is mainly personal to the tenant, rather than something that attaches to the property he occupies. However, it is possible that some of it will rub off on the property, particularly in the case of shops, if a business of a particular kind has been carried on in the same location for a long time. A new tenant, who wanted to operate the same type of business, might well be prepared to pay extra in rent to secure that particular property. This is therefore a feasible component of the market rent, but it would be unfair at rent review to charge extra to the tenant who had provided that goodwill in the first place.

Even if not expressly stated, this disregard may be implied from the previous one, ie the disregard of the effect of the tenant being in occupation[1].

(3) *Tenant's improvements.* We saw at the beginning of the section, as illustrated in the case of *Goh Eng Wah v Yap Phooi Yin*, why it was right to disregard the effect of tenant's improvements (especially if, as in that case, the improvement involved erecting an entire building): it is unfair that a tenant should be charged for improvements twice, once when he pays the capital cost of them, and then again in the form of a higher rent. Section 34 of the 1954 Act qualifies this by requiring the value of improvements carried out under a lease obligation to the landlord to be disregarded, and this exception is usually also included in rent review clauses.

The *Goh Eng Wah* case is not an isolated one. In the leading case of *Ponsford v HMS Aerosols Ltd*[2] a factory was leased for 21 years with rent reviews at 7-year intervals. A year after the lease began, the premises burned down and were rebuilt by the landlords from

1 *Prudential Assurance Co Ltd v Grand Metropolitan Estate Ltd* [1993] 32 EG 74.
2 [1979] AC 63, [1978] 2 All ER 837.

the insurance money. However the tenants, with the landlords' permission, decided to take the opportunity afforded by the rebuilding process to incorporate substantial improvements in the building, which they paid for themselves at a cost of £31,780. When the rent came to be reviewed, the tenants claimed that any value added to the premises by them should not be taken into account in assessing the new rent. But nothing was said about this in the lease. It merely said that the tenant should pay a 'reasonable' rent for the relevant period. The House of Lords confirmed, by a majority of three to two, that this did not mean the improvements should be disregarded in assessing the rent.

In *Ravenseft Properties Ltd v Park*[1] the tenants in question erected a supermarket, half on their own land, half on land leased from someone else. It was held that the rent of the leased portion should include the value of the part of the building erected there. There are other cases of tenants suffering a similar fate[2].

Where there is no specific disregard, the tenant may nevertheless be saved by other provisions in the lease; for example, where a lease consistently distinguished between the land and the buildings erected on it, it was held that rent should be payable only in respect of the land[3] and a similar decision resulted from the rent being described in the lease as a 'ground rent'[4].

However, such phraseology should not be relied upon. The disregard of the value of tenant's improvements is probably the most important of all the valuation instructions and should always be expressly included in rent review clauses as an essential component of the hypothetical lease. A few additional points are worth noting:

(a) If a tenant enters a new lease with the same landlord, it should be made clear in that new lease that the value of improvements made during the currency of the original lease should also be disregarded. In *Brett v Brett Essex Golf Club Ltd*[5], the tenants (ie the golf club) laid out the land as a golf course and built a clubhouse. Later they entered into a completely new lease of the property with the same landlord. As the course and clubhouse were already incorporated in the property when the new lease was entered, it was held that their

---

1 [1988] 50 EG 52.
2 *Sheerness Steel Co plc v Medway Ports Authority* [1992] 12 EG 138; *Laura Investments v Havering* [1992] 24 EG 136.
3 *Ipswich Town Football Club Co Ltd v Ipswich Borough Council* [1988] 32 EG 49.
4 *Guildford Borough Council v Cobb* [1994] 16 EG 147.
5 (1986) 52 P & CR 330, 278 EG 1476, CA; see also *Panther Shop Investments Ltd v Keith Pople Ltd* (1987) 282 EG 594.

considerable value could not be disregarded as a tenant's improvement when the rent came up for review. This seems less hard on the golf club company in light of the fact that, at the time the work was done, the company was virtually owned by the landlord, Mr Brett, who held three quarters of the shares, and that these had been sold by him prior to the new lease being entered into. However, it should be noted that this was *not* a relevant legal consideration in the case and was not taken into account in reaching the decision. A limited company is a distinct legal person from its shareholders, no matter who owns the shares. The message to tenant's advisers is therefore clear: the rent review clause should provide for *all* the tenant's improvements to be disregarded, whether they were made during the current lease or an earlier one between the same parties.

(b) It is a usual provision in leases that tenants must obtain the landlord's permission before carrying out any alterations or improvements. Also, in rent review clauses it is common to qualify the disregard of improvements to the effect that the landlord's permission must have been obtained for them. Such a provision was included in the lease in *Hamish Cathie Travel England Ltd v Insight International Tours Ltd*[1]. The tenant failed to get the landlord's consent to alterations he made and it was held that their value could not be disregarded at the rent review.

(c) In *Orchid Lodge (UK) Ltd v Extel Computing Ltd*[2], the tenants carried out alterations of a very high standard (described by the landlords' lawyer as a 'Rolls-Royce job'). It was agreed that the standard disregard of tenant's improvements (incorporated from the 1954 Act) meant that the full value of these could not be taken into account; however, since it was also to be assumed that the premises were fit for use and occupation, the landlords argued that the rent should include the value of whatever hypothetical improvements (of a lower standard than those actually carried out) would have been necessary to make the premises fit for occupation for the tenants' use. The Court of Appeal held that *all* improvements, actual or hypothetical, had to be discounted; to do anything else would have involved the surveyor valuing a 'hypothetical building in a dreamland of his own'[3].

---

1 [1986] 1 EGLR 244.
2 [1991] 32 EG 57; see also *Iceland Frozen Foods plc v Starlight Investments Ltd* [1992] 07 EG 117.
3 [1991] 32 EG 57 at 59 per Dillon LJ.

(d) It should be noted that the improvements disregard does not always work in the tenant's favour: it can be in the landlord's interest also to have it included. The reason for this is that it cannot be assumed that alterations made to the property will always add to its value. They may be to a poor standard. Or they may have the effect of adapting the premises for the specialised business of the tenant, which could lower their market value to other tenants with different types of business. It would obviously be unfair to the landlord if this had the effect of lowering the rent he could charge at review. In the light of this, it would perhaps be more accurate to refer in the disregard to 'alterations' or 'alterations and improvements' rather than merely 'improvements' carried out by the tenant. This ensures a situation that is fair to both parties. Another way of dealing with this point is to include an assumption that no work has been carried out by the tenant that has diminished the rental value of the premises[1].

(4) *Effect of a licence.* This may refer to a betting or gaming licence, or a licence to sell alcohol. The theory is that any effect on rent caused by the fact that the tenant holds such a licence should be disregarded, presumably because this value is personal to the tenant and not an attribute of the property. This can be important, as it is a field where a lot of money may be involved. In *Cornwall Coast Country Club v Cardrange Ltd*[2], which related to a casino in Mayfair, the case hinged on, among other things, the precise effect of a lease provision for the disregard of the tenants' gaming licence. The tenants' estimate of the market rent was £180,000, whereas the landlords thought it should have been £3,000,000. Obviously this is an area where the stakes are high!

Excluding the effect of future reviews

We saw above that there is generally included an assumption that the hypothetical let will be on the same terms as the original let. In many clauses there has been added a qualification that the terms will be the same 'other than those relating to rent'. The obvious reason for this is that the valuer should be free to depart from the original rent stated in the lease when fixing a new rent at review.

1 See *Ross & McKichan* para 6.25.
2 [1987] 1 EGLR 146, (1987) 282 EG 1664; see also *Daejan Investments v Cornwall Coast Country Club* (1985) 273 EG 1122, 82 LS Gaz 3085 and *Ritz Hotel (London) Ltd v Ritz Casino Ltd* [1989] 46 EG 95.

However, there have been cases where it has been held that a qualification in these terms also excludes the rent review terms[1]. This can confer an unexpected (and undeserved) windfall upon the landlord. It means, for example, that a lease with rent reviews will be valued as if there were no reviews at all, and the landlord will be able to charge a premium (as much as 20 per cent in some cases) on the untrue assumption that he will have no further opportunity to raise the rent before the end of the lease.

The British Gas *rules.* In *British Gas Corporation v Universities Superannuation Scheme Ltd*[2] the Vice-Chancellor, Sir Nicholas Browne-Wilkinson made an admirable attempt to steer such interpretations back into the realms of reality. Pointing out that the logical conclusion of excluding *all* provisions relating to rent would be an absurd situation in which the valuer had to ignore the tenant's obligation to pay the rent and the landlord's remedies for non-payment, he went on to produce rules of thumb to assist interpretation in such cases:

> '(a) words in a rent exclusion provision which require *all* provisions as to rent to be disregarded produce a result so manifestly contrary to commercial common sense that they cannot be given literal effect;
>
> (b) other clear words which require the rent review provision (as opposed to all provisions of the lease) to be disregarded . . . must be given effect to, however wayward the result, and
>
> (c) subject to (b), in the absence of special circumstances it is proper to give effect to the underlying commercial purpose of a rent review clause and to construe the words so as to give effect to that purpose by requiring future rent reviews to be taken into account in fixing the open market rental under the hypothetical letting[3].'

In *Equity & Law Life Assurance plc v Bodfield Ltd*[4] the Court of Appeal approved the guidelines but emphasised that they were not mechanistic rules of construction to be applied rigidly in every case. Priority had always to be given to the actual wording of the

---

1 See eg *National Westminster Bank v Arthur Young McLelland Moores & Co* (1985) 273 EG 402.
2 [1986] 1 All ER 978, (1986) 277 EG 980.
3 [1986] 1 All ER 978 at 984.
4 [1987] 1 EGLR 124, (1987) 54 P & CR 290.

individual lease, and in that particular case and in some others sub-sequent to the *British Gas* decision, the wording was nevertheless held to be sufficiently clear to exclude the effect of future reviews[1]. There are other cases, however, where the guidelines have been successfully applied[2].

Presumption of reality. The *British Gas* case may not have been com-pletely successful in solving the above problem, but it was an impor-tant stage in a developing principle (to be applied to rent review clauses in general) that the court should apply a presumption of real-ity: in other words, unless the lease wording clearly provides other-wise, the commercial purpose of the rent review clause should prevail[3]. This welcome bias in favour of common sense may operate even where the effect of future reviews has been clearly excluded. In *Prudential Assurance Co Ltd v Salisburys Handbags Ltd*[4] the effect of this exclusion was potentially very serious for the tenants since, fol-lowing the first review in 1982, the unexpired term of the lease was 85 years. Thus the tenants faced the possibility that, at 7-yearly inter-vals throughout the currency of the lease, the rent would be deter-mined on the preposterous assumption that there would be no reviews for almost a century! It was held that such a lease was 'so far outside the experience and expertise of an ordinary valuer as to be properly regarded as extinct[5]'. Fortunately there was no express provision that the term of the hypothetical let should be the actual unexpired term of the lease; in such circumstances it was held inappropriate to assume this, and instead it was held preferable to assume a much shorter term, which might vary at each review at the discretion of the valuer, depending upon the prevailing market conditions. This would pre-sumably have the effect of the tenants paying a more realistic rent, both at the current review and those in the future.

Effect of lease restrictions

If the provisions of a lease are particularly onerous, it can have the effect of depressing the level of rent that may be fixed at a rent

---

1 *General Accident Fire & Life Assurance Corpn plc v Electronic Data Processing Co plc* (1987) 53 P & CR 189, 281 EG 65; *Prudential Assurance Co Ltd v Salisburys Handbags Ltd* [1992] 23 EG 117.
2 *British Home Stores plc v Ranbrook Properties Ltd* (1988) 16 EG 80; *Prudential Assurance Co Ltd v 99 Bishopsgate Ltd* [1991] 03 EG 120.
3 See also section on 'The effect of rent-free periods and inducements' below.
4 [1992] 23 EG 117.
5 [1992] 23 EG 117 at 119 per Mr Justice Chadwick.

review. This is because a restrictive lease is a less marketable commodity than one which is not. In a real market situation there will be fewer potential tenants willing to take it on. The same will therefore be true of the hypothetical letting, provided that it is on the same terms as the actual lease; and, as we saw above, this is normally assumed to be the case. Problems in this area have generally related to restrictive use (or user) clauses or restrictive provisions regarding alienation (ie assignation), but other onerous restrictions can have a similar effect.

This means that, when a lease is being drafted, a landlord may have to balance two conflicting priorities. From the point of view of estate management, he will want to have lease conditions that maximise his control of the situation, particularly regarding how the property may be used and to whom it may be assigned. However, if his control is too tight, this policy may rebound upon him financially when the rent comes to be reviewed.

Use clause. In *Plinth Property Investments v Mott, Hay & Anderson*[1] a lease provided that the property could only be used as an office for the purpose of the tenant's business of consulting civil engineers. The court held that, at a rent review, the arbitrator was justified in fixing a rent considerably lower than the full market rental (£89,000 instead of £130,455). This was because the lease was theoretically only assignable to other civil engineers and therefore had a lower market value than if the use had not been thus restricted. The landlords argued that if the tenants ever wanted to assign, they would be willing to waive the restriction, but this was held to be irrelevant; the tenant was entitled to assume that the landlord would insist upon his legal rights. Alternatively, if he agreed to a change he might insist on the tenant paying some financial consideration in return.

A landlord cannot get round this difficulty by unilaterally imposing a wider range of uses on the tenant purely to justify a rent increase at the rent review. In *C & A Pensions Trustees Ltd v British Vita Investments Ltd*[2] it was held that the landlords were not entitled to impose upon the tenants an additional number of authorised uses which they neither requested nor wanted.

On the other hand, if the landlord goes even further and restricts the use, not just to a narrow category, but to one named person (ie the tenant himself) it will *not* have the effect of depressing the rent

1 (1978) 38 P & CR 361.
2 (1984) 272 EG 63.

payable at review. This would create a hypothetical lease with only one possible tenant, which is incompatible with an open market simulation, and the court will be forced to amend the lease to make the rent review provisions workable. In *Law Land Co Ltd v Consumers Association Ltd*[1] the Court of Appeal held in these circumstances that the hypothetical lease should have a use clause in which the tenant's name had been deleted, thereby opening up the hypothetical market by freeing it of any use restrictions at all. However, any use restriction which is less total, and is compatible with some kind of hypothetical market, however restricted, will have a similar effect to that in the *Plinth* case[2].

Alienation. A restrictive alienation clause (eg an absolute prohibition against assignation without the landlord's consent) will have a similar effect as a restrictive use clause in depressing rent level at a review[3]. Like the latter clause, it restricts the number of potential tenants in the hypothetical market.

Avoiding the effects of restrictions on use and/or alienation. There are several methods by which a landlord may seek to avoid the above difficulty:

(1) By a provision that the landlord's consent to an assignation or subletting or (as the case may be) to a change of use 'will not be unreasonably withheld'. This will probably open up the restriction sufficiently to allow the full market rent to be charged[4].

(2) By widening the category of permitted uses. While a landlord of a shopping centre (for example) may want to limit each tenant to a particular business in order to control the trade mix, it is arguable whether this is really necessary for other types of commercial property. One way to achieve a broader control is to limit the tenant to a use within a particular class of the Town and Country Planning (Use Classes) (Scotland) Order 1989. This could (for example) prevent a change from shop to office use, or from light to heavy

---

1 (1980) 255 EG 617, CA; see also *Orchid Lodge (UK) Ltd v Extel Computing Ltd* [1991] 32 EG 57 and *Post Office Counters Ltd v Harlow District Council* [1991] 36 EG 151.

2 *James v British Crafts Centre* (1987) 282 EG 1251; *SI Pension Trustees Ltd v Ministerio de Marina de la Republica Peruana* [1988] 13 EG 48.

3 *Post Office Counters Ltd v Harlow District Council* [1991] 36 EG 151 (a reduction of 7.5 per cent); see also *Fiveways Properties Ltd v Secretary of State for the Environment* [1990] 31 EG 50 (a reduction of 5.5 per cent).

4 *Tea Trade Properties Ltd v CIN Properties Ltd* [1990] 22 EG 67.

industry, without restricting the hypothetical market in a way that would depress the rent[1].

(3) By maintaining restrictions in the use clause or alienation clause of the actual lease, but assuming more liberal provisions in the hypothetical lease for the purposes of rent review. Such an arrangement may be enforceable[2]. However, the lease wording will have to make the situation absolutely clear in order to overcome the presumption of reality, ie that the terms of the hypothetical lease will be the same as those of the actual one[3].

Other lease restrictions. Onerous provisions other than those relating to use or alienation can also have the effect of narrowing the hypothetical market. In *Norwich Union Life Insurance Society v British Railways Board*[4] the tenants' repairing obligation included a liability to 'rebuild, reconstruct or replace' the property when necessary. As the lease was for 150 years, it was held that such rebuilding by the tenants might well prove necessary and this was considered sufficiently onerous to justify a rent reduction of 27.5 per cent.

Effect of rent-free periods and inducements

Even though commercial leases tend to be lengthy, we could be forgiven for hoping that, over the years, rent review headaches might ease somewhat, as the leases which have caused all the problems are gradually replaced by the products of a new generation of lease drafters, alert to the snares of review timetables and the need for a sophisticated hypothetical letting. This may well be so, but we are involved in a subject with a possibly infinite capacity to unearth new complications. The fast-developing topic of rent-free periods and inducements provides a good illustration.

Period for fitting out etc. It has for a long time been common for landlords, at the beginning of a lease, to allow a tenant a period free of rent. Traditionally this would be for at least three months, or even

---

1 For examples of this method and some associated problems see *Wolff v Enfield London Borough Council* (1987) 281 EG 1320 and *Brewers' Company v Viewplan plc* [1989] 45 EG 153.
2 *Bovis Group Pension Fund Ltd v GC Flooring & Furnishing Ltd* (1984) 269 EG 1252; *Sheerness Steel Co plc v Medway Ports Authority* [1992] 12 EG 138.
3 *Basingstoke & Deane Borough Council v the Host Group Ltd* (1987) 284 EG 1587; *Postel Properties Ltd v Greenwell* [1992] 47 EG 106.
4 (1987) 283 EG 846.

longer, and it acknowledged the fact that there would be an initial period when the tenant would not be earning money from the property and might even be incurring some expense. If he was intending to occupy the property himself, he would need to spend some time and money fitting it out to meet his business requirements; in the case of a larger property, it might be his intention to sublet part or all of it, in which case he would need time to find subtenants.

As we have seen, the purpose of the hypothetical letting is to simulate a market situation, ie apply the valuation criteria for a new let to a mid-term rent review. It could be argued from this (and some tenants did) that, following a review, a tenant would be entitled to the same rent-free period as he would normally enjoy at the beginning of a lease; he might not be allowed a gap in his rental payments, but would be due the equivalent benefit in the form of a rent reduction. There is some logic in this, but it does not accord with reality, as a tenant, after a rent review, would not in fact normally have to fit out the property or find subtenants. Nevertheless, in *99 Bishopsgate v Prudential Assurance Co Ltd*[1] it was held by the Court of Appeal that the standard assumption of vacant possession[2] had precisely this effect:

> 'On the review of the rent of a 30-storey office building in the City, the arbitrator found that the most likely tenant would have wanted only part of the building for his own use and would have sublet the rest. He would have bargained for a rent-free period to cover the time needed to find subtenants and the rent-free period he would have to allow them to fit out their premises. Having regard to the size of the building in relation to the general supply of similar office space in the City, he would have been able to secure a 16-month rent-free period on a 14-year letting. The arbitrator therefore found that if one had to assume that the building was empty one would have to discount the rent which would have been paid by a tenant whose activities were already up and running[3].'

The judge at first instance and the Court of Appeal both agreed that this necessarily followed from the assumption of a letting with vacant possession.

1 [1985] 1 EGLR 72, (1984) 270 EG 950.
2 See above.
3 *99 Bishopsgate Ltd v Prudential Assurance Co Ltd*, as paraphrased by Hoffman LJ in *Co-operative Wholesale Society Ltd v Prudential Assurance Co Ltd* [1995] 01 EG 111 at 112.

'Fit for immediate occupation and use'. It was predictable that land-lords would not take the above lying down, and they sought to get round the problem by including an assumption that the property was 'fit for immediate occupation and use', or some such phraseology. Then some landlords tried to argue that this assumption not only had the intended effect of denying a tenant a deduction in lieu of a rent-free period, but also allowed the landlord to charge more than the market rate! After all, if the hypothetical tenant in the hypothetical open market was entering premises that were already fitted out to suit him, then maybe he should be prepared to pay more as a result. However, the courts have not been prepared to go along with this, and have held that the effect of the assumption is (as originally intended) to deprive the tenant of the right to a dis-count, without giving the landlord a bonus to which he should not be entitled[1]. This is obviously fair and reflects the reality of the sit-uation.

Inducements and headline rents. Landlords have sought other ways of getting round the above problem, eg by including an assumption 'that any rent-free period or concessionary rent or any other inducement . . . which may be offered in the case of a new letting in the open market at the relevant date of review shall have expired or been given immediately before the relevant date of review[2]'. In due course, however, such assumptions also proved to have an unin-tended effect, in this case to the advantage of landlords.

The leases which have most recently come before the courts for scrutiny were entered into before the property market went into recession towards the end of the 1980s. When they were drafted, rent-free periods were generally only granted for the reasons given above, ie to allow tenants time for fitting out and/or to find sub-tenants, and it was right that this should not allow them to claim equivalent concessions at rent review. However, with the recession the practice grew up of landlords granting extended rent-free peri-ods for a quite different reason. In order to maintain rent levels at a time when market forces might have caused them to fall, land-lords often persuaded tenants of new lets to pay 'headline' rents, above the real market level, in return for which tenants would be

---

1 *London & Leeds Estates Ltd v Paribas Ltd* [1993] 30 EG 89; see also *Iceland Frozen Foods PLC v Starlight Investments Ltd* [1992] 07 EG 117 and *Pontsarn Investments v Kansallis-Osake-Pankki* [1992] 22 EG 103.

2 *Co-operative Wholesale Society Ltd v National Westminster Bank PLC* [1995] 01 EG 111.

granted substantial rent-free periods. The length of these would vary according to the state of the market or the length of the lease, but were frequently for a period of years. The question then arising was this: could a clause designed to deny a tenant a discount at review in respect of a rent-free period for fitting-out etc, also deprive him of a discount for the other type of rent-free period? If it did, a tenant at a rent review could be saddled with a headline rent, substantially above the market level, and the landlord would receive an undeserved windfall. The reviewed rent would be fixed in comparison with those agreed for new lets, but without the benefit of any inducement that might have persuaded a new tenant to pay over the odds.

As usual, individual cases differed according to the wording of the particular leases, but it soon became clear that tenants *could*, in some circumstances, end up paying a headline rent. Several cases where this happened were taken to the Court of Appeal, which recently gave a joint judgment in respect of four of them[1]. In only one of these, where the wording allowed no other conclusion, was the tenant left paying a headline rent[2]. In its construction of the clauses, the court applied the 'presumption of reality', the principle that had been developing in recent rent review cases[3], ie that courts should favour the construction most likely to give effect to the commercial purpose of the lease:

'So, in the case of rent-free periods, it is easy to see why the parties should not wish to allow the tenant a reduction simply because the fiction of vacant possession entails that the incoming tenant would have the expense of moving in and fitting out. A clause which excludes the assumption that he would have this expense is more in accordance with the presumption of reality than one which does not. On the other hand, a clause which deems the market rent to be the headline rent obtainable after a rent-free period granted simply to disguise the fall in the rental value of the property is not in accordance with the basic purpose of a rent review clause. It enables a landlord to obtain an increase in rent without any rise in property values

---

1 *Co-operative Wholesale Society Ltd v National Westminster Bank plc; Scottish Amicable Life Assurance Society v Middleton Potts & Co; Broadgate Square plc v Lehman Brothers Ltd;* and *Prudential Nominees Ltd v Greenham Trading Ltd* [1995] 01 EG 111.
2 *Broadgate Square plc v Lehman Brothers Ltd* supra.
3 Eg *British Gas Corporation v Universities Superannuation Scheme Ltd* [1986] WLR 398; see also section on 'Excluding the effect of future reviews' above.

or fall in the value of money, but simply by reason of changes in the way the market is choosing to structure the financial packaging of the deal.

It therefore seems to me that, in the absence of unambiguous language, a court should not be ready to construe a rent review clause as having this effect[1].'

However, if the terms of a lease clearly oblige a tenant to pay a headline rent, this will be enforced, even if such an outcome was not foreseen at the time the lease was entered. A bargain is not changed because of subsequent events that were not anticipated. 'The tenant cannot complain because in changed market conditions [the lease] is more onerous than anyone would have foreseen[1]'.

This topic is still developing, but the latest formulation of the 'presumption of reality' promises to be a useful principle for the construction of rent review clauses generally.

'Upwards or downwards' valuation

One important valuation instruction remains to be considered. It is normal for landlords to include in rent review clauses a provision that any rent review should be upwards only, or, at the very least, that the rent should not fall below the current level. Until a few years ago this was not something that tenants were likely to quibble about: in the mid-1970s, when inflation was soaring, the suggestion that rental levels might sometimes fall would have seemed to be firmly in the realm of fantasy. More recently, however, there has been a severe recession in the property market. This is a timely reminder that when we are drafting a commercial or industrial lease we are producing a contract that may determine the parties' rights and obligations many decades into the future. It would be a rash person who would try to predict the economic circumstances likely to prevail over such a period. The rent review clause, as well as the rest of the lease, should be framed as flexibly as possible, so as to cope with as many different types of circumstances as possible.

With this in mind, the tenant should insist that any reviews may be either upwards _or_ downwards. It has recently been held that the

---

1 _Co-operative Wholesale Society v National Westminster Bank plc_ [1995] 01 EG 111 at 113 per Hoffman LJ.

inclusion of such a provision in a new lease is not unfair[1]. A corollary of this is that the tenant, as well as the landlord, should have the right to call for a review at the review date; otherwise, if rent levels were to fall, the landlord might conveniently 'forget' about the review. Landlords, of course, may resist the inclusion of these modifications, but tenants should do their best to insist.

4. SETTLING OF DISPUTES: ARBITER OR EXPERT

If nothing else has been gained from the preceding sections, the reader will at least be stripped of any illusion that drafting a rent review clause could be a simple and uncomplicated matter. If we do not have valuation instructions, for example, we are liable to produce a rent that in some sense may be a market rent, but is liable to be unfair to at least one of the parties. However, without such instructions, we would still have a rent review clause that was operational. It would still produce a result, however inequitable. On the other hand, without some formula for deciding between the parties in the event of disagreement, we are in danger of producing a rent review clause that is totally unenforceable. The courts are liable to declare it void from uncertainty. Arguably, then, the machinery for independent determination of the rent is the single most important element in any rent review clause.

It seems incredible that there might actually have been cases where clauses provided for a rent to be 'agreed between the parties' and left it at that. Nothing is more predictable than that the landlord and tenant are liable to disagree about this, so where do they go from there? Yet there have been several such cases in England, both in relation to options to renew and mid-term rent reviews. Sometimes such a provision has been held void from uncertainty[2], sometimes a workable formula has been written into the contract by the court[3], and sometimes the rent has been left as it was[4].

In the Scottish case of *Crawford v Bruce*[5] a 10-year lease provided that the rent should be £3,250 'with a review of the rent at the

---

1 *Forbouys v Newport Borough Council* [1994] 24 EG 156.
2 *Kings Motors (Oxford) Ltd v Lax* [1969] 3 All ER 665, [1970] 1 WLR 426.
3 *Brown v Gould* [1972] Ch 53; *Beer v Bowden* (1975) 237 EG 41; *Thomas Bates & Son Ltd v Wyndhams (Lingerie) Ltd* (1979) 39 P & CR 517.
4 *King v King* (1980) 41 P & CR 311, 255 EG 1205.
5 1992 SLT 524.

expiry of each three-year period'. After reviewing the English authority, the court decided that it could only amend the contract on the ground of necessity, in order to give it efficacy. Here, although the above rent review provision was void from uncertainty, there was no hiatus or gap that had to be filled by the court in order to make the contract workable. It was consistent with the terms of the lease that the initial rent, if unaltered by a review, should remain payable for the full term of the lease.

Yet again we have a situation where the moral is plain: it is absolutely essential to have some means of fixing the rent independently of the parties themselves.

In the context of a hypothetical letting this is usually achieved by providing for disputes to be referred either to an arbiter or an expert. Sometimes a lease will allow a landlord to choose either. What is the difference between them?

The first point to note is that we are not talking about different types of individual. In rent review cases, each is likely to be a chartered surveyor. The difference lies in the role that he is called upon to play. In neither case is it advisable for a lease to name a particular individual: the person selected may have retired or died even before the first rent review, and if not will require considerable longevity to survive to the last rent review of some leases. There should therefore be some formula for selecting a person. The most common one is to provide that the parties will select an arbiter or expert and that, failing their agreement, he will be selected by the Chairman for the time being of the Scottish Branch of the Royal Institution of Chartered Surveyors.

The difference between an arbiter and an expert is that an arbiter performs a quasi-judicial function, hearing submissions and expert testimony put forward by both parties. An expert, on the other hand, is simply asked to carry out the professional task of making a valuation. Using an expert has the advantage of comparative speed and cheapness. However, there is a danger of choosing what has come to be called an 'eccentric expert', who may reach a valuation far removed from what either the landlord or the tenant contemplated. There will normally be no appeal against his decision[1], although it is possible that he could be sued for professional negligence[2]. The

---

1 *Nikko Hotels (UK) Ltd v MEPC plc* [1991] 28 EG 86; *Pontsarn Investments v Kansallis-Osaki-Pankki* [1992] 22 EG 103. But see also *Postel Properties & Daichilire (London) v Greenwell* [1992] 47 EG 106.
2 *Campbell v Edwards* [1976] 1 All ER 785, [1976] 1 WLR 403, CA; regarding the liability generally of arbiter and expert, see *Ross & McKichan* para 6.48.

reason for a bad decision by an expert may be incompetence, or simply the fact that he was not sufficiently acquainted with the area in question. This may also be true of an arbiter, but at least the nature of the arbitration process is liable to ensure that he is properly informed before he reaches a decision.

This at any rate is the distinction as it is normally formulated in relation to England. It is often assumed that the position in Scotland is roughly the same. However, we must not forget about the considerable differences in the arbitration law of the two countries[1]. In England, arbitrations are almost entirely regulated by statute[2]. In Scotland, however, although there are certain areas where statutory arbitrations occur (under the Agricultural Holdings (Scotland) Act 1991, for example), it is mainly a common law matter, with some relatively minor statutory intrusions[3]. It has been suggested by some commentators that the nature of arbitration under Scots law is such that, in rent review clauses in Scottish leases, a reference to a decision by an expert is a *de facto* arbitration, unless the expert's role is limited absolutely to that of valuer, without any power to decide between conflicting sets of facts or on points of law[4]. Nevertheless, the distinction between arbiter and expert appears to be recognised in practice in Scotland.

As mentioned earlier[5], there is a limited right in Scottish arbitrations to appeal by stated case to the Court of Session on points of law. However, this can only be done during the course of the arbitration, not after the arbiter's decision has been made. Moreover, this right can be contracted out of, and often is[6]. Apart from that, an arbiter's award can sometimes be challenged on grounds other than the merits of the case, eg where the arbiter has an interest or there has been a procedural irregularity[7]. Unlike an expert, an arbiter cannot normally be liable for professional negligence[8].

In *Grahame House Investments Ltd v Secretary of State for the Environment*[9], a surveyor agreed to act as an arbiter in a rent review

---

1 See pt 1 above.
2 Arbitration Acts 1950 and 1979.
3 Arbitration (Scotland) Act 1894; Administration of Justice (Scotland) Act 1972, s 3.
4 See ED Buchanan, 'Rent Review Clauses in Commercial Leases', Journal of the Law Society of Scotland (Workshop Section) p 369 (July 1983); *Ross & McKichan* para 6.46.
5 See pt 1 above.
6 Administration of Justice (Scotland) Act 1972, s 3; see also pt 1 above.
7 See *Fountain Forestry Holdings Ltd v Sparkes* 1983 SLT 853.
8 See *Ross & McKichan* para 4.68.
9 1985 SLT 502.

dispute having, on the same day, accepted an appointment to act as an independent expert in relation to other premises owned by the same landlord in the same office building. In a stated case, the tenants challenged the arbiter's impartiality, as he began the arbitration having already issued his decision as expert for the other premises. It was held that he was not disqualified from acting as arbiter. In England it has been held that the findings of another arbitrator are hearsay and therefore inadmissable as evidence in an arbitration[1].

5. PROBLEMS OF CONSTRUCTION

In the introduction to this chapter, we noted that it is difficult to generalise about rent review case law because every case is in essence concerned with interpreting the wording of an individual lease, and in theory it is possible for no two leases to have wording that was exactly the same. And so, while we have rightly concentrated so far on those areas where some general principles *can* be drawn, there remain a large number of rent review cases which turned upon unique points of construction relating to the wording of the lease in question[2]. Since, by their nature, such cases have limited value as precedents, little would be gained by cataloguing them at length. However, before moving on we will briefly look at a couple of examples, if only to illustrate how devoting insufficient care to the wording of a rent review clause can have bizarre and sometimes disastrous consequences.

In *Holicater Ltd v Grandred Ltd*[3] the rent review clause provided *inter alia*:

'Unless the landlord and tenant shall agree by not later than three months prior to the review date the market rent payable from a review date such market rent shall be determined . . . by a person acting as an Expert . . . on the application of either the Landlord or the Tenant made at any time before the said next review date or the expiration of the term as the case may be (time being of the essence).'

---

1 *Land Securities v Westminster City Council* [1992] 44 EG 153.
2 See eg *GRE Compass v Master and Wardens and Brethren and Sisters of the Guild of Fraternity of the Blessed Mary the Virgin of the Mystery of Drapers of the City of London (a body corporate)* [1994] EGCS 97.
3 [1993] 23 EG 129.

The tenants contended that the landlords had lost their right to review because they failed to refer the dispute to an expert by the review date. While this was probably in accordance with the lease draftsman's intention, the Court of Appeal held that, in relation to the phrase 'the said next review date', the word 'said' had to be rejected as meaningless, and so the landlord had until the next review date to refer to the expert, ie another five years.

The above result was not exactly disastrous for either party, though there is certainly something odd about time being declared to be of the essence in relation to a five-year deadline! However, more serious consequences followed from the decision in *Stedman v Midland Bank plc*[1], where the lease was for a period of 71 years and the disputed part of the rent review clause read as follows:

> 'PAYING therefor during the first year of the said term the yearly rent of eight hundred pounds rising by annual increases of Ten pounds each to eight hundred and forty pounds in the fifth year and thereafter at a rent to be agreed or in default of agreement to be fixed by an Arbitrator to be appointed by the parties hereto.'

The landlord claimed that, after the first five years, for which the increases had already been determined, there were to be annual reviews throughout the lease. Once again, this was probably what the hapless lawyer responsible for the wording had intended. However, the Court of Appeal decided that the actual words used could only mean that there would be a once-and-for-all review at year 5, after which the rent would stay the same for the remaining 66 years of the lease!

6. ALTERNATIVE METHODS OF RENT REVIEW

Having now seen the scope for unforeseen complication, untoward expense and general grief inherent in the rent review procedures we have examined so far, it is tempting to look for some other method, for some magical formula that will calculate the new rent without worry or fuss, and without any room for disagreement between the parties. Is such a thing possible? If so, why has it not been adopted wholesale by landlords and tenants, abandoning the hypothetical let and all its paraphernalia to masochists and madmen? The

---

1 [1990] 03 EG 767.

answer is that there *are* other methods but, as usual, they also have drawbacks. Let us look at two such alternatives, which sometimes crop up in Britain, but more often abroad.

Index linked rents

This is a method by which the rent is varied simply by reference to a published index, such as the Retail Price Index. It is therefore jacked up automatically in line with inflation, in a completely mechanistic way, without there being any scope for ambiguity or argument. What could be simpler? Gone are the complex valuation instructions of our hypothetical let and their endless problems of interpretation; gone is the delay, worry and expense of resorting to arbiter or expert. Instead, we make a simple mathematical calculation and the job is done.

Unfortunately, if we substitute for a system involving fallible human judgment one in which there is no human judgment involved at all, the result is not necessarily better. First of all, rent increases may not always be in line with the general level of inflation: sometimes rents lag behind other prices, at other times they shoot ahead. But there is no government index that measures only property values. There are several privately produced indexes that do this, but even they are not sufficiently sophisticated to take into account, except in very broad terms, all the regional variations and other local factors that could affect the market value of a particular property. The result, therefore, may be easy to calculate, but it is probably not the market rent. Certainty has been achieved at the expense of accuracy.

Moreover, to frame a clause that works properly involves some sophistication of drafting; index linking, therefore, does not offer immunity from litigation over the meaning of clauses[1]. If there are few reported cases, it is probably because such clauses are still fairly rare. On the other hand, index-linking of rents is quite common in some other countries, including several of Britain's partners in the European Community.

Turnover rents

This is a method by which the rent is linked to a percentage of the tenant's gross turnover in his business. The landlord's 'cut'

---

1 For a brief review of some of the decided cases, see HW Wilkinson 'Rents and the Retail Price Index', New Law Journal March 27 1987, p 288; see also *Wyndham Investments Ltd v Motorway Tyres & Accessories Ltd* [1991] 30 EG 65.

therefore varies according to whether the tenant is doing well or badly. Turnover rents are common in America and are increasingly being used in Britain too.

This method can also be criticised for not necessarily achieving a market rent. It could result, for example, in an anomalous situation where there were two adjoining identical shops with quite different rents, simply because one tenant was trading more successfully than the other. The one paying more might well feel that he was being unfairly penalised for his success. On the other hand, even the most competently-run business can hit bad times, and a turnover rent can cushion the effect of a difficult period by easing the rent burden when takings are down. Nor is it necessarily correct to think of the landlord's percentage as unearned income. Having a stake in their tenants' success provides landlords with an incentive to provide better services and generally be more interested in looking after their tenants' interests.

Another problem with turnover rents is the difficulty of obtaining an accurate estimate of a tenant's turnover: apart from procedural problems (what to do about returned goods, for example) the tenant has an obvious motive to falsify the figures. This problem has been resolved in some modern shopping centres, where the presence of all the tenants within one building allows their tills to be linked to a common computer, monitored by the landlord.

It has also been observed that the use of turnover rents in America can lead to the rather ruthless practice of linking the level of turnover to the landlord's right to terminate a lease prematurely: in other words, if the tenant's performance is not satisfactory, he can be replaced by one who provides the landlord with a bigger cut. It has been pointed out in England that the protection of the Landlord and Tenant Act 1954 might prevent this practice. It should no longer be necessary to add that this protection does not apply in Scotland, so perhaps tenants north of the Border should regard turnover rents with more caution.

Finally, we should note that it is not the normal practice for rents to be calculated *entirely* by reference to turnover. Usually there is a base rent which will be topped up by a percentage of the tenant's turnover. Since the base rent will probably be subject to review by the normal method, this means that turnover rents are not really an alternative method of calculation, but merely a supplementary one. They may have their attractions, but they are not going to avoid the incidence of disputes and the need to resort to arbitration, and sometimes, also to litigation.

7. CONCLUSION

The reader, if he has stayed the course so far, will probably by now be contemplating an alternative career, or will at least have retreated to some area of the law where he need never have to draft a rent review clause. Fortunately, the lease drafter is not entirely without assistance. Model rent review clauses have been drawn up to assist him. In England, two such models have been provided by the Royal Institution of Chartered Surveyors (in conjunction with the English Law Society), and by the Incorporated Society of Valuers and Auctioneers respectively. However, these clauses should be regarded with some caution in Scotland: they contain much terminology that is peculiarly English, and of course they have taken no account of the significant differences in Scots law which we have noted in this chapter. Better alternatives for the Scottish lawyer would be the styles of commercial lease (including rent review provisions) produced by Messrs Ross and McKichan and by Professor Halliday[1].

---

1 *Ross & McKichan* Appendix 1; Halliday *Conveyancing Law and Practice* Vol III (1987), paras 29.41–29.43.

11 Service Charges

1. GENERAL

Nature of service charges

Service charges arise in properties where a number of tenants share common areas, facilities or parts of a building, and the landlord provides common services for them. The kinds of service that can be involved are extensive, but typically include things like insurance, cleaning of common parts, provision of staff, gardening, heating and air conditioning, security, fire prevention, refuse disposal, maintenance and provision of car parks, toilet facilities and administration and management[1].

Most of the above are what one might expect from the meaning of the word 'service'. However, items normally included in service charges extend some way beyond this usual meaning. We have seen that the most common type of commercial and industrial lease nowadays is the full repairing and insuring lease, one of the main reasons for this being the desire of financial institutions investing in property to keep their rental income as free as possible of overheads. Where the property is self-contained, this can be achieved simply by making the tenant responsible for repairs, insurance and any other outgoings. In the case of properties in multiple occupation, however, it would be quite impractical for the tenants to be responsible for maintaining the fabric of the property in a piecemeal fashion.

It therefore makes sense for the landlord, not only to provide common services of the type mentioned in the first paragraph, but also to undertake the maintenance and repair of the common parts

---

1 For a more detailed consideration of service charges from the Scottish viewpoint, see Ross & McKichan *Drafting and Negotiating Commercial Leases in Scotland* (2nd edn, 1993) ch 11.

of the property. Thereafter he will recover a proportion of the cost of these services and repairs from each tenant. We are not therefore dealing with a negligible item of a tenant's expenditure, and it is necessary to include a properly drafted provision in the lease to regulate the situation.

Properties subject to service charges

Service charges can arise in different types of property. In England they occur regularly in residential property, ie in blocks of flats. In Scotland there is little tradition of long leases of residential property, and, as we have already seen, new residential leases of more than twenty years have not been possible since 1974[1]. However, we may find service charges in Scotland in residential lets of shorter duration. They also occur regularly in industrial estates and in office blocks, where services undertaken by the landlord help to provide a pleasant working environment for the tenants and their staff. However, service charges are probably most important in shopping centres. There the services are being provided, not just for the tenants and their workers, but predominantly for members of the public visiting a centre. A high standard of service is therefore required to attract the public into a centre, with the result that service charges for tenants in shopping centres tend to be relatively high.

A number of important issues need to be dealt with in drafting a service charge clause. These include the tenant's obligation (including the method of apportionment between tenants and the method of collection), the landlord's obligation and, finally, whether or not a sinking fund should be set up.

2. THE TENANT'S OBLIGATION

Types of service charge

The clause will usually specify the types of service the tenant will have to pay for – insurance, cleaning, heating etc – and will also typically give the landlord discretion in determining the standard of service provided. They will also include a 'sweeper' clause (eg 'any other services provided by the landlord from time to time', etc), to

---

1 Land Tenure Reform (Scotland) Act 1974, s 8; see also ch 6, pt 4 above.

cover any services that might have been omitted. This is reasonable, as it is often difficult to predict in advance every service that might in the future be necessary or desirable. The tenant would be advised, however, to make sure that the 'sweeper' clause is not too general in nature and is suitably qualified so as not to give the landlord unlimited discretion in extending the scope of charges. For example, the 'sweeper' clause could be limited to those services that are 'reasonably necessary' or 'in keeping with the principles of good estate management'. It is advisable for some such limitation of the landlord's discretion to be included in the clause; however, if it were to be omitted, some protection may be provided by the law. In *Finchbourne Ltd v Rodrigues*[1], the court implied a term into the lease that the service charges recoverable from the tenant should be 'fair and reasonable'. 'In my opinion,' said Cairns LJ, 'the parties cannot have intended that the landlords should have an unfettered discretion to adopt the highest conceivable standard and to charge the tenant with it[2].' On the other hand, in the Scottish case of *WW Promotions (Scotland) Ltd v De Marco*[3], where the certificate of the landlord's surveyor was declared in the lease to be final, it was held that it was therefore up to the surveyor to decide on reasonableness, and that his certificate could not thereafter be challenged by the tenant on the ground that the charges were unreasonable. It is safer for the tenant, therefore, to try and get his protection from unreasonable charges built into the lease terms.

Apportionment of service charges

One of the most problematic areas concerns the method of apportioning the service charges among the various tenants in the property. One common method is to base it on the floor area occupied by each tenant, and another is to tie it to the rateable values of the various units. The former has the disadvantages that it could lead to disputes regarding measurement, and also complaints from tenants of larger units that the extra amount they pay is disproportionate to the extra benefits they receive from the provision of the services. The rateable value system caters for this in that larger

---

1 [1976] 3 All ER 581, CA; see also *Jacob Isbiski & Co Ltd v Goulding & Bird Ltd* [1989] EG 236 and *Lloyd's Bank plc v Bowker Orford* [1992] 31 EG 68.
2 [1976] 3 All ER 581, CA at 587.
3 1988 SLT (Sh Ct) 43; see also *Victor Harris (Gentswear) Ltd v the Wool Warehouse (Perth) Ltd* 1995 SCLR 577.

units are valued proportionately less. However, a system of apportionment based upon rateable value has other drawbacks. In a new development, the rateable values will not be known at the outset and may have to be estimated. Also, they would be subject to individual appeals by tenants, which could lead to uncertainty and confusion. A third method, which combines the virtues and avoids some of the difficulties of the above, is to apportion according to 'weighted' floor area. This involves basing the apportionment on floor area, but incorporating a formula whereby larger areas are given a 'discount' and thereby pay proportionately less.

Instead of including a formula in the lease for working out the proportion, the landlord may wish to avoid uncertainty by stating a fixed percentage of total services for which the tenant is liable. He may have worked this out on the basis of floor area or rateable value or otherwise, but the tenant will have agreed to the percentage when signing the lease and so (theoretically) there should be no grounds for dispute. However, the inflexibility of this may itself lead to problems, eg if the landlord should later want to add to the property. In *Pole Properties Ltd v Feinberg*[1], the defendant, a tenant in a block of flats, was due according to his lease to pay two-sevenths of any increase in the cost of central heating fuel. The landlords later extended the property by building a new block of flats on an adjoining site and making the central heating system common to both blocks. A new proportion had therefore to be worked out for the tenant's share, which he contested because it took no account of the fact that the new flats were more intensively heated, with radiators in more of their rooms. The court held that the situation had so radically altered that the terms of the lease no longer applied. The tenant would have to pay what was fair and reasonable in the circumstances, ie according to the heating facilities provided for him. Incidentally, this pinpoints a criticism that could be made of all the apportionment methods mentioned above: that they do not necessarily reflect the amount of the services which the respective tenants actually use or enjoy.

Methods of collection

The lease will also require to specify the method of collection. This can either be done by the landlord charging a higher rent, to include the provision of services, or by providing that the cost of

1 (1982) 43 P & CR 121, 259 EG 417, CA.

services may be recovered as a separate charge. The former method has the attraction of simplicity and is used widely in England, as it makes it easier to enforce the English remedy of forfeiture for non-payment of rent. This does not apply in Scotland, but including service charges as part of rent would at least make the landlord's hypothec available for their recovery[1]. However, for accounting and tax purposes, it is probably better from the landlord's point of view to have service charges shown as a separate item.

Certificate by surveyor or accountant

Finally, it is common for landlords to specify in the clause relating to service charges that the amount of the charge will be as certified by his surveyor or accountant. It is sometimes also provided that his surveyor will settle any disputes regarding service charges. Both of these practices, as well as being possibly unfair to the tenant, can be dangerous for the landlord. In *Finchbourne Ltd v Rodrigues*[2], the surveyors' certificates were held to be invalid because the surveyors were essentially the same persons as the lessors. This is not quite the same as the landlord having the certificates issued by a firm of surveyors who have been engaged as his agents. As we saw above, in *W W Promotions (Scotland) Ltd v De Marco*[3], the Scottish courts at any rate are prepared to hold such certificates to be valid; the Sheriff Principal in that case suggested that it might have been better for the surveyor to have been more independent, but did not express his opinion more strongly than that. However, it is probably safer for the landlord, as well as fairer on the tenant, to have certificates issued by someone other than the firm of surveyors who manage the property.

These cases concerned leases where the surveyor's function was to certify the *amount* of the charge. If the lease goes even further and provides for the landlord's surveyor to settle disputes the position is less clear. In *Re Davstone Estates Ltd's Leases*[4], such a provision was held to be void because it involved the surveyor in interpretation of the lease terms; that was a question of law, which was properly the jurisdiction of the courts. On the other hand, in

1 See ch 4, pt 2 above.
2 [1976] 3 ALL ER 581, CA; see also *Concorde Graphics Ltd v Andromeda Investments Ltd* (1982) 265 EG 386 and *Skilleter v Charles* [1992] 13 EG 113.
3 1988 SLT (Sh Ct) 43.
4 [1969] 2 Ch 378, [1969] 2 All ER 849.

Nikko Hotels (UK) Ltd v MEPC plc[1] (a rent review case) it was held that an accountant acting as an independent expert *did* have the power to decide questions of lease construction, and the *Davstone* decision was criticised as being too wide in its application.

3. THE LANDLORD'S OBLIGATION

Provision of services

The tenant's agent should ensure that the lease, as well as obliging the tenant to pay for services, actually contains an undertaking by the landlord to provide the services in the first place. One would have thought that this would be implied – it does not make much sense to charge the tenant for services he may not have received – but this is not necessarily the case. In the *Duke of Westminster v Guild*[2], the lease obliged the tenant to contribute to the maintenance of a drain, but there was no corresponding obligation on the part of the landlord actually to do the maintenance, and the court refused to imply a condition to this effect into the lease. It will depend, of course, on the wording of the lease in each individual case, but it is better if the tenant's agent makes sure that the landlord's obligation is clearly stated.

Unfair Contract Terms Act

It is also worth noting that the Unfair Contract Terms Act 1977 applies to the provision of services by landlords. The Act does not apply to leases in general, but *does* specifically apply to services connected with the use of land[3]. This means that if the landlord purports in the lease to exempt himself from the breach of any obligation, arising from the express or implied terms of the contract, to take reasonable care or exercise reasonable skill in his provision of services, such a disclaimer may be ineffective. If his breach relates to death or personal injury, the exemption clause will be totally void; in other cases, the court will only enforce it if it considers the

---

1 [1991] 28 EG 86; see also *Pontsarn Investments v Kansallis-Osake-Pankki* [1992] 22 EG 103.
2 [1985] QB 688, [1984] 3 All ER 144, CA.
3 Unfair Contract Terms Act 1977, s 15.

exemption to have been fair and reasonable when the contract was entered into[1].

A tenant's agent, however, should not rely on the effect of the Act, which may be uncertain in view of the court's discretion to determine when a clause is fair and reasonable. Instead, he should resist any attempt of the landlord to include such disclaimers in his service charge clause.

4. SINKING FUNDS

Some leases provide for the establishment of a sinking fund, ie a common fund to which all tenants contribute and from which service charges are paid. This can be advantageous to tenants in that it will spread the load of charges evenly over a number of years. It is also fairer where there is a turnover of tenants. It means that one particular tenant will not have to bear the whole of a particularly heavy expense because he happens to be the one in occupation at the time it occurs; for example, in the case of repairs, it is reasonable that his predecessors and successors in the property should also contribute. A sinking fund can also provide the landlord with a build-up of capital to pay for major replacement work in the premises: it is obviously easier to pass such costs on to the tenant if it is done in a piecemeal fashion.

However, from a landlord's point of view, sinking funds also have disadvantages. The landlord may be liable for income tax or corporation tax on the sinking fund payments. This can be partially avoided by setting up a trust fund, but even then any income on the trust may be taxable. As a result of these tax complications, sinking funds have not been widely used in relation to commercial properties[2].

---

1 Ibid s 16.
2 For a more detailed discussion of sinking funds and their tax implications, see *Ross & McKichan* paras 11.24–11.32.

12 Agricultural Holdings

1. INTRODUCTION

Since the late nineteenth century, leases of agricultural holdings have been subject to statutory control by a series of enactments generally known as the Agricultural Holdings Acts. The broad object of this legislation is to encourage tenants to farm well and to make any necessary improvements to their holdings, while at the same time ensuring that the landlords receive a proper economic rent. At common law, if a tenant carried out any improvements to his holding, eg adding new buildings or draining fields, these would accrue to the landlord at the end of the lease[1] The lease contract might provide for him to be compensated for improvements, but there was no automatic right to this. As a result of this, in the last years of his lease, the tenant had no real incentive to farm well: not only might he be reluctant to add necessary improvements to the holding, but he would be tempted to overwork the land, leaving it infertile for his successor. It was therefore in the interests of both landlords and tenants for the matter to be regulated in some way.

This is mainly achieved by giving tenants, in many cases, the statutory right to stay in occupation beyond the expiry date contracted for in the lease, even where the landlord wants to regain possession of the farm; in other words, the tenant is granted extended security of tenure. In certain other cases, the landlord *will* be able to regain possession when the lease is due to end, but the tenant will be entitled to compensation for any improvements he has made to the holding. Because he is being forced to move, he will often (though not always) also have the right to disturbance compensation, as well as various other compensation claims.

The rights to security of tenure and to compensation form the foundation of the tenant's statutory protection. However, the legislation affects the landlord/tenant relationship in several other

1 See ch 7, pt 4 above.

respects. As well as regulating the terms of farm leases in a number of important ways, it provides comprehensive rules for the settlement of disputes by arbitration. Finally, it is recognised that much of the benefit that a tenant has worked for may be lost if the lease is terminated by his premature death; and so there is provision, in certain circumstances, for the tenancy of a holding to be inherited after his death by a member of the tenant's family. All of these matters are given consideration below.

Crofts and other small landholdings, although not expressly excluded, are primarily regulated by their own separate legislation. These provisions are rather complex, but a brief outline of them is given at the end of the chapter.

The law of agricultural holdings is broadly the same in both England and Scotland, although Scotland has its own separate legislation. The various Acts affecting Scotland have now been consolidated in the Agricultural Holdings (Scotland) Act 1991.

There would not be much point in providing the tenant with such extensive statutory protection if it was possible for a farm lease to include a clause contracting out of the provisions of the Act. Contracting out is not universally prohibited, but is expressly forbidden in respect of many of the Act's more important functions; in some other cases, although there has been no express prohibition, the courts have held that the mandatory wording of the provision has precluded contracting out. It was suggested by the House of Lords in *Johnson v Moreton*[1], that, in the latter cases, the underlying distinction is between those provisions that affect only the private contractual interests of the parties (where contracting out is allowed), and those that involve the public interest, in the welfare of the tenant and in the proper farming of the land (where contracting out is forbidden). Contracting out is prohibited, for example, in respect of the provisions for a written notice to quit[2], entitlement to compensation[3], arbitration[4], and most importantly of all, security of tenure[5].

As well as the wide scope which the Act provides for reference of disputes to arbitration, considerable jurisdiction is given to the Scottish Land Court. This is a court of special jurisdiction, which also has wide jurisdiction in relation to crofts and small landholdings, which were the main reason for its creation in 1911. The

1 [1980] AC 37, [1978] 3 All ER 37, HL
2 Agricultural Holdings (Scotland) Act 1991, s 21(1).
3 Ibid s 53.
4 Ibid s 61(1).
5 *Johnson v Moreton* [1980] AC 37, [1978] 3 All ER 37, HL.

Scottish Land Court should *not* be confused with the Lands Tribunal for Scotland, which is an administrative tribunal with quite different functions, eg variation of land obligations[1] and settlement of disputes over compulsory purchase claims. The legislation relating to the constitution and proceedings of the Scottish Land Court has now been consolidated in the Scottish Land Court Act 1993.

Definition of agricultural holding

The statutory definition may be broadly summed up as a lease of land used for agriculture as part of a trade or business[2]. Leases where the tenant is an employee of the landlord are excluded. 'Agriculture' is given a very comprehensive definition, but generally includes all arable, pastoral and livestock-raising activity[3]. 'Lease' is defined as 'a letting of land for a term of years, or for lives, or for lives and years, or from year to year[3]. Market gardens are included, but are subject to certain special provisions regarding compensation and fixtures[4].

The Act does not allow agricultural leases for a term of less than a year. If an agricultural lease is entered into purporting to be for less than a year, and it is one to which the Act would otherwise apply, it will take effect as a lease from year to year, bringing it within the ambit of the Act. There are one or two limited exceptions to this, namely grazing or mowing lets for a specified part of the year, or where the Secretary of State has granted permission for a let of less than a year. In these cases the Act will not apply, either to these excepted tenants or to any of their subtenants[5]. Also, if the lease is an informal one for an unspecified term, there is a possibility that the Act may be excluded because the lease does not meet the statutory definition of a lease in this context[6].

The Secretary of State is only likely to give permission for leases of less than a year, thereby excluding the Act, if the public interest is in some way involved, or if granting a longer lease is in some way unreasonable or impracticable. For example, in a new town, it is normal for the development corporation to begin acquiring land

---

1 See ch 6, pt 3 above.
2 Agricultural Holdings (Scotland) Act 1991, s 1.
3 Ibid s 85(1).
4 Ibid ss 40–42.
5 Ibid s 2.
6 *Stirrat v Whyte* 1967 SC 265, 1968 SLT 157; but see also *Morrison-Low v Paterson* 1985 SLT (HL) 255 and *Gairneybridge Farm Ltd and King, Applicants* 1974 SLT (Land Ct) 8.

within its designated area well in advance of the land being actually developed. Since much of this is likely to be farmland, it makes sense to lease it back to the farmers until such time as it is required; however, it would rather negate the point of this if the farmers could eventually claim security of tenure or lodge large compensation claims. In such a case, the Secretary of State will grant permission for the development corporation to grant farm leases for less than a year. There is no reason why such a lease cannot be renewed if the land is still not required by the termination date, provided the original term is for less than a year (eg 364 days) and a notice to quit is sent; if it is allowed to run on by tacit relocation, the Act will probably apply.

2. GENERAL PROVISIONS REGARDING LEASE TERMS

Written leases[1]

Where there is no written lease embodying the terms of a tenancy, either party may require the other to enter into a written agreement for this purpose. This should include the basic terms included in Schedule 1 of the 1991 Act, as well as the provisions regarding maintenance of fixed equipment (see below). If, therefore, there is a written lease, but it does not incorporate these terms, either party may likewise require the other to enter into an amended lease that does. Six months written notice should be given by the party requiring the lease, or the amendment, failing which the terms of the lease will be referred to arbitration. In the case of *Grieve & Sons v Barr*[2], it was held that improbative writings validated by homologation or *rei interventus* amounted to a written lease for the purpose of the Act[3].

The basic lease terms laid down by Schedule 1 are as follows:

(1) The names of the parties.

(2) Particulars of the holding, with sufficient description to identify its extent, by reference to a map or plan of the fields and other parcels of land.

(3) The duration of the let, or durations if different for different parts of the holding.

1 Agricultural Holdings (Scotland) Act 1991, s 4.
2 1954 SC 414, 1954 SLT 261.
3 But see ch 2, pt 1 above.

(4) The rent and the dates on which it is payable.

(5) An undertaking by the landlord to reinstate or replace any building on the holding damaged by fire, if this is required by the rules of good estate management. The landlord is also required to insure all such buildings for their full value. The insurance requirement does not apply to government departments or other landlords who, with the approval of the Secretary of State, have made provision for defraying the cost of such reinstatement; the reason for this is that landlords, such as the government, who own a large amount of property, may find that bearing the cost of any fire damage themselves is cheaper than paying the necessary insurance premiums.

(6) An undertaking by the tenant, so far as required by the rules of good husbandry, to return the full equivalent manurial value of any harvested crops destroyed by fire, which were grown on the holding for consumption there. The tenant is also required to insure all such harvested crops, as well as dead stock, though there is a similar exemption as in (5) where the tenant is a government department or the Secretary of State's permission has been given.

The first four of these conditions, of course, are basically the essential provisions that any lease must have at common law[1]. They would therefore have been legally necessary, even if the Act had not specifically included them.

Maintenance of fixed equipment[2]

The Act provides for certain maintenance provisions to be included in every lease of an agricultural holding. The landlord is bound, before the commencement of the lease, to put the fixed equipment in a thorough state of repair and to provide the necessary buildings and other equipment. 'Fixed equipment' is defined in s 85(1) of the 1991 Act and, broadly speaking, means all permanent buildings or structures necessary for the holding, including farm buildings, fences, hedges and dykes, gates, ditches, drains, service roads and electrical equipment, among others. Both landlord and tenant have maintenance obligations in relation to the fixed equipment. The landlord is bound to make such replacement or renewal of the fixed equipment as is made necessary by natural

---

1 See ch 2, pt 2 above.
2 Agricultural Holdings (Scotland) Act 1991, s 5.

decay or fair wear and tear. Otherwise, the maintenance obligation falls upon the tenant, ie to keep it in a good state of repair, fair wear and tear excepted.

Either party may agree to be responsible for the other's obligations regarding the fixed equipment, though any provision in a lease requiring the tenant to pay the whole or part of a fire insurance premium in respect of the fixed equipment will be null and void.

Rent reviews[1]

As with any other kind of lease, if its contractual duration is of any length, the landlord will have included provision for rent reviews at regular intervals. However, as we have already noted, it is one of the main purposes of the Act that the tenant may be granted security of tenure beyond the termination date stated in his lease. In such cases, the provision of rent reviews will thereafter be regulated by the Act.

Where a lease is due to expire and the Land Court has decided that it should continue under the security of tenure provisions[2], either the landlord or the tenant may serve a written demand on the other to have the question of rent referred to arbitration. The rent will be fixed by the arbiter on an open market value basis and may become effective as at the date of expiry of the original lease or at any time thereafter. Certain valuation criteria are laid down; for example the value of tenant's improvements should be disregarded, as well as the fact that the tenant is in occupation of the holding. Any deterioration caused to the holding by the tenant should also be discounted. After a new rent has been thus fixed, a further application cannot be made by either party until a period of three years has elapsed. If the original lease was for less than three years, no variation in rent can be made until three years have elapsed since the commencement of the tenancy.

This means in effect that a lease continuing under the security of tenure provisions is subject to three-yearly rent reviews. For a general discussion of relevant valuation considerations see the undernoted references[3].

1 Ibid s13.
2 See pt 3 below.
3 *Aberdeen Endowments Trust v Will* 1985 SLT (Land Ct) 23; *Dunbar and Anderson, Joint Applicants* 1985 SLCR 1.

Apart from the above provisions, the rent may also be increased in certain circumstances when improvements to the holding have been made by the landlord[1].

Tenant's right to remove fixtures[2]

We saw above that the necessary buildings and other basic equipment necessary to run the farm have to be provided by the landlord as fixed equipment. However, the tenant, if he wishes, may add fixtures to the holding at his own expense. Since these are provided by him, he is entitled to remove them, either during the tenancy or within six months after the lease has ended. A fixture is defined as 'any engine, machinery, fencing or other fixture'. The same right applies to buildings erected by the tenant, other than ones for which he is entitled to compensation for improvements.

The tenant is entitled to remove a fixture or building only if he is up to date with his rent and has performed all other obligations of the lease. Also, before exercising his right, he must give the landlord one month's written notice of his intention, which will give the landlord the option of buying the fixture at its value to an incoming tenant of the holding. If the fixture is in fact removed, the tenant must make good all damage caused by its removal.

Record of holding[3]

Since disputes may arise, either during a tenancy or at its termination – regarding, for example, who provided certain fixtures, or whether neglect to a holding was inherited by the tenant or largely caused by him – it is useful to have some independent evidence by which to establish the facts. The Act therefore provides for written records of certain aspects of a holding to be made, some of them compulsory, some optional. Such a record is to be made by a person appointed by the Secretary of State, at the joint expense of the parties. The following are the types of record that may be made:

(a) A record of the condition of the fixed equipment. This *must* be made at the beginning of the tenancy and is deemed to form part of the lease.

1 Agricultural Holdings (Scotland) Act 1991, s 15.
2 Ibid s 18.
3 Ibid ss 5 and 8.

(b) A record of the condition of cultivation of the holding and of the condition of the fixed equipment. This may be made at any time during the currency of the lease, but is not compulsory unless *either* the landlord *or* the tenant demands it.

(c) Any improvements made by the tenant, or fixtures or buildings which he is entitled to remove (see the preceding section). This only needs to be made if the *tenant* demands it.

In relation to (b) and (c), the parties may agree to make a record of only part of the holding, or of the fixed equipment only.

Removal for non-payment of rent[1]

It is important to remember that the security of tenure issues discussed below relate only to the tenant's position at the *end* of his lease. Like the tenant in any lease, whether or not it is one subject to statutory control, an agricultural tenant has a contractual right to remain in the property until the lease is due to expire, and the statutory provisions determine only whether he has the right to stay on *beyond* that date.

However, as with other types of lease, an agricultural lease can be terminated prematurely on one of the grounds (eg irritancy) specified in chapter 7. To this the Act has added another ground of termination, which can apply either during the contractual duration or after the security of tenure provisions have been invoked. Where six months' rent is due and unpaid the landlord can raise an action in the sheriff court for the tenant's removal at the next term of Whitsunday or Martinmas, ie 28 May or 28 November[2]. The sheriff will grant decree against the tenant unless the tenant can either pay the rent due or find sufficient security, to the sheriff's satisfaction, for the rent due and an additional one year's rent. A lease terminated in this way will be treated as if it had expired naturally at that term. The tenant will therefore be entitled to the usual waygoing rights such as compensation for improvements. He will not, however, be entitled to compensation for disturbance.

In effect, this provision amounts to a legal irritancy, imposed by statute, which can be purged by the tenant in the manner described above (ie by paying the rent, etc).

---

1 Ibid s 20.
2 Term and Quarter Days (Scotland) Act 1990, s 1.

Miscellaneous provisions regarding lease terms

Apart from those mentioned above, the 1991 Act makes a number of other provisions regulating the relationship of landlord and tenant. These include the right of either party to refer to arbitration the question of whether or not the amount of permanent pasture on the holding should be reduced[1], the right of the tenant to adopt his own method of cropping and to dispose of the produce of the holding as he pleases[2], and the right of the landlord at any reasonable time to enter the holding to view its condition or carry out his responsibilities[3].

3. SECURITY OF TENURE

As mentioned above, one of the main purposes of the 1991 Act is to provide greater security of tenure for agricultural tenants. Like the tenant in any other kind of lease, the tenant of an agricultural holding has the contractual right to stay on in the property until the expiry date of his lease. Like other tenants, he can only be removed before then in extraordinary circumstances, for example if he has committed a breach justifying irritancy, or the property has been destroyed. When the lease is due to end, the tenant may be able to stay on if the landlord agrees to a new lease, or if the old one is allowed to be renewed automatically by tacit relocation. However, in leases where the common law applies, a landlord who wants his tenant out at the expiry date has an absolute right to evict him, provided he sends a notice to quit in time[4].

On the other hand, where the 1991 Act applies, a landlord who wants to remove a tenant at the end of his lease may be legally prevented from doing so. In certain cases the tenant will have the right to stay on in the property indefinitely, long after the contractual term of his lease has expired. This extended security of tenure is not automatic. In some exceptional cases the landlord will have an absolute right to remove the tenant, provided that he follows the correct statutory procedure. In all other cases the tenant will have the right to refer the matter to the Land Court. Once that happens, it will be in the hands of that court to decide whether or not the

---

1 Agricultural Holdings (Scotland) Act 1991, s 9.
2 Ibid s 7.
3 Ibid s 10.
4 See ch 7, pt 2 above.

tenant should be granted security of tenure. There are certain statutory criteria which they should have regard to when reaching their decision, but they are not bound by them and have a wide discretion in each individual case.

The Act does not contain a specific prohibition against contracting out of the security of tenure provisions, but in *Johnson v Moreton*[1] the House of Lords held that the mandatory wording of the provisions precluded this. In a moving pastoral eulogy, Lord Hailsham spoke at some length of the tenant's 'years (sometimes generations) of patient and self-abnegating toil and investment to put heart into soil' and otherwise develop the holding. 'These are not simply matters of private contracts . . .' he concluded. 'It is a public interest introduced for the sake of the soil and husbandry of England of which both landlord and tenant are in a moral, though not of course a legal, sense the trustees for posterity. Silence is not an argument, particularly when the words are prima facie mandatory, for excusing a term in a contract introduced for the purpose of annulling the protection given to the tenant by s 24[2].'

Since the Scottish provision is virtually identical to the one considered in that case, it seems likely that the soil of Scotland is similarly protected.

Notice to quit

As in other types of lease, the tenant cannot be removed at all unless either party serves a notice to quit for the requisite period before the end of the lease. A landlord's notice should be as prescribed either by the Removal Terms (Scotland) Act 1886 or by the Sheriff Courts (Scotland) Act 1907[3]. In the case of tenancies subject to the 1991 Act, the statutory period of notice is not more than two years or less than one year before the date of expiry[4]. This provision cannot be contracted out of, ie any clause in the lease substituting a longer or shorter period of notice would not be enforceable[5]. If notice is not served, or is not served in time, the lease will continue from year to year by tacit relocation until proper

---

1 [1980] AC 37, [1978] 3 All ER 37, HL.
2 *Johnson v Moreton* [1980] AC 37 at 59 and 60, [1978] 3 All ER 37, HL.
3 Agricultural Holdings (Scotland) Act 1991, s 21(5); *Rae & Cooper v Davidson* 1954 SC 361,1955 SLT 25. See also *Gemmell v Andrew* 1975 SLT (Land Ct) 5 and *Taylor v Brick* 1982 SLT 25.
4 Agricultural Holdings (Scotland) Act 1991, s 21(3).
5 Ibid s 21(1); *Duguid v Muirhead* 1926 SC 1078.

notice is served; this is, of course, the common law rule for all leases, but in the case of agricultural lets it is given statutory reinforcement[1]. The operation of tacit relocation cannot be contracted out of[2].

Exceptions to security of tenure[3]

If any of the grounds of removal listed below applies, the landlord has an absolute right to remove the tenant without the tenant being able to refer the matter to the Land Court. The notice to quit must expressly state which of the six grounds of removal applies. Otherwise the notice, although it may be valid for other purposes, will not be effective in excluding the jurisdiction of the Land Court and the matter may be referred to them by the tenant serving a counter-notice on the landlord (see below). Where recourse to the Land Court *has* been excluded, the tenant nevertheless has the right, within one month, to refer the matter to arbitration. However, if the landlord's stated ground does exist, this will do the tenant no good: the function of arbitration in this context is merely to determine whether the landlord was within his rights in claiming that one of the grounds of removal applies.

The seven grounds of removal are as follows:

(1) The landlord has let permanent pasture to the tenant for a definite period to use as arable land on condition that the tenant sows grass again at the end of the let.

(2) The land is required for a use other than agriculture for which planning permission has been granted or is not required.

(3) Within the last nine months an application has been made to the Land Court and the Court has granted a certificate that the tenant was not fulfilling his responsibilities to farm in accordance with the rules of good husbandry[4].

(4) The tenant is in arrears with his rent or is in breach of another term of the lease which is remediable. The landlord must have

1 Agricultural Holdings (Scotland) Act 1991, s 3.
2 Ibid; see also ch 7, pt 2 above.
3 Ibid s 22(2).
4 *Luss Estates Co v Firkin Farm Co* 1985 SLT (Land Ct) 17; *Cambusmore Estate Trust v Little* 1991 SLT (Land Ct) 33.

given the tenant two months' notice to pay the rent arrears or a reasonable period of notice to remedy the breach[1].

(5) The landlord's interest has been materially prejudiced by the tenant's breach of a term of the lease which could not be remedied in reasonable time and at economic cost.

(6) The tenant is bankrupt.

(7) The tenant is the successor of a deceased tenant, other than a near relative[2].

If the ground of removal is breach of a lease condition (ie (4) or (5) above), that condition must not be inconsistent with the tenant's fulfilment of his responsibilities to farm in accordance with the rules of good husbandry. In other words, if the lease imposes an obligation which it would be bad farming practice for the tenant to obey, he cannot be removed for failure to observe it. The rules of good husbandry are defined as 'maintaining a reasonable standard of efficient production, as respects both the kind of produce and the quality and quantity thereof, while keeping the unit in a condition to enable such a standard to be maintained in the future'[3]. Specific mention is made of maintenance of grassland, handling of arable land, proper keeping of livestock, pest control, maintenance of equipment etc.

In all of the above cases except (2) (ie where the land is required for a use other than agriculture) and (7) (where the tenant is the successor of a deceased tenant), the tenant loses his right to compensation for disturbance, although he retains other rights on removal, such as his right to compensation for improvements.

Examination of the above grounds of removal will show that in each case there is some justification for depriving the tenant of his right to appeal to the Land Court. In cases (3)–(6) listed above the tenant is at fault in some way, being a bad farmer, in breach of contract or bankrupt. Case (1) listed above is a special case where the landlord wishes to renew the soil by the transfer of grazing land to arable for a limited period, and presumably the tenant knew the position when he took the lease on.

In case (2) listed above, where the land is required for a non-agricultural use, the tenant is probably not at fault: it is just that the

1 *Macnabb v A & J Anderson* 1955 SC 38, 1955 SLT 73.
2 See pt 6 below.
3 Agriculture (Scotland) Act 1948, Sch 6.

merits of the alternative use are considered to outweigh the needs of the tenant. However, here the tenant is in a better position. As we saw above he retains his right to compensation for disturbance. Also, where a planning application is being made in respect of land subject to an agricultural tenancy or tenancies, there is a statutory requirement for the applicant to serve notice of his application on all agricultural tenants on the land[1]. And so, even though it is too late for the tenant to challenge the landlord after planning permission has been obtained, he will have an opportunity at an earlier stage to lodge objections and in some cases there may even be a public enquiry regarding the proposals.

Security of tenure

In all cases other than (1)–(7) listed above the tenant may, within one month of receiving a notice to quit, serve a counter-notice on the landlord referring the matter to the Land Court[2]. The court will consent to the tenant's removal only where it is established that one of the following circumstances applies[3].

(1) The carrying out of the purpose for which the landlord seeks to terminate the tenancy is desirable in the interests of good husbandry.

(2) The carrying out is desirable in the interests of sound estate management[4].

(3) The carrying out is desirable for the purposes of agricultural research, experiment, education etc.

(4) Greater hardship would be caused by withholding than by giving consent to the operation of the notice[5] or

(5) The landlord's purpose is to employ the land for a use other than agriculture for which planning permission is required but has not been granted.

---

1 Town and Country Planning (Scotland) Act 1972, s 24.
2 Agricultural Holdings (Scotland) Act 1991, s 22(1); see also *Kildrummy (Jersey) v Calder* 1994 SLT 888.
3 1991 Act, s 24(1)
4 *Altyre Estate Trs v McLay* 1975 SLT (Land Ct) 12.
5 *Somerville v Watson* 1980 SLT (Land Ct) 14; see also *Hutchison v Buchanan* 1980 SLT (Land Ct) 17; *Prior v J & A Henderson Ltd* 1984 SLT (Land Ct) 51, 1983 SLCR 34 (a case where an attempt to remove the tenant failed under (a), (b) and (d) above); *Lindsay-Macdougall v Peterson* 1987 SLCR 59; and *Lovie v Davidson* 1988 SLCR 13.

The onus of proof is on the landlord to establish that one or more of the above grounds exists[1]. And even where the landlord succeeds in discharging that onus, the Land Court still have the discretion to refuse the landlord's application if it appears to them that a fair and reasonable landlord would not insist on possession[2].

It would be an unwise landlord who found himself in the Land Court arguing for repossession on number (5) of the above grounds. Where his alternative use requires planning permission, he should obtain that permission first, before sending his notice to quit. In that way he will qualify under the second exception to security of tenure and he will have an absolute right to remove the tenant, with the latter having no right to take him to the Land Court. If he serves his notice to quit *before* obtaining planning permission, the tenant may refer the matter to the Land Court and, because of the court's ultimate discretion, the outcome will be uncertain.

Where the tenant is the near-relative successor of a deceased tenant, there are additional grounds of removal[3].

Notice to quit part of the holding

In some cases, the landlord may only want back part of the holding, and be happy for the tenant to remain on in the remainder. He may therefore serve on the tenant a notice to quit part of the holding at the lease's termination date. However, this may not suit the tenant, who may prefer to move elsewhere, or to retire, rather than farm a reduced holding. Furthermore, the smaller area may not be economically viable. Since the contractual period of the tenant's lease will be about to end, he will of course be perfectly entitled legally to call it a day: the effect of the 1991 Act only gives a *tenant* the right to extend his lease, without a landlord having a reciprocal right to hold a tenant beyond the end of his lease term. And so, irrespective of the Act, the tenant's basic right, if he so wishes, is to end the lease at its natural termination date by serving the landlord with at least a year's notice. If he receives sufficient notice of the landlord's intention to take back part of the holding, there will be no problem.

However, what if the landlord were to send his notice a bare year

1 *McLaren v Lawrie* 1964 SLT (Land Ct) 10.
2 Agricultural Holdings (Scotland) Act 1991, s 24(2); see also *Altyre Estate Trs v McLay* 1975 SLT (Land Ct) 12.
3 See pt 6 below.

before the end of the lease? It would be unfair if the tenant were held by tacit relocation for a further year to only part of the holding, which he might not want on its own. Furthermore, we will see below that where a tenant is denied his security of tenure he generally has a right to compensation for disturbance of up to two years' rent. If a reduced holding is no use to him, would it be fair for him to get disturbance only for the part that the landlord wanted back? This is where the Act steps in to give the tenant further rights in such circumstances.

Where the landlord serves a notice to quit for part of the holding the tenant, within twenty-eight days, may serve a counter-notice making the landlord's notice take effect for the full holding[1]. This allows the tenant to claim the compensation payable on his removal from the whole farm, should he not consider it desirable to continue in occupation of the reduced holding. However, if the part claimed back by the landlord is less than one-fourth of the holding either in area or rental value and the diminished holding is reasonably capable of being farmed as a separate unit, compensation for disturbance will be restricted to the part included in the landlord's notice to quit[2]. This means that the tenant, if he wants, can leave the whole holding; however, only if a significant part is being reclaimed by the landlord will he get a disturbance payment for all of the holding rather than just the part the landlord wants back.

Of course, to take the money and run is not the tenant's only option. Instead of giving in to the landlord by leaving the holding, he will usually have the alternative of referring the matter to the Land Court. It is therefore possible that they will grant him security of tenure for the whole holding, despite the landlord's notice.

4. TENANT'S COMPENSATION RIGHTS

Under the 1991 Act there are a number of compensation rights which a tenant may be entitled to claim from his landlord at the termination of his let. The oldest and most fundamental statutory right of the agricultural tenant, dating back from the very first Act in 1883, is to receive compensation for any improvements that he has made to the holding. Even the right to security of tenure came much later. In the case of compensation for improvements, it does

---

1 Agricultural Holdings (Scotland) Act 1991, s 30.
2 Ibid s 43(7).

not matter that it may have been the tenant's fault that he was removed from the holding. Even if he has been removed prematurely for non-payment of rent he will be entitled to his compensation. The reason for this is quite obvious. If he has added to the value of the holding, he is due reimbursement for that, whatever else he may have been guilty of.

However, that is not the end of the story. If the tenant has to be moved through no fault of his own, it is right that he should also receive some compensation for the inconvenience and expense of this. Thus he will sometimes also be entitled to compensation for disturbance. In addition, the Agriculture (Miscellaneous Provisions) Act 1968 (the relevant provisions of which are now incorporated within the 1991 Act)[1] added a further substantial payment for reorganisation of the tenant's affairs, to which he will be entitled in certain limited circumstances. It is a prerequisite for payment of this that the tenant is entitled to compensation for disturbance; however, it is not payable in all situations where disturbance is due.

These three heads of compensation are the main possible claims a tenant can make at the end of his lease if he is denied extended security of tenure. In some cases he may get all three; in other cases he may be denied some or all of them, if he has made no improvements, for example, or has been in breach of his lease. There are, however, certain other compensation rights, which will be noted briefly at the end of the section.

With a few limited exceptions, none of these rights can be contracted out of: in other words, any clause in an agricultural lease depriving the tenant of his rights of compensation, or any of them, will generally not be given effect to[2].

(1) Compensation for improvements

An agricultural tenant is entitled at the termination of his lease to obtain from the landlord a sum which fairly represents the value of certain improvements he may have made to the property[3]. In some cases the tenant will require to serve adequate notice on the landlord of his intention to carry out the improvements and in other cases he will require the landlord's written consent before carrying

1 Agricultural Holdings (Scotland) Act 1991, ss 54 and 55.
2 Ibid s 53.
3 Ibid s 34.

them out. If the tenant fails to comply with these requirements in the cases where they are necessary, he will lose his right to compensation[1]. Note that this right of compensation (unlike the ones which follow) can arise even if it is the tenant who gives the notice to quit: as observed above, he has added to the value of the holding, whatever the circumstances of his departure.

The amount of compensation payable will be calculated on the basis of the value of the improvements to an incoming tenant as agreed between the parties. Failing agreement, the compensation will be fixed by arbitration[2].

The provisions described here relate to improvements begun on or after 1 November 1948. In respect of improvements carried out before then, the provisions are slightly different[3]. There are also special compensation provisions for agricultural holdings that qualify as market gardens[4].

There are three categories of improvement that may qualify for compensation. The following is a brief selection of some of the types of improvement under each category; for the full list, the reader is referred to the Act[5].

(a) *Permanent improvements.* To be entitled to compensation, the tenant must have obtained the landlord's written consent before carrying out the improvements. The category of permanent improvements includes laying down permanent pasture, making water meadows or works of irrigation and the planting of orchards or fruit bushes.

(b) *Drainage and associated improvements.* The tenant will not be due compensation unless he has given the landlord prior written notice of his intention to carry out the improvements, not less than *three months* before he proceeds with them.

Included in this category are land drainage, making or improvement of farm access or service roads, making or removal of permanent fences (including hedges, stone dykes and gates), erection, alteration or enlargement of buildings and repairs to fixed equipment. It should be noted in particular that the erection of buildings comes under this category, as it might have seemed more logical to

---

1 Ibid s 37.
2 Agricultural Holdings (Scotland) Act 1991, s 60.
3 Ibid s 33 etc.
4 Ibid ss 40–42.
5 Ibid Sch 5.

regard it as a permanent improvement. If the landlord objects to the improvement, there is provision for the matter being determined by the Land Court[1].

(c) *Temporary improvements.* Here neither the consent of, or notice to, the landlord is required. Temporary improvements include protecting fruit trees against animals, eradication of bracken, whins or broom, application to the land of purchased manure and laying down of temporary pasture.

(2) Compensation for disturbance[2]

Subject to certain exceptions noted below, compensation for disturbance is paid where the tenant has left the holding in the following circumstances:

(1) The landlord has given the tenant notice to quit the holding. If it is the other way around and the tenant has given the landlord notice, the tenant will not be entitled to compensation for disturbance. He can hardly claim for the inconvenience of having to move if he is doing so on his own initiative.

(2) The landlord has given the tenant notice to quit *part* of the holding and the tenant has served a counter-notice requiring the notice to quit to take effect for the full holding. We saw above that, provided the part claimed is sufficiently substantial, the tenant can claim disturbance for the whole holding. This does not mean that he will be denied disturbance compensation if the landlord only wants less than a quarter of the holding, or if he decides to accept the landlord's notice and stay on in the reduced holding. In such cases, he will be entitled to reduced compensation, proportionate to the area which the landlord has reclaimed[3].

The minimum amount of compensation payable is one year's rent at the rate payable immediately before the termination of the tenancy (subject to certain minor deductions). If the tenant can prove additional loss directly attributable to his removal, he can claim additional compensation up to a maximum total compensation of two years' rent.

Compensation for disturbance is excluded in the following circumstances:

---

1 Ibid s 39; *Renwick v Rodger* 1988 SLT (Land Ct) 23.
2 Agricultural Holdings (Scotland) Act 1991, s 43.
3 Ibid s 49.

(1) In all cases (with one exception) where the landlord has an absolute right to remove the tenant without being taken to the Land Court[1]. As we saw earlier, the exception is the second of the cases, ie where the land is required for a use other than agriculture for which planning permission has been granted or is not required.

(2) In certain cases where the tenant is the successor of a deceased tenant[2].

(3) Sum for reorganisation of tenant's affairs[3]

Where (and only where) compensation for disturbance is payable, the landlord may also have to pay, in certain circumstances, a sum to assist in the reorganisation of the tenant's affairs. The amount of this sum is four times the annual rent of the holding at the rate payable immediately prior to the termination of the tenancy. Where compensation for disturbance is only payable in respect of *part* of the holding, the sum is four times the appropriate portion of the annual rent. In *Copeland v McQuaker*[4], it was held that the sum for reorganisation was payable even although additional loss could not be proved; it was not compensation as such, but a fixed sum which, if it was applicable, was paid regardless of loss.

The provisions which govern when the sum for reorganisation is payable are rather complex. However, broadly speaking, it appears that the sum need only be paid where the landlord wants the land for some use other than agriculture. In all other cases payment can be avoided, provided that the landlord states in his notice to quit the reason why he requires to resume possession. The reasons he may give roughly correspond to the Land Court's four other criteria for removal (ie interests of good husbandry, interests of sound estate management, required for agricultural research etc, hardship to the landlord)[5]. There is therefore an onus on the landlord to ensure that he words his notice to quit correctly if he wants to avoid making an unnecessary payment. Even so, if the matter has gone to the Land Court, he may still be required to pay the sum

1 See pt 3 above.
2 See pt 6 below.
3 Agricultural Holdings (Scotland) 1991, ss 54 and 55.
4 1973 SLT 186.
5 See pt 3 above; see also *Barns-Graham v Lamont* 1971 SC 170, 1971 SLT 341 and *Copeland v McQuaker* 1973 SLT 186.

if the Court is satisfied that the land *is* required for a use other than agriculture, even though the landlord stated another ground as the basis of his right to terminate[1].

In the situation where the lease can be terminated without the tenant being able to refer the matter to the Land Court, the sum for reorganisation will likewise only be payable when the land is required for a use other than agriculture. The reason for this is simply that the sum for reorganisation is only paid along with disturbance, and no disturbance compensation is payable in the other six cases where the Land Court's jurisdiction can be excluded[2].

(4) Other compensation rights

At end of lease. Other waygoing rights to which a tenant may sometimes be entitled at the end of his lease include compensation for continuous adoption of a special standard of farming[3], additional payments where the holding has been compulsorily acquired[4] and compensation for milk quota[5].

At other times. Where the landlord, in exercise of a provision in the lease, resumes (ie takes back from the tenant) part of the holding for non-agricultural purposes, the tenant is entitled to compensation for early resumption[6]. In certain circumstances, a tenant may claim compensation for damage caused to his crops by game[7].

Landlord's compensation. In certain circumstances the landlord may be due compensation from the tenant, notably where the tenant has been responsible for a deterioration in the holding[8] and for failure to repair or maintain fixed equipment[9].

---

1 Agricultural Holdings (Scotland) Act 1991, s 55(2)(b).
2 See pt 3 above.
3 Agricultural Holdings (Scotland) Act 1991, s 44.
4 Ibid ss 56 and 57.
5 Agriculture Act 1986, s 14 and Sch 2.
6 Agricultural Holdings (Scotland) Act 1991, s 58.
7 Ibid s 52.
8 Ibid s 45.
9 Ibid s 46.

5. ARBITRATION UNDER THE AGRICULTURAL HOLDINGS ACT

Section 60 of the 1991 Act contains a blanket provision that, except where the Act provides to the contrary (and subject to a right of the parties to jointly submit a dispute to the Land Court instead)[1], that disputes relating to agricultural holdings should be submitted to arbitration.

This means that virtually every dispute between the parties, with very few exceptions, must be referred to arbitration. Recourse must even be had to arbitration where the dispute relates to the landlord's attempt to remove the tenant, by irritancy or otherwise[2]. Arbitration is excluded where the dispute relates to liability for rent and also where it relates to valuations of sheep stocks, dung, fallow, straw, crops, fences and other property of an outgoing tenant, which is being taken over by the landlord or an incoming tenant[3]. The courts also have jurisdiction, rather than an arbiter, when the issue is whether there is a landlord/tenant relationship at all[4].

Procedure

Arbitrations are to be heard by a single arbiter[5] selected from a panel appointed by the Lord President of the Court of Session[6]. The choice of arbiter is made by the parties; if they cannot agree on the choice, it will be made by the Secretary of State[6] or (where the Secretary of State is a party to the dispute) by the Land Court[7]. Where the arbiter is selected by agreement, this must be done in a formal deed signed by both parties and an exchange of letters is not sufficient[8].

The procedure for arbitrations is set out in Schedule 7 of the 1991 Act[9]. Provisions are made regarding submission of particulars of a

---

1 Agricultural Holdings (Scotland) Act 1991, s 60(2).
2 *Houison-Craufurd's Trs v Davies* 1951 SC 1, 1951 SLT 25; *Brodie v Ker* 1952 SC 216, 1952 SLT 226.
3 Agricultural Holdings (Scotland) Act 1991, s 61(7).
4 *Cormack v McIldowie's Exrs* 1974 SLT 178.
5 Agricultural Holdings (Scotland) Act 1991, s 61(1).
6 Ibid s 63(1).
7 Ibid s 64.
8 *Chalmers Property Investment Co Ltd v MacColl* 1951 SC 24, 1951 SLT 50.
9 Agricultural Holdings (Scotland) Act 1991, Sch 7.

claim[1], the production of evidence[2] and the making of the award, which must normally be done within three months of the arbiter's appointment[3].

Appeals

Apart from disputes relating to rent reviews which now have their own special rules (treated separately below), the rights of appeal from an arbiter's award are fairly limited. The arbiter's decision is binding on points of fact but, at any stage of the proceedings, a stated case may be made to the sheriff on points of law arising during the course of the arbitration. This can either be made as a result of a direction by the arbiter, or by the sheriff himself on the application of either the landlord or the tenant[4]. It should be noted that the wording of this provision means that the appeal by stated case can only be made during the proceedings and not after the issue of the arbiter's award; once made, the award is final and binding on both parties[5]. However, in those cases which have gone to the sheriff, a further appeal may be made from the sheriff's decision to the Court of Session[6]. After a decision in law has been made by the sheriff court or Court of Session, the arbiter is bound to apply it, or he will be guilty of misconduct[7].

In the case of disputes relating to rent reviews, an exception to the above rules was introduced by the Agricultural Holdings (Amendment) (Scotland) Act 1983[8]. It was felt that, because of the large sums at stake in rent review disputes, the decision should not rest on a single arbiter alone. In such cases, therefore, there is introduced a new right of appeal from the arbiter's award on any question of fact or law[9]. This right of appeal is to the Land Court, and must be made within two months of the award[10]. There is still provision for a stated case on points of law to be made before the issue of the award, but in rent review cases it must now be made to the

1 Ibid Sch 7, para 5.
2 Ibid Sch 7, paras 6 and 7.
3 Ibid Sch 7, para 8.
4 Ibid Sch 7, para 20.
5 Ibid Sch 7, para 15.
6 Ibid, Sch 7, para 21.
7 *Mitchell-Gill v Buchan* 1921 SC 390.
8 Now incorporated in the Agricultural Holdings (Scotland) Act 1991, s 61 and Sch 7.
9 Ibid s 61(2).
10 Ibid s 61(3).

Land Court. In both of these instances, the Land Court's decision is final[1]. This seems rather odd, in view of the fact that appeals can be made from the sheriff to the Court of Session in other types of dispute.

It should also be noted that these provisions in respect of rent review disputes only apply when the arbiter has been appointed by the Secretary of State or by the Land Court, not when he has been appointed by the parties themselves. In the latter case, appeals in rent review arbitrations are still subject to exactly the same rules as any other type of arbitration under the 1991 Act (ie stated case to the sheriff on points of law before the issue of the award). In rent review disputes, therefore, even where the parties can agree on a choice of arbiter, it might be in their interest to have him appointed by the Secretary of State, so that they can enjoy the wider rights of appeal introduced in 1983.

6. SUCCESSION TO AGRICULTURAL TENANCIES

Introduction

We saw in chapter 7 that a lease may be inherited either under testate succession (where the tenancy has been bequeathed in the tenant's will) or under intestate succession (where the tenant has either not left a will, or has left one but has failed to dispose of the lease in it)[2]. We also saw that, in some cases, the landlord could object to the succession and prevent the transmission to the new tenant. The same is broadly true of succession to agricultural holdings; however, the matter is here entirely regulated by statute and is, unfortunately, a little more complex.

Bequest of lease (testate succession)[3]

The tenant of an agricultural holding is entitled to bequeath his lease under his will. Since a bequest is virtually a form of assignation, this therefore forms an exception to the common law rule that agricultural leases, other than those of unusual duration, cannot be

---

1 Ibid sch 7, para 22.
2 See ch 7, pt 1 above.
3 Agricultural Holdings (Scotland) Act 1991, s 11.

assigned without the landlord's consent[1]. However, this particular provision is one where there is no express prohibition against contracting out. And so in *Kennedy v Johnstone*[2] it was held that it *could* be contracted out of, and that a provision in a lease expressly excluding the tenant's legatee was valid.

Moreover, the Act does not give a tenant the right to bequeath his lease to anyone at all, but only to a person selected from a limited class of individuals. It must be bequeathed to someone who, had the tenant not left a will, might have been entitled to succeed him under the law of intestate succession; alternatively, it may be bequeathed to either his son-in-law or his daughter-in-law. Apart from these last two relatives by marriage, this mainly means that it must be left to a blood relative, probably a child, but possibly also a brother or sister or even a parent or more remote member of the family. It may also be left to the tenant's wife or husband[3]. The bequest does not have to be to the first person in line of succession, as long as it is to someone among the class of possible intestate successors. For example, even though he has children, he could leave the lease to his brother, or bypass his blood relatives entirely and leave it to his son-in-law.

It is of course possible that the legatee may not be a willing recipient; after all, a lease, like any other contract, involves responsibilities as well as benefits. If the legatee wants the tenancy, therefore, he must notify the landlord of this within twenty-one days of the tenant's death, unless he is prevented from doing so by some unavoidable cause. In *Coats v Logan*[4], the legatee failed to notify the landlord in time and was prevented from acquiring the tenancy; moreover, since he had actually accepted the bequest and this fact had been recorded in the confirmation, the tenant's executors were unable to dispose of the tenancy as intestate estate. The result was that the landlords were able to regain possession of the holding. However, in *Morrison-Low v Paterson*[5], the tenant's two sons carried on in occupation of the holding for six years after their father's death, continuing to pay rent and otherwise interacting with the landlord. It was held that a tenancy had been constituted by the actings of the parties.

The landlord may object to the bequest by sending, within one

---

1 See ch 5, pt 1 above.
2 1956 SC 39, 1956 SLT 73.
3 Succession (Scotland) Act 1964, s 2.
4 1985 SLT 221.
5 1985 SLT (HL) 255.

month of the legatee's notice, a counter-notice referring the matter
to the Land Court. The Land Court will thereafter either confirm
the bequest or, if it thinks that the landlord has a reasonable objection, it may declare the bequest to be null and void.

Intestate succession

The lease of an agricultural holding may also be inherited under
the rules of intestate succession. As stated above, this will apply if
the tenant has either not left a will, or has left one but has failed to
dispose of the lease under it. However, the lease may also pass
under the rules of intestacy where there has been a bequest, but the
legatee has declined to accept it or the landlord's objection to him
has been upheld by the Land Court[1]. As with other types of lease,
the lease will initially pass to the executor, who has power to transfer it to any of the people entitled to succeed the tenant under the
rules of intestate succession[2]. This does not mean that the executor
has as much scope as a tenant making a bequest under his will,
where the lease could be bequeathed to any possible intestate successor, not necessarily the first in line of succession. The executor
has to choose one of the class of people who are first in line of succession, eg one of the tenant's children. The reason why he is given
the right to choose only one out of that class is to avoid creating a
joint tenancy among two or more successors.

The executor's right to transfer the tenancy applies even where the
lease contains an express or implied prohibition against assignation[3].

The landlord has a right to object to the new tenant, very much
along the same lines as in the case of a bequest. Within twenty-one
days of acquiring the lease, the new tenant must notify the landlord
of the fact, and the landlord may within one month send a counter-
notice referring the matter to the Land Court. The Land Court has
power, similar to that which it has with bequests, to either confirm
the succession or terminate the tenancy[4].

Security of tenure

What we have been discussing so far are situations where the tenant dies before the contractual term of his lease has ended. What

1 Agricultural Holdings (Scotland) Act 1991, s 11(8).
2 Succession (Scotland) Act 1964, s 16.
3 Ibid s 16(1) and (2).
4 Agricultural Holdings (Scotland) Act 1991, s 12.

the successor inherits, therefore, whether by bequest or through intestacy, is the unexpired portion of the lease. However, if the original tenant had survived, he might well have had a statutory right to claim extended security of tenure beyond the lease's contractual expiry[1]. The question that now arises is whether a tenant by inheritance has a similar right when the expiry date arrives.

Because of a number of changes in the law the position is somewhat complex, and it may be more easily understood if we first take a brief look at the history of these changes. Originally a successor tenant had the same right to claim security of tenure as the original tenant. This was changed by the Agriculture Act 1958, which deprived the original tenant's successor of any right to security of tenure when the lease expired. The situation was partially reversed by the Agriculture (Miscellaneous Provisions) Act 1968, which distinguished two categories of successor, a near relative successor (the tenant's child or spouse), and all others. The right to claim security of tenure was reinstated for near relative successors, but was still denied to the others. However, being granted security of tenure was made harder for the near relative successor than it would have been for the original tenant; in addition to the normal Land Court criteria for terminating a lease, the 1968 Act provided additional grounds of termination which applied only in the case of near relative successors. Finally, the Agricultural Holdings (Amendment) (Scotland) Act 1983 made it even more difficult for a near relative successor to be granted security of tenure by placing further legal hurdles in his way; however, in order not to spoil the reasonable expectations of existing tenants and their families, these additional rules were only made applicable to new leases, granted on or after 1 January 1984.

This leaves us at present with three categories of successor tenant, each in a separate legal position regarding his right to claim security of tenure when the lease expires: (1) a successor who is not a near relative; (2) a near relative successor to a lease granted *before* 1 January 1984, and (3) a near relative successor to a lease granted *on or after* 1 January 1984. In each of these cases, the tenant may either have succeeded through a bequest or under intestacy. In all of them, a landlord, who may have objected unsuccessfully to the succession when the original tenant died, will now get a second bite at the cherry at the end of the lease. His chances of success will vary depending upon which of the above categories the original tenant's successor falls into.

---

1 See pt 3 above.

Successors other than a near relative[1]

The most straightforward situation is where the successor is other than a near relative. The tenant (subject to a minor qualification noted below) has no right to security of tenure beyond the lease's termination date and no right to refer the matter to the Court. The fact that he is the original tenant's successor but not a near relative is one of the grounds which gives the landlord an absolute right to terminate the lease at the expiry date stated in the notice to quit[2]. This will be the original termination date of the lease if the lease had more than two years to run when the successor acquired the tenancy. However, if there was two years or less of the lease left at that date, the tenant may be able to stay on a little longer. In such a case, the notice to quit may terminate the tenancy at a subsequent anniversary of the original expiry date, as long as the new date is not less than one or more than three years after the successor's acquisition of the tenancy. This means that the successor tenant cannot be removed before the original expiry date, but may have it extended for a period of up to two years. In practice, however, if the landlord really wants the tenant out, he will be able to terminate the lease, at the latest, by the first anniversary of the termination date: even if the new tenant succeeded to the tenancy in the last year of the lease, there will be time to give him the statutory minimum of one year's notice and get him out only a year late.

It should be noted that the operative date from which these time limits run is the successor's *date of acquisition* of the tenancy, *not* the date of the tenant's death.

This last provision will apply in situations where, prior to the tenant's death, the original lease had expired and was continuing on a yearly basis by tacit relocation. Its effect is to ensure that the successor tenant is assured of his minimum year's notice to quit.

Near relative successors – old leases[3]

The term 'old leases' relates to holdings let prior to 1 January 1984. 'Near relative' means a surviving spouse or child, including an adopted child[4]. Here the landlord does not have an absolute right to end the tenancy at the expiry date of the lease. If he attempts to

---

1 Agricultural Holdings (Scotland) Act 1991, s 25(1) and (2)(a), (b) and (d).
2 See pt 3 above.
3 Agricultural Holdings (Scotland) Act 1991, s 25(3) and Sch 2, pt I.
4 Ibid Sch 2, pt III.

terminate by sending a notice to quit, the successor tenant has the same right as the original tenant would have had to send a counter-notice within one month, referring the matter to the Land Court. However, in addition to the usual grounds, the Land Court has additional criteria which it may invoke to terminate the lease[1].

(1) The tenant has neither sufficient training in agriculture nor sufficient experience in the farming of land to enable him to farm the holding with reasonable efficiency[2].

(2) The holding is not a two man unit (ie not big enough to provide work for two or more men) and the landlord, within two years, wants to amalgamate it with another holding, which he specifies[3].

(3) The tenant is himself the occupier of a separate two man unit, which he has occupied since before the death of the tenant whom he succeeded[4]. 'Occupier' has been interpreted as referring to the occupation of an individual, and the Land Court have refused to terminate a lease under criterion (3) where the tenant was a partner of a firm that occupied other holdings[5]. This remains the case for leases entered prior to 1 January 1984, but has now been changed in the case of new leases (see section below).

Where the successor acquired the lease within two years of its date of expiry, the termination date in the notice to quit is worked out along the same lines as with successors who are not near relatives (see above). This means that if security of tenure is refused, there may still be a right to a slight extension beyond the original termination date.

Near relative successor – new leases[6]

The term 'new leases' relates to holdings let *on or after* 1 January 1984. Broadly speaking, the successor is in a similar position to that of a successor under an older lease, with the same right to refer the matter to the Land Court on receiving the landlord's notice to quit. However, the termination grounds have been considerably tightened

---

1 Ibid Sch 2, pt I.
2 *Macdonald v Macrae* 1987 SLCR 72.
3 *Mackenzie v Lyon* 1984 SLT (Land Ct) 30, 1983 SLCR 22; *Trustees of the Main Calthorpe Settlement v Calder* 1988 SLT (Land Ct) 30.
4 *Mackenzie v Lyon* 1984 SLT (Land Ct) 30, 1983 SLCR 22.
5 *Haddo House Estate Trs v Davidson* 1982 SLT (Land Ct) 14.
6 Agricultural Holdings (Scotland) Act 1991, s 25(3) and Sch 2, pt II.

up, making it even harder for a successor to be granted security of tenure. All the termination grounds applying to older leases apply here also. In addition, the following significant changes have been made:

(1) A new termination ground has been added, ie that the tenant does not have sufficient financial resources to enable him to farm the holding with reasonable efficiency.

(2) In the case of ground (1) above and also where the ground is the tenant's lack of training or experience, the Land Court's discretion is curtailed. Until now there has always been a proviso that the court should withhold their consent to a termination if it appeared to them that a fair and reasonable landlord would not insist on possession. With regard to the two grounds mentioned above, this proviso has been removed.

(3) In the case of three of the grounds, the burden of proof has now been shifted to the tenant. We saw above that the onus is normally on the landlord to establish that one or more of the termination grounds exists[1]. Now, in all of the cases except where the landlord desires to amalgamate holdings (ie tenant's lack of financial resources, insufficient training or experience, tenant also the tenant of a separate two man unit), it is now the tenant who has to satisfy the court that the termination ground does not apply.

(4) Where the ground is the tenant's insufficient training and experience, the ground will not apply where the tenant has, since the death of the original tenant, been involved in a course of agricultural training which he is expected to complete satisfactorily within four years. He must also have made satisfactory interim arrangements for the farming of the holding. This, alone out of all the changes, operates in the tenant's favour.

(5) Where the ground is that the tenant already occupies a separate two man unit, occupation is defined to include cases where the other unit is occupied by a company controlled by the tenant or by a firm of which he is a partner[2]. This negates the case of *Haddo House Estate Trs v Davidson*[3] in respect of new leases (see preceding section).

Where the successor acquired the tenancy within two years of the tenancy's termination date, the same rules apply as before with regard to the termination date in the notice to quit.

---

1 *McLaren v Lawrie* 1964 SLT (Land Ct) 10.
2 Agricultural Holdings (Scotland) Act 1991, Sch 2, pt III.
3 *Haddo House Estate Trs v Davidson* 1982 SLT (Land Ct) 14.

7. CROFTS AND SMALL LANDHOLDINGS

Introduction

If an agricultural unit is small enough, or the rent is very low, it will in some cases be subject to the legislation for crofts and small landholdings. The law relating to these is rather complex, and to examine it in depth would take much more space than is available here[1]. However, an attempt will be made to outline the basic principles involved.

One of the reasons for the complexity is that there are at least four different types of small landholders, each subject to different rules, in some cases to separate legislation. These are (a) small landholders, (b) statutory small tenants, (c) crofters and (d) cottars. To understand how this disparity came about, we must first take a very brief look at the history of the relevant legislation.

The first Act, the Crofters Holdings (Scotland) Act 1886, had as its purpose the alleviation of hardship suffered by crofters in the highlands and islands of Scotland. It applied only to the crofting counties in the highlands, ie Argyll, Caithness, Inverness, Orkney, Ross and Cromarty, Sutherland and Zetland. It conferred on a crofter a statutory right to a fair rent, security of tenure, compensation for improvements at the end of his lease and the right to bequeath the tenancy to a member of his family. Although parallel rights are now enjoyed by agricultural tenants generally, the 1886 Act went far beyond the scope of the agricultural holdings legislation at that time. There was also set up a body known as the Crofters Commission to implement the Act.

The next stage occurred in 1911, when the Small Landholders (Scotland) Act 1911 extended this statutory protection beyond the crofting counties to the whole of Scotland. A distinction was made between a small landholder and a statutory small tenant, the former enjoying more legal privileges because he (or his predecessors) had provided most of the buildings and permanent improvements on the holding. Also, the Crofters Commission was replaced by the newly set up Scottish Land Court.

Finally, the special needs of the crofting counties were recognised again when they were given separate legal status by the Crofters (Scotland) Act 1955. Among other things, this abolished,

---

1 See McCuish & Flyn *Crofting Law* (1990) and 1 *Stair Memorial Encyclopaedia* paras 797–860 'Crofting and Smallholdings'.

in the crofting counties, the distinction between small landholders and statutory small tenants. However, the distinction persists in the rest of Scotland, in respect of which the earlier legislation, as amended, remains in force.

The main Acts now in force are (for the whole of Scotland apart from the crofting counties) the Crofters Holdings (Scotland) Act 1886, as amended by the Small Landholders (Scotland) Act 1911, the Land Settlement (Scotland) Act 1919 and the Small Landholders and Agricultural Holdings (Scotland) Act 1931. The legislation applicable to the crofting counties is now consolidated in the Crofters (Scotland) Act 1993. It will be noticed that, paradoxically, while the 1886 Act originally applied only to crofts, it has been replaced with regard to them by the later crofting legislation, but remains as the basis of the law relating to other small landholdings.

Before looking more closely at this interesting selection of different tenures, it may help us to get things into perspective and alleviate confusion if we first gain some idea of how often the various tenures are encountered in practice. If we take the number of reported Land Court cases as a guide, we get the impression that crofting tenure is the only one that remains anything like a vital force. While there is a steady annual stream of crofting decisions, there have been only a handful of reported cases on small landholders and statutory small tenants since the crofting legislation went its separate way in 1955. It would appear, therefore, that while the phenomenon of small holdings remains widespread in the crofting counties of the highlands, it is much more of an anachronism elsewhere in Scotland. Even so, the legislation on small landholdings remains in force and the occasional case still turns up[1].

Small landholders

Definition. For a tenant to be a small landholder, his holding must have had a rent of not more than £50 a year in April 1912 *or* must be not more than twenty hectares in extent[2]. Also, the tenancy

---

1 For example, *Clark v Moffat's Exrs* 1982 SLCR 137; *Arran Properties Ltd v Currie* 1983 SLCR 92.
2 Small Landholders (Scotland) Act 1911, s 26 (as amended by the Agriculture (Adaptation of Enactments) (Scotland) Regulations 1977).

must have already been in existence in 1911[1]. This could be the case if the present holder inherited the holding from the original tenant or a member of his family; alternatively the tenant (or his predecessor) may have been registered subsequently as a new holder[2]. It is necessary for the landholder to cultivate the holding by himself or with his family, with or without hired labour[3]. Finally, the tenant or his predecessor in the same family must have provided or paid for the whole or greater part of the buildings and permanent improvements on the holding; otherwise, he will be a statutory small tenant[4].

Small landholder's rights. The small landholder enjoys the right to a fair rent[5], security of tenure[6], compensation for improvements[7], and the right to bequeath his tenancy[8]. These are of course similar to the rights of agricultural tenants generally, though they differ on points of detail. For example, the landholder can lose his security of tenure for opening a public house without the landlord's consent. The landlord, with the Land Court's consent, has the right to resume the holding for some reasonable purpose[9]. The landholder has no general power to assign or sublet without the landlord's consent, though a limited right to assign may be granted by the Land Court[10].

Statutory small tenants

As indicated above, the statutory small tenant is someone who would have qualified as a small landholder, except that neither he

---

1 Small Landholders (Scotland) Act 1911, s 2(1) (as amended by the Agriculture (Adaptation of Enactments) (Scotland) Regulations 1977).
2 Small Landholders (Scotland) Act 1911, s 7 (as amended by the Land Settlement (Scotland) Act 1919, s 9).
3 Small Landholders (Scotland) Act 1911, s 10(1).
4 Ibid s 2(1)(iii).
5 Crofters Holdings (Scotland) Act 1886, s 6.
6 Ibid s 1 (as amended by the Small Landholders (Scotland) Act 1911, s 10).
7 Crofters Holdings (Scotland) Act 1886, s 8 (as amended by the Small Landholders and Agricultural Holdings (Scotland) Act 1931, s 12).
8 Crofters Holdings (Scotland) Act 1886, s 16 (as amended by the Small Landholders (Scotland) Act 1911, s 20 and the Succession (Scotland) Act 1964, Sch 2.
9 Crofters Holdings (Scotland) Act 1886, s 2 (as amended by the Small Landholders (Scotland) Act 1911, s 19).
10 Small Landholders (Scotland) Act 1911, s 21 (as amended by the Succession (Scotland) Act 1964, Sch 2, para 15).

nor a predecessor in the same family provided the greater part of the buildings and permanent improvements on the holding[1]. He is denied most of the rights enjoyed by the small landholder, though he may apply to the Land Court for a renewal of his lease at the end of his tenancy, and either he or the landlord can apply to the Land Court to fix an 'equitable' rent; the formula for this suggests that it should be worked out on more of a market basis than the fair rent enjoyed by the small landholder[2]. The Small Landholders and Agricultural Holdings (Scotland) Act 1931 gave the statutory small tenant the option of converting his status to that of landholder, for the sake of becoming entitled to compensation for improvements[3].

Crofters

Definition. The Crofters (Scotland) Act 1955 reintroduced crofts as a separate form of tenure in respect of the crofting counties only. All holdings occupied by small landholders or statutory small tenants immediately prior to the Act now became crofts. Provision was made for the creation of new crofts by order of the Land Court followed by registration under the 1955 Act; this system was abolished by the Crofters (Scotland) Act 1961, after which new crofts could be created by direction of the Secretary of State until that measure was in turn repealed by the Crofting Reform (Scotland) Act 1976. The current definition is now contained in the 1993 Act and covers holdings originating in all of the above ways[4]. If the landowner and the crofter agree, the croft may later be enlarged by the addition of non-crofting land, provided the total area (exclusive of common pasture or grazing) is not more than thirty hectares and the rent more than £100; these limits may be exceeded (though not substantially) by the Crofters Commission on a joint application of the parties[5].

The 1955 Act revived the Crofters Commission, but only for the administration of the crofting system. Judicial and other legal jurisdiction remained, and still remains, with the Land Court.

Crofters' rights. Like the small landholder, the crofter has the right to a fair rent[6], compensation for improvements[7], security of

---

1 Small Landholders (Scotland) Act 1911, s 2(1)(iii).
2 Ibid s 32.
3 Small Landholders and Agricultural Holdings (Scotland) Act 1931, s 14.
4 Crofters (Scotland) Act 1993, s 3.
5 Ibid s 4.
6 Ibid s 6.
7 Ibid, ss 30–35.

tenure[1], and the right to bequeath his lease[2]. The provisions are broadly similar to those applying to the small landholder but differ in detail. In particular, the crofter now has greatly improved compensation rights in respect of permanent improvements, and in the event of the croft being resumed by the landowner.

Common grazings. Crofters who share common grazings may appoint a grazings committee[3], whose duties include maintaining and improving the grazings[4] and making regulations with regard to them[5]. Trees may be planted on common grazings with the consent of the Crofters Commission and the landlord[6].

Acquisition right[7]. The Crofting Reform (Scotland) Act 1976 gave a crofter the right to buy his croft from the landowner. If terms cannot be agreed with the owner, the matter will be dealt with by the Land Court. His right to buy the house and any garden ground is absolute, but whether or not he can acquire the rest of the land is at the discretion of the Land Court.

Cottars

A cottar enjoys a special kind of tenure which, like crofts, occurs only in the crofting counties. A cottar is someone who occupies a house, with or without garden ground, either rent free, or under a yearly tenancy at a rent of not more than £6 per year[8]. The difference between a cottar who pays no rent and a squatter is that the former has the landowner's permission to occupy the property[9]. If he is removed from the property, a cottar is entitled to compensation for permanent improvements[10]. Since 1976, a cottar has had the same right as a crofter to buy the house he occupies from the landowner[11].

---

1 Ibid s 5
2 Ibid s 10
3 Ibid s 47.
4 Ibid s 48.
5 Ibid s 49.
6 Ibid s 50.
7 Ibid ss 12–19.
8 Ibid s 12(5).
9 *Duke of Argyll's Trs v MacNeill* 1983 SLT (Land Ct) 35, 1982 SLCR 67.
10 Crofters (Scotland) Act 1993, s 36.
11 Ibid s 12.

13 Residential Leases: The Private Sector

1. INTRODUCTION: THE RENT ACTS

We now come to the area of lease law where statutory control of leases has for long been at its most prolific and confusing. Since the middle of the 1914–18 war, lets of dwellinghouses by private landlords have been largely subject to a series of statutes known originally as the Rent Restriction Acts and, more recently, as the Rent Acts. It is a field that has traditionally been fraught with difficulty and controversy. 'Even the most casual inspection of any recent volume of the King's Bench Reports will disclose the inhuman bondage in which the Rent Acts hold the legal profession'. These words of RE Megarry[1] have for long summed up the opinion of lawyers on the subject; this view was held not least by judges, who have described the Acts as 'this chaotic series of Acts' or 'that chaos of verbal darkness', to mention only two of the more flattering descriptions[2].

In 1967 Paton and Cameron quoted no less than eighteen Rent Acts that were wholly or partly in force at that time[3]. Since then the legislation has twice been consolidated, in 1971 and, most recently, by the Rent (Scotland) Act 1984. However, this welcome simplification proved to be somewhat short-lived, and fundamental changes to the system were made by the Housing (Scotland) Act 1988.

The purpose of the Rent Acts was to protect tenants of dwellinghouses in the private sector from exploitation by landlords. This was attempted mainly by means of rent control and by providing the tenant with security of tenure; to these there has been more recently added protection from harassment and unlawful eviction.

1 R E Megarry *The Rent Acts* (10th edn, 1967), quoting the preface to the 6th edn, 1951.
2 Lord Justice Mackinnon quoted in *Megarry*, introduction to 10th edn and in Paton & Cameron *Landlord and Tenant* (1967) p 497.
3 *Paton & Cameron* pp 497–498.

The first Act was introduced (as a temporary measure!) in 1915, because of an acute shortage of houses for working-class people during the 1914–18 war. This shortage was caused partly by the diversion of resources away from house building and into the war effort, and partly by the widespread migration of workers from rural areas into the towns to work in munitions factories. Since then, however, housing shortages have never quite gone away, and neither have the Rent Acts; unfortunately, neither did the illusion that they were temporary measures, and so after the first consolidating Act in 1920, there was no further consolidation until 1968 (in England) and 1971 (in Scotland). This accounts for much of the traditional confusion in this area.

But much more of the blame derives from the fact that, virtually from the start, the subject of rent control has been something of a political football. Conservative governments have tended to favour the position of the landlord and to relax restrictions; Labour governments, on the other hand, have been more inclined to favour tenants and to reimpose controls. This has, arguably, created a situation in which neither landlord nor tenant has been done full justice.

Few people would disagree that it is desirable to protect tenants from exploitation of housing shortages by unscrupulous landlords. But even the stoutest defenders of the Rent Acts will acknowledge that the Acts have not, in the long run, been an unqualified success, and that their well-intentioned intervention has had a counter-productive effect. The imposition on landlords of low rents, which for many years were allowed no adjustment to take account of inflation, meant that essential repairs and maintenance were often not carried out, hastening the decline of properties into slum condition. These rent levels, and the inability of landlords to regain possession of their properties when they wanted them, meant that owners who might otherwise have leased their properties were disinclined to do so; and those who did lease them were liable, when the properties eventually became vacant, to sell them off rather than relet them. Finally, private investment in this area virtually came to a halt, so that few new houses were built for letting by the private sector.

This situation was recognised by the then Labour government in 1965 when they substantially overhauled the system by introducing a system of fair rents that were designed to meet the needs of both landlords and tenants. This remained the basis of the system until 1988, when legislation was passed to replace it with a system of market rents.

To properly see the matter in perspective, however, we must

remember that the decline in private sector house letting over the course of the century was accompanied by an unprecedented increase, particularly since the last war, in the provision of public sector houses for let. When the first Rent Act was introduced in 1915, most people leased their dwellinghouse from a private landlord. Now the situation is quite different, with public sector land housing association tenancies being the dominant tenures, along with a rise in the incidence of owner-occupation. Nevertheless, the private sector element remains substantial, particularly in the realm of bedsits and other temporary furnished accommodation. The purpose of the most recent legislation was to reverse the trend by attracting private investment back to the house letting market.

We can sum up our historical outline, therefore, by dividing the legislation into three main phases:

(1) Controlled tenancies

The system of controlled tenancies was the main system from the onset of rent control until the system of regulated tenancies was introduced in 1965. However, the two systems continued in parallel until controlled tenancies were abolished in 1980. The tenant paid a standard rent which was not subject to increase except in very limited circumstances, eg where the landlord had carried out improvements. The result was that, especially in the years after the second world war, the rents paid under controlled tenancies became very low in real terms, being very far below market value. In 1957 the then Conservative government abolished rent control for all new tenancies and de-controlled all existing tenancies, apart from those with fairly low rateable values (those below £40 in London and below £30 elsewhere)[1]. The latter remained controlled, but for the standard rent there was substituted one linked to gross annual value. Many of those existing controlled tenancies, though gradually dwindling in number, continued in existence for some years, before being transformed into regulated tenancies in 1980[2].

Controlled tenancies are therefore now obsolete, and we need concern ourselves with them no further; this alone makes our task considerably easier, as it was in the heyday of controlled tenancies that the Rent Acts were at their most prolific and confusing. It should be said that the above brief account of controlled tenancies is an extremely general and simplified one: it is, thankfully, no

1 Rent Act 1957, s 11(1).
2 Tenants Rights Etc (Scotland) Act 1980, s 46.

longer necessary to consider their considerable complexities in further detail.

(2) Regulated tenancies

Regulated tenancies were introduced in 1965 by the Labour government in power at that time[1]. The massive decontrol in 1957 had led to many cases of poor tenants being exploited by slum landlords; one such landlord, a certain Mr Rachman, was even given the dubious honour of having his name incorporated into the English language, and the word 'rachmanism' came to stand for such exploitation. The Labour government, therefore, decided to reimpose controls, but sought to avoid the mistakes of the past by changing the system in a fundamental way. Tenants of dwellinghouses once again enjoyed security of tenure and freedom from eviction. In place of the old 'standard rent' there was introduced a system of 'fair rents', to be fixed in individual cases by the local rent officer, a government official appointed for the purpose, and with rights of appeal to a rent assessment committee. The fair rent was intended to provide a balance between the needs of landlords and tenants, by giving landlords a reasonable return on their investment, but ignoring any market forces caused by housing shortages. It also allowed for rents to be periodically reviewed to take account of inflation. There are still regulated tenancies in existence, mainly tenancies that were entered into prior to 1989. It will therefore be necessary to include some coverage of the law regarding them, but only after consideration of assured tenancies, which is now the dominant tenure.

(3) Assured tenancies

Since 2 January 1989 (when the appropriate part of the Housing (Scotland) Act 1988 came into force), there can, apart from a few limited exceptions to cover transitional cases, be no new regulated tenancies. Instead, new tenancies of dwellinghouses are subject to a system of assured tenancies, although existing regulated tenancies continue to be subject to the old system. Security of tenure remains, though the grounds of repossession have been modified somewhat in favour of landlords. However, the right of either the landlord or the tenant to apply to the rent officer to have a fair rent fixed was abolished; instead, the parties now negotiate a market

1 Rent Act 1965.

rent. The rent assessment committees continue to have a function in hearing appeals; however, in relation to assured tenancies they are fixing, not fair rents under the old formula, but market rents. Would-be private landlords are also given encouragement by a system of **short assured tenancies,** where security of tenure may be limited to no more than six months.

Application to Scotland

The original Rent Acts were United Kingdom statutes, dispensing their horrors indiscriminately both north and south of the Border. In more recent years, Scotland has had its own separate legislation, although the law has remained substantially the same in both countries, and the decisions of English courts in this field remain highly persuasive. The present Scottish law is mainly contained in the Rent (Scotland) Act 1984 and the Housing (Scotland) Act 1988.

Terminology

A number of different terms are used to describe the types of tenancy that fall within the ambit of the Rent Acts. The term 'regulated tenancy' has already been introduced as the general term for tenancies under the system introduced in 1965 and now governed by the Rent (Scotland) Act 1984[1]. This distinguishes it from the now obsolete 'controlled tenancy' and the 'assured tenancy' introduced by the 1988 Act. Within the broad definitions of 'regulated tenancy' and 'assured tenancy', however, there are several sub-categories. The term 'protected tenancy' is used generally for a tenancy that satisfies the criteria set out below for entitlement to security of tenure and rent regulation under the 1984 Act; it specifically applies to tenancies where the expiry date of the lease has not arrived, or where it has arrived and the lease is continuing under tacit relocation[2]. The term 'contractual tenancy' is sometimes used instead here, since it describes the period when the tenant's right to occupy the property derives from the lease contract, as with any other lease. However, as soon as the security of tenure provisions actually require to be invoked (ie when the landlord has served a notice to quit), the tenancy is described instead as a 'statutory tenancy'[3]. The

---

1 Rent (Scotland) Act 1984, s 8.
2 Ibid ss 1 and 2.
3 Ibid s 3.

terms 'contractual tenancy' and 'statutory tenancy' are used in a similar sense in relation to assured tenancies.

2. ASSURED TENANCIES: GENERAL

Definition

As we saw earlier, new tenancies which would formerly have been regulated tenancies, will be classified as assured tenancies if they were created after 2 January 1989, when Part II of the Housing (Scotland) Act 1988 came into force.

The general qualification for an assured tenancy is that a house is let as a separate dwelling[1]. It does not matter if some of the accommodation is shared with other tenants as long as there is a part that is occupied exclusively by the tenant[2]. Where land is let along with the house (other than agricultural land of more than two acres), the land will be included within the assured tenancy provided that the main purpose of the letting is the provision of a home for the tenant[3].

The definition of 'separate dwelling' includes flats as well as self-contained dwellinghouses[4]. It may also include part of a house, possibly no more than a single room, if it is let as a separate dwelling[5]. On the other hand, where the house which is the subject of let contains a number of units of habitation (which may be sub-let by the tenant), then the leased property is not a separate dwelling but a number of dwellings[6].

It is also a requirement for an assured tenancy that the tenant (or at least one of them if there are joint tenants) must occupy the house as his only or principal home[7]. In relation to regulated tenancies, it has been held that a tenant may qualify in this respect even although he only resides in the house part of the time, though if his absence is prolonged the onus is on him to establish an intention to return, and the court will look with particular care at two-home cases[8]. A

1 Housing (Scotland) Act 1988, s 12(1).
2 Ibid s 14; see also s 21 for situations where the right to shared accommodation may be terminated or varied.
3 Ibid s 13; Sch 4, para 5.
4 *Langford Property Co Ltd v Goldrich* [1949] 1 KB 511, [1949] 1 All ER 402, CA.
5 *Cole v Harris* [1945] KB 474, [1945] 2 All ER 146, CA.
6 *Horford Investments Ltd v Lambert* [1976] Ch 39, [1976] 1 All ER 131, CA; *St Catherine's College v Dorling* [1979] 3 All ER 250, [1980] 1 WLR 66, CA.
7 Housing (Scotland) Act 1988, s 12(1).
8 *Brickfield Properties v Hughes* (1988) 20 HLR 108, CA.

tenant who sublets his property in its entirety[1], or allows someone else (eg a mistress) to occupy in his place while living elsewhere himself[2], will not be considered to be in occupation. However, a tenant who sublets part of the property, while remaining in occupation of the rest, will not lose his right to security of tenure, provided that he intends at some future date to reoccupy the part sublet[3]. A corollary to the requirement that the tenant must occupy the property as his only or principal home is that, for there to be an assured tenancy, the tenant (or, in the case of joint tenants, at least one of them) must be a human being (and not, for example, a limited company).

Excepted categories

There are thirteen categories which do not qualify as assured tenancies. These are all identical, or substantially similar, to cases that were excluded from regulation under the Rent (Scotland) Act 1984[4], and so many of the cases on regulated tenancies are likely to be highly persuasive.

Schedule 4 of the Housing (Scotland) Act 1988 lists the following types of tenancy that cannot be assured tenancies. The numbers correspond to the paragraph numbers in the Schedule:

1. *A tenancy entered into before, or pursuant to a contract made before, Schedule 4 came into force.* This is a transitional provision that allows existing regulated tenancies to remain subject to the older system.

2. *Tenancies at a low rent.* These are tenancies where either no rent is payable, or the rent is less than £6 a week (or its equivalent, if the payment period is different)[5]. This limit may be varied in the future in a further order made by the Secretary of State. In determining the appropriate level, sums payable by the tenant in respect of services, repairs, maintenance or insurance are to be disregarded.

3. *A tenancy to which the Tenancy of Shops (Scotland) Act 1949 applies*[6]. Under the old system, a sublet of a residential element of a

---

1 *Menzies v Mackay* 1938 SC 74, 1938 SLT 135.
2 *Colin Smith Music Ltd v Ridge* [1975] 1 All ER 290, [1975] 1 WLR 463, CA.
3 *Regalian Securities Ltd v Ramsden* [1981] 2 All ER 65, [1981] 1 WLR 611, HL.
4 See pt 6 below.
5 Assured Tenancies (Tenancies at a Low Rent) (Scotland) Order 1988, SI 1988/2069.
6 See ch 8 above.

shop tenancy could be protected[1]. That proviso does *not* apply in the case of assured tenancies.

4. *Licensed premises.* The lease of a public house may include a dwellinghouse for the use of the person or persons operating the pub (an arrangement perhaps more common in England than it is in Scotland). This will not be an assured tenancy, presumably because the dwellinghouse element is an adjunct of a commercial let.

5. *Tenancies of agricultural land.* These are tenancies under which agricultural land exceeding two acres is let along with the house. Such tenancies, of course, are likely to enjoy the alternative protection of the Agricultural Holdings (Scotland) Act 1991[2].

6. *Tenancies of agricultural holdings.* This refers to tenancies under which the house is comprised in an agricultural holding within the meaning of the Agricultural Holdings (Scotland) Act 1991[3], and it is occupied by the person responsible for farming the holding; the latter may be either the tenant himself or his servant or agent. It is not immediately obvious which cases this would include that were not already caught by category 5. Presumably it would extend the exclusion to agricultural holdings of under two acres, eg some market gardens.

7. *Student lets, where the landlord is the student's educational institution.* This is a sensible provision that allows universities and colleges to remove ex-students from their properties in order to make way for new students. A student who leases directly from a private landlord has, of course, the same rights as any other tenant; only where his university or college is the landlord is he denied the status of assured tenant.

A list of educational establishments that qualify under this exception is contained in the Assured Tenancies (Exceptions) (Scotland) Regulations 1988[4].

8. *Holiday lets.* Obviously someone who takes a lease of a holiday cottage for two weeks or a month should not have the right to claim

---

1 Rent (Scotland) Act 1984, s 10(2).
2 See ch 12 above.
3 See ch 12, pt 1 above.
4 SI 1988/2068 (as amended by the Assured Tenancies (Exceptions) (Scotland) Amendment Regulations 1993, SI 1993/995).

extended security of tenure. However, the word 'holiday' is not defined in the relevant legislation, and the concept of a holiday let has been extended by the courts to cover some rather unlikely holiday situations. In *McHale v Daneham*[1] the tenants of premises in Maida Vale were foreign visitors working in London and the tenancy had endured for over six months before repossession was claimed. The court held that it was nevertheless a holiday let and the tenants were denied protection as a regulated tenancy. Nevertheless, the court will not necessarily confirm a let to be a holiday let merely because the lease says so, if there is other evidence to show that this is a sham by the landlord to evade the effects of the legislation.

9. *Where the landlord is resident.* The wording of this provision is somewhat lengthy and complex, but basically it means that security of tenure is denied where the landlord and tenant occupy the same house or flat. A similar exception has existed for regulated tenancies for some time, but the definition of resident landlord has been amended several times to exclude unintentional interpretations. The wording of the provision relating to assured tenancies is therefore designed to make it clear that a landlord is *not* regarded as resident (a) where he and the tenant occupy separate flats within a custom-built block of flats and (b) where they occupy separate flats within a single house that has been converted into self-contained flats. This is done by including a condition that, for a landlord to be considered resident, he must have some means of access through the tenant's house or vice versa[2].

For the tenancy to escape being an assured tenancy, the landlord must have been resident when the tenancy was granted and have continued to be resident thereafter. Where there is a change of landlord, as a result of death or otherwise, but the new landlord is also resident, there is a limited exception to the continuous residency requirement[3]. Where the tenancy is granted by joint landlords, only one needs to be resident to fall within this exception[4].

10. *Crown tenancies.* There is no assured tenancy where the landlord is the Crown or a government department, with the exception of property under the management of the Crown Estate Commissioners.

---

1 (1979) 249 EG 969.
2 Housing (Scotland) Act 1988, Sch 4, para 9(1)(c).
3 Ibid, Sch 4, para 9(3) and (4).
4 *Cooper v Tait* (1984) 271 EG 105, (1984) 48 P & CR 460, CA.

11. *Public sector tenancies.* Until now these have included the tenancies of regional, islands and district councils and in future will include tenancies of the new single tier councils that, after local government reorganisation, will replace the former[1]. Also included are the tenancies of water and sewage authorities[1], new town and urban development corporations, Scottish Homes and co-operative housing associations. These (with the exception of housing associations) all qualify for the more substantial protection conferred by a secure tenancy under the Housing (Scotland) Act 1987[2].

Also denied the status of assured tenancy are tenancies granted on a temporary basis by local authorities in fulfilment of their duty to provide accommodation for homeless persons[3].

12. *Shared ownership agreements.* This means any tenancy under a shared ownership agreement within the meaning of the Housing Associations Act 1985[4]. This refers to a situation where a tenant has an 'equity share' in the property, ie as well as paying a periodic rent he has paid a capital sum and remains entitled to a percentage of the house's value; in effect, therefore, he is part tenant, part owner. For people who cannot yet afford to take the full plunge into owner-occupation this arrangement provides a useful halfway stage between tenancy and ownership. Such agreements will not be assured tenancies, though presumably the tenant's equity share (if not the terms of the agreement) will give him a measure of security, as the tenancy could not be terminated without him being paid his share of the property's value.

13. *Transitional cases.* These are (a) protected tenancies under the Rent (Scotland) Act 1984; (b) housing association tenancies, and (c) secure tenancies[5]. Tenancies in these categories which commenced prior to 2 January 1989 (when the Housing (Scotland) Act 1988 came into force) continue to enjoy their existing status, ie private sector lets are regulated tenancies and housing association lets are secure tenancies. Housing association tenancies entered subsequently are assured tenancies[6], though new public sector lets in

1 Local Government etc (Scotland) Act 1994, Sch 13, para 157(7).
2 See ch 14, pt 2 below.
3 Housing Act 1988, Sch 7, para 90.
4 Housing Associations Act 1985, s 106 (as amended by the Housing (Scotland) Act 1988, Sch 9, para 9).
5 See ch 14, pt 2 below.
6 See however *Milnbank Housing Association v Murdoch* 1995 SLT (Sh Ct) 12.

general continue to be secure tenancies and cannot really be considered as transitional cases.

3. ASSURED TENANCIES: SECURITY OF TENURE

Statutory assured tenancies

An assured tenant's right to remain in occupation of the dwelling-house will not initially derive from the statutory provisions; as with any other tenant, it will depend upon the contractual period of his lease, and any extension to that term by the process of tacit relocation. It is only when the landlord has attempted to terminate the tenancy by sending a notice to quit that the statutory provisions for security of tenure come into force. Unless the landlord can establish one of the stated grounds of removal the tenancy will become a statutory assured tenancy, which will give the tenant the right to stay on in the property indefinitely.

Although these security of tenure provisions appear to offer a similar degree of protection to that enjoyed by regulated tenants and by secure tenants in the public sector[1], this protection is considerably weakened in the case of assured tenancies by the landlord's option of granting a short assured tenancy instead, which may not give the tenant any security of tenure at all, beyond a minimum period of six months[2].

Notice to quit

The contractual period of the tenancy (ie the period specified in the lease document) can only be terminated by the landlord serving a notice to quit at least four weeks prior to the termination date[3]. This notice will be invalid unless it contains certain specified information informing the tenant of his legal rights[4]. The tenant under an assured tenancy who remains in possession of the house after the contractual period of his lease has been thus terminated, will continue to have the assured tenancy of the house[5]. He can only be

1 See ch 14, pt 2 below.
2 See pt 5 below.
3 Rent (Scotland) Act 1984, s 112.
4 Assured Tenancies (Notices to Quit Prescribed Information) (Scotland) Regulations 1988, SI 1988/2067.
5 Housing (Scotland) Act 1988, s 16(1).

removed if the landlord obtains a court order by the sheriff, based on one of the grounds set out in Schedule 5 of the Act[1]. Although these grounds primarily apply to the termination of statutory assured tenancies, certain of them also apply during the contractual period of the lease, provided that the tenancy terms allow it[2].

Notice of proceedings for repossession

The tenant must also be given prior written notice of the repossession proceedings and the notice must state and give particulars of the ground of repossession[3]. The period of notice depends upon the ground that is being used. In respect of grounds 1, 2, 5, 6, 7, 9 and 17 below it is two months, and in the case of all the other grounds it is only two weeks. In certain circumstances the sheriff has discretion to dispense with the need for a notice[4]. The required form of the notice is laid down by the Assured Tenancies (Forms) (Scotland) Regulations 1988[5].

It will be noted that two separate notices are involved, a notice to quit, which has the function of bringing the contractual period of the lease to an end and preventing the onset of tacit relocation, and another notice intimating the landlord's intention to raise proceedings for repossession. There seems to be no reason why the two may not be sent at the same time, provided that the minimum period of notice for each is observed, as well as other legal requirements. Of course, a notice of proceedings for possession could also be sent at another time, eg if a repossession ground only arose later on during the statutory period of the tenancy.

Position of subtenants

If a property subject to an assured tenancy has been lawfully sublet, also under an assured tenancy, then the subtenant's tenancy will not be terminated along with that of the principal tenant; instead the subtenant will take the principal tenant's place under the main tenancy[6].

1 Housing (Scotland) Act 1988, s 16(2).
2 Ibid s 18(6).
3 Ibid s 19(2) (as amended by the Housing Act 1988, Sch 17, para 85).
4 Housing (Scotland) Act 1988 s 19.
5 SI 1988/2109 (as amended by the Assured Tenancies (Forms) (Scotland) Amendment Regulations 1993, SI 1993/648).
6 Housing (Scotland) Act 1988, s 28.

Mandatory grounds of repossession[1]

In these cases the sheriff, if he is satisfied that the ground exists, *must* give possession back to the landlord[2]. In respect of grounds (1) to (5) the tenant must have been given prior written notice that possession might be required under the ground in question; however, in the case of the first two of these grounds, the sheriff has the discretion to dispense with the need for such notice if he thinks it reasonable. The numbers of these mandatory grounds (and of the discretionary ones below) correspond to the paragraph numbers in Schedule 5 of the 1988 Act:

(1) *Occupancy by landlord.* The landlord formerly occupied the house as his only or principal home; alternatively he did not formerly occupy it, but now requires it for himself or his spouse and did not buy the property subject to the sitting tenancy.

(2) *Mortgage default.* The house is subject to a heritable security granted before the creation of the tenancy and, as a result of the debtor's default, the creditor requires to sell the house with vacant possession. The obvious example of this is where the house is repossessed because of the landlord's mortgage arrears.

(3) *Holiday property.* Off-season lets of holiday premises for a period not exceeding eight months. This should be distinguished from holiday lets, which are not assured tenancies at all[3]. If a property used for holiday lets is leased outwith the holiday season, it may qualify as an assured tenancy. For obvious reasons, however, extended security of tenure cannot be given.

(4) *Student accommodation.* A short lease between student lettings for a period not exceeding twelve months. This would cover lets during vacation time of properties normally let to students by their educational institution; as we saw above, the actual lets to the students themselves are *not* assured tenancies[3].

(5) *Ecclesiastical lets.* The house is required for a minister or a full-time lay missionary.

---

1 Ibid Sch 5, pt I.
2 Ibid s 18(3).
3 See pt 2 above.

(6) *Redevelopment*. The landlord intends to demolish or reconstruct the whole or a substantial part of the house, or to carry out substantial works on the house, or a building of which it forms part. This ground will not apply where the landlord or his predecessor bought the property for value after the creation of the tenancy. In other words, a landlord who bought the house subject to the sitting tenancy with the purpose of redeveloping the property will not be able to get vacant possession under this ground. It is also a condition of the ground applying that the work cannot be done without the tenant vacating the property; alternatively, it will apply if it is necessary for the tenant to accept a tenancy of only part of the house, or some other variation of his tenancy terms, and he has refused to agree to this. Where a tenancy is terminated under this ground (or under ground (9) below) the landlord is required to pay the tenant's removal expenses[1].

(7) *Inherited tenancy*. The tenant inherited the tenancy from a former tenant. The proceedings for recovery of possession must be begun not later than twelve months after the death of the former tenant, or within twelve months after the date when (in the sheriff's opinion) the landlord became aware of the former tenant's death. Mere acceptance of rent by the landlord after the death of the former tenant will not create a new tenancy, unless he has agreed in writing to change the level of rent, the duration of the let or some other term of the tenancy. This ground was first introduced along with assured tenancies, which have more restricted succession rights than regulated tenancies.

(8) *Three months rent arrears*. Both at the date of the service of the notice relating to the repossession proceedings and at the date of the hearing, the tenant is at least three months in arrears with rent. In the case of regulated tenancies, rent arrears is always a discretionary ground, but is mandatory for assured tenancies, provided that there are at least three months arrears. This means that, even where there are mitigating circumstances, the sheriff has no power to delay the proceedings to give the tenant time to pay; in theory, eviction could be mandatory even in circumstances where it was not the tenant's fault at all, eg if there was a delay in payment of housing benefit. The only leeway allowed the tenant is the opportunity to bring his arrears below the three months level during the period between the service of the landlord's notice and the date of the hearing; however, since this is one of the grounds where only two weeks' notice is required before the landlord can begin proceedings, this is not giving the tenant very much room for manoeuvre.

1 Housing (Scotland) Act 1988, s 22.

Discretionary grounds

Where one of the grounds in Part II of Schedule 5[1] is established, the sheriff is not to grant an order for possession unless he considers it reasonable to do so[2]. The sheriff has the power in the case of a discretionary ground to delay the proceedings, including the power to adjourn the case[3]. In addition he is required to impose conditions with regard to the payment of any rent arrears, and also with regard to payment of rent or other payments relating to the tenant's occupation of the property after the termination of the tenancy, or any other conditions he thinks fit; however, he has the discretion not to impose such conditions if he considers that to do so would cause exceptional hardship to the tenant or would otherwise be unreasonable[4]. In the case of regulated tenancies, it has been held that the court has a duty to take the question of reasonableness into account even if the issue was not pleaded or raised by the tenant[5].

(9) *Alternative accommodation.* Suitable alternative accommodation is available for the tenant or will be available for him when the order for possession takes effect. What is meant by suitable alternative accommodation is set out in Part III of Schedule 5. Factors to be taken into account include the proximity to the tenant's place of work, the rent level and the extent and character of the accommodation. The alternative accommodation must be under an assured tenancy or one giving an equivalent degree of security of tenure; a short assured tenancy or one subject to termination under grounds (1) to (5) above does not qualify as suitable. A certificate by the relevant local authority, new town or by Scottish Homes that they will rehouse the tenant is sufficient evidence that suitable alternative accommodation is available. Where a tenancy is terminated under this ground (or under ground (5) above) the landlord is required to pay the tenant's removal expenses[6]. In relation to regulated tenancies, it has been held that environmental factors such as noise or smell may make a property unsuitable[7]. However, the alternative accommodation only requires to be reasonably suitable to the needs of the tenant, and it is not necessary for him to be kept

---

1 As amended by the NHS and Community Care Act 1990, Sch 8, para 11.
2 Housing (Scotland) Act 1988, s 18(4).
3 Ibid s 20.
4 Ibid s 20(3).
5 *Smith v Poulter* [1947] KB 339, [1947] 1 All ER 216.
6 Ibid s 22.
7 *Redspring Ltd v Francis* [1973] 1 All ER 640, [1973] 1 WLR 134, CA.

in the style to which he has become accustomed. Thus in *Hill v Rochard*[1] the tenants, an elderly married couple, had the tenancy of a period country house with many spacious rooms, a staff flat, outbuildings, a stable, and one-and-a-half acres of land, including a paddock, where the tenants kept a pony. It was held that a house with a mere four bedrooms, occupying a paltry eighth of an acre and having no stable or paddock, was nevertheless suitable alternative accommodation, and the landlords were granted possession.

(10) *Tenant's notice to quit.* The tenant has given a notice to quit to the landlord and has remained in possession of the house after the expiry of the notice. Proceedings must be begun by the landlord within six months of the expiry of the notice. Also, the landlord will be precluded from using this ground if the tenant has been granted a new tenancy of the house in the meantime. In the case of regulated tenancies there was a requirement that the landlord, on the strength of the tenant's notice, must have committed himself in some way, eg by contracting to sell or relet the house. In the case of assured tenancies there is no such requirement.

(11) *Rent persistently late.* The tenant has persistently delayed paying rent which has become lawfully due. This ground applies whether or not there are actually any rent arrears due on the date when repossession proceedings are begun.

(12) *Rent arrears.* Some rent is unpaid on the date when repossession proceedings are begun. There also must have been unpaid rent on the date when notice of the proceedings was served on the tenant, unless it is a case where the sheriff has used his discretion to dispense with such a notice[2].

(13) *Other breach.* Any other obligation of the tenancy has been broken or not performed. The fact that this is a discretionary ground suggests that the breach would normally have to be relatively serious.

(14) *Deterioration of house.* The condition of the house or any of the common parts of the building has deteriorated because of the neglect of the tenant, or any one of joint tenants, or anyone living with the tenant. The tenant may only be removed for the act or

---

1 [1983] 2 All ER 21, [1983] 1 WLR 478, CA; see also *Siddiqui v Rashid* [1980] 3 All ER 184, [1980] 1 WLR 1018, CA.
2 Housing (Scotland) Act 1988, s 19(1)(b).

default of a lodger or subtenant where he has failed to take any reasonable steps to remove the person concerned. In relation to regulated tenancies, this ground has been held to include neglect of a garden attached to the house[1].

(15) *Nuisance etc.* There has been conduct in the house which is a nuisance or annoyance to adjoining proprietors, or there is a criminal conviction for using the house for an immoral or illegal purpose. It is not necessary that there should be a specific reference to using the premises in the criminal charge, provided that sufficient evidence is produced to show that the house was in fact used for the crime[2]. In the case of nuisance it may be either the tenant or some other person occupying the house who is responsible, and in the latter case it is probably not necessary that the tenant should have been aware of any conduct constituting a nuisance, eg where it was caused by the tenant's wife while he was in prison[3]. Also, the adjoining proprietors only need to be nearby (eg in the same building) and not necessarily physically contiguous[4].

(16) *Deterioration of furniture.* In the case of a furnished let there has been deterioration in the condition of the furniture because of ill treatment by the tenant or anyone living with him. As with ground (14) above, the tenant may only be removed for the act or default of a lodger or subtenant where he has failed to take any reasonable steps to remove the person concerned.

(17) *Ex-employee tenant.* The house was let to the tenant in consequence of his employment by the landlord, or a previous landlord, and the tenant has ceased to be in that employment. In the case of regulated tenancies, it was also necessary for the landlord to require the house for another employee. In relation to assured tenancies, that requirement has been dropped.

4. ASSURED TENANCIES: OTHER PROVISIONS

Rents under assured tenancies

As we have already observed, it is in relation to the rent level that an assured tenancy differs most fundamentally from its predeces-

1 *Holloway v Povey* (1984) 271 EG 195, (1984) 15 HLR 104, CA.
2 *Abrahams v Wilson* [1971] 2 QB 88, [1971] 2 All ER 1114, CA.
3 *Scottish Special Housing Association v Lumsden* 1984 SLT (Sh Ct) 71.
4 *Cobstone Investments v Maxim* [1985] QB 140, [1984] 2 All ER 635, CA.

sor, the regulated tenancy. A tenant no longer has the right to have a fair rent registered with the rent officer. Instead, a market rent is payable, although rent assessment committees still have a role to play in settling disputes[1].

Where the period of let specified in the lease contract is still unexpired, or where the lease is continuing on tacit relocation, the rent will be as stated in the lease document. Since it will presumably be at a level negotiated between the parties, and since the tenant will have no right to go to the rent officer to have it altered, this means that it is likely to be at a market level. After the expiry of the lease contract, when the tenancy is continuing as a statutory assured tenancy, the landlord may at any time serve a notice on the tenant proposing a new rent[2]. If the length of the tenancy was six months or more, the period of notice is six months; if the length was less than six months, the period will be the duration of the tenancy, though not less than one month[3]. After the rent has been increased, it may not be raised again until after a year has passed[4].

The new rent will take effect unless the tenant refers the matter to a rent assessment committee, or the parties negotiate a different level of rent. Section 25 sets out the rent assessment committees' guidelines for fixing a market rent. Since the tenant may feel that the landlord has proposed a rent above the market level, it may well be worth his while to refer the matter to a committee. The appropriate level of rent is that at which the committee considers that the house might reasonably be expected to be let in the open market by a willing landlord under an assured tenancy. It is to be assumed that the tenancy begins at the period when the new rent is to take effect and that the house has been let on terms (other than those relating to rent) that are the actual terms of the tenancy. If a notice or notices have been given that possession might be recovered under grounds (1) to (5) of Schedule 5, that should also be taken into account[5]. There should be disregarded any effect on the rent attributable to (a) the granting of a tenancy to a sitting tenant; (b)

---

1 For a more detailed discussion of the fixing of rents for assured tenancies and the role of rent assessment committees see Peter Robson *Residential Tenancies* (1994) pp 125–136.
2 Housing (Scotland) Act 1988, s 24(1) (as amended by the Local Government and Housing Act 1989, Sch 11, para 100). For the prescribed form of such a notice, see Assured Tenancies (Forms) (Scotland) Regulations 1988, SI 1988/2109 (as amended by the Assured Tenancies (Forms) (Scotland) Amendment Regulations 1993, SI 1993/648).
3 Housing (Scotland) Act 1988, s 24(2).
4 Ibid s 24(4).
5 Ibid s 25(1).

an improvement carried out by the tenant or a predecessor in title, unless the improvement was carried out in pursuance of the terms of the tenancy, and (c) the failure by the tenant to comply with any terms of the tenancy[1].

Other tenancy terms

Alteration of terms. During the contractual period of an assured tenancy, the terms will be those in the lease document. Once the tenancy has become a statutory one, the terms (other than those relating to termination of the tenancy or increasing the rent) will initially remain the same as before[2]. They will only be changed if the landlord, within a year of the termination of the contractual tenancy, serves a notice on the tenant proposing different terms[3]. The tenant may refer the notice to a rent assessment committee, which may confirm the new terms or fix other terms that it considers reasonable[4]. If the notice is not referred to a committee, the new terms will take effect three months after the service of the notice, or after such longer period as the notice specifies[5]. Either the landlord in his notice, or the rent assessment committee if the matter is referred to it, may make an adjustment of the rent to take account of the new terms[6]. There are prescribed forms for both the landlord's and the tenant's notices[7].

Assignation and subletting[8]. It is an implied term of every assured tenancy that, except with the consent of the landlord, the tenant shall not (a) assign the tenancy (in whole or in part) or (b) sublet or part with possession of the whole or any part of the house. This provision only applies if there is no provision in the lease dealing with assignation or subletting.

---

1 Ibid s 25(2).
2 Housing (Scotland) Act 1988, s 16(1) (as amended by the Local Government and Housing Act 1989, Sch 11, para 99).
3 Housing (Scotland) Act 1988, s 17(2). For the prescribed forms of notice for both landlord and tenant under this section, see the Assured Tenancies (Forms) (Scotland) Regulations 1988, SI 1988/2109 (as amended by the Assured Tenancies (Forms) (Scotland) Amendment Regulations 1993, SI 1993/648).
4 Housing (Scotland) Act 1988, s 17(4).
5 Ibid s 17(3).
6 Ibid s 17(5).
7 Assured Tenancies (Forms) (Scotland) Regulations 1988, SI 1988/2109 (as amended by the Assured Tenancies (Forms) (Scotland) Amendment Regulations 1993, SI 1993/648).
8 Housing (Scotland) Act 1988, s 23.

Access for repairs[1]. It is an implied term of every assured tenancy that the tenant will afford the landlord reasonable access to the house and all reasonable facilities for carrying out any repairs the landlord is entitled to execute.

Written lease and rent book[2]. The landlord under an assured tenancy has a duty to draw up a formal document containing or referring to the tenancy terms, and to give a copy of it to the tenant. This should all be free of charge to the tenant. If the landlord fails to draw up such a document, or to adjust the terms of an existing document where necessary, the tenant can refer the matter to the sheriff. Where the rent is payable weekly, the landlord has a duty to provide a rent book, and a landlord failing to do so will be liable to a fine. The rent book must contain certain information informing the tenant of his legal rights[3].

5. SHORT ASSURED TENANCIES[4]

Nature

This is a special type of tenure under which the landlord has an absolute right to possession of the house when the period stated in the lease contract comes to an end. In such cases, therefore, the tenant is denied the right to extended security of tenure as a statutory assured tenant. In order to qualify for this exemption, the term of the let must be at least six months and the tenant must have been given written notice in advance that the tenancy was to be a short assured tenancy[5]. If the tenant is granted a renewal of the lease, or it continues by tacit relocation, no fresh notice will be required to qualify the tenancy as a short assured tenancy[6]. The landlord, however, is entitled to convert such a renewed lease into an ordinary assured tenancy by serving on the tenant a notice to that effect[7]. There are prescribed forms for both of the above notices[8].

1 Ibid s 26.
2 Ibid s 30.
3 Assured Tenancies (Rent Book) (Scotland) Regulations 1988, SI 1988/2085 (as amended by the Assured Tenancies (Rent Book) (Scotland) Amendment Regulations 1993, SI 1993/649).
4 Housing (Scotland) Act 1988, ss 32–35.
5 Ibid s 32 (1) and (2).
6 Ibid s 32(3).
7 Ibid s 32(4).
8 Assured Tenancies (Forms) (Scotland) Regulations 1988, SI 1988/2109 (as amended by the Assured Tenancies (Forms) (Scotland) Amendment Regulations 1993, SI 1993/648).

Termination of short assured tenancies

The same grounds of repossession apply to short assured tenancies as with other assured tenancies. In addition, the sheriff is bound to give an order for possession if he is satisfied (a) that the short assured tenancy has reached its ish (ie its expiry date); (b) that tacit relocation is not operating; (c) that no further contractual tenancy is in existence; and (d) that the landlord has given a notice stating that he requires possession of the house[1]. The period of notice is two months, or such longer period as the lease specifies[2].

The 1988 Act does not make the function of such a notice entirely clear. It cannot be a notice to quit in the normal sense, as it is expressly stated that it may be served before, at or after the termination of the tenancy to which it relates[3]. However, the sheriff cannot grant the landlord possession where tacit relocation is operating, and the common law relating to notices to quit and tacit relocation is expressly saved by s 52. It will therefore be necessary for the landlord to send a notice to quit at least 28 days prior to the expiry date of the tenancy to prevent the onset of tacit relocation[4]. Unlike the situation with ordinary assured tenancies, there is no prescribed form for the notice requiring possession of the house, and the 1988 Act does not even state that such a notice needs to be in writing[5]. Needless to say, a written notice is highly advisable and is definitely a legal requirement if the notice is also to fulfil the function of a notice to quit[6].

There seems to be no reason why the two notices cannot be combined in one, provided that their respective functions are met by the single notice. However, although a 28-day notice will stop tacit relocation operating, the landlord cannot raise repossession proceedings until he has given the required notice of at least two months. This means that if the landlord wants to be able to raise proceedings as soon as the lease has ended, he will require to serve his combined notice at least two months before the expiry date.

Advantages and disadvantages

Since the general provisions relating to assured tenancies apply to short assured tenancies as well there seems no reason for landlords

1 Housing (Scotland) Act 1988, s 33(1).
2 Ibid s 33(2).
3 Ibid s 33(3).
4 Rent (Scotland) Act 1984, s 112; see also ch 7, pt 2 above.
5 Housing (Scotland) Act 1988, s 33; see also *Robson* p 181.
6 Rent (Scotland) Act 1984, s 112(1).

not to adopt the latter as the preferred form of tenure. If landlords opt for short assured tenancies of the minimum length, the greatest security that any tenant will enjoy is for the initial period of six months. If the landlord grants a renewal, it can be for a shorter period[1]. There therefore seems no reason why a landlord could not, for example, grant a lease of six months, followed by one of a shorter period, which could thereafter proceed by tacit relocation until the landlord decided to terminate it or put up the rent. Such a let, however, would still require two months' notice of termination.

There are, however, some disadvantages that a landlord will suffer by opting for a short assured tenancy. For example, if the tenant thinks that his rent is too high, he can refer it to a rent assessment committee to have a market rent fixed during the contractual period of his lease[2]. In the case of a normal assured tenancy, on the other hand, he is stuck with the rent in the lease until the lease has ended and the tenancy has become a statutory one; then, if the landlord serves a notice of increase, the tenant can refer the matter to a rent assessment committee. The right of a tenant under a short assured tenancy to have a market rent fixed by a rent assessment committee is qualified in two ways: (1) there must be a sufficient number of similar houses in the locality let on assured tenancies for the committee to use as comparisons[3]; and (2) the right can be discontinued in particular areas, or in other specified circumstances, if the Secretary of State makes an order to that effect[4].

One possible advantage to a landlord of opting for a normal assured tenancy, therefore, is that he may be able to get a tenant to agree to a rent above the level that a rent assessment committee is likely to fix as a market rent. In such a case the tenant will be held to that rent until the lease has expired, and even after that, provided that the landlord has not served a notice of increase. The landlord's penalty is that the tenant will get extended security of tenure.

In general, however, there seems to be more incentive for landlords to opt for the short assured tenancy, which means that the security of tenure offered by a normal assured tenancy may be more apparent than real.

1 Housing (Scotland) Act 1988, s 32(3).
2 Ibid s 34.
3 Ibid s 34(3).
4 Ibid s 35.

6. REGULATED TENANCIES: GENERAL

As we saw at the beginning of the chapter, the system of regulated tenancies is intended eventually to become obsolete. However, existing regulated tenancies entered into before Part II of the Housing (Scotland) Act 1988 came into force (ie 2 January 1989) continue to have protection under the Rent (Scotland) Act 1984, and to enjoy a system of fair rents. Also, new regulated tenancies can be created in certain special circumstances[1]: (a) where the tenancy is entered in pursuance of a contract made before 2 January 1989; (b) where, immediately before the tenancy was granted, the tenant was the protected or a statutory tenant of the same landlord (ie not only where an existing regulated tenancy is being renewed, but also where the same landlord grants a tenancy of a different property); and (c) where the tenant was entitled to alternative accommodation on the termination of a previous regulated tenancy (or of a secure tenancy from a public sector landlord - see chapter 14); this provision would apply, for example, where the availability of alternative accommodation had been the ground of repossession. It is therefore still necessary to give an account of the main provisions relating to regulated tenancies.

Protected tenancies

Rateable value limit. The Rent (Scotland) Act 1984 applies only to houses under a certain rateable value limit. The relevant limit is such, however, that it includes most houses likely to come on the normal letting market. The result is that only properties at the very top end of the market (apart from those excluded for one of the other reasons stated below) will be free from statutory protection. In most cases the relevant rateable value limit is not the current rateable value of the property, but a historic one, ie its rateable value when the system of regulated tenancies was first introduced by the Rent Act 1965. If, therefore, the property in question was in existence in 1965, any subsequent tenancy of it will be protected if it had a rateable value of under £200 on 23 March 1965 (the date when the Rent Act 1965 came into force), irrespective of its rateable value now.

As we saw in the introductory section above, one effect of the Rent Acts has been that few new dwellinghouses have been built by the private sector for letting. This means that most of the houses on

1 Housing (Scotland) Act 1988, s 42(1).

the private letting market are older properties which were in existence in 1965 and which appeared on the valuation roll at that date. In most cases, therefore, the property will have a historic rateable value, and reference to this will determine whether or not a tenancy comes within the limit for protection. But it is nevertheless possible that properties built since 1965 may be let and may be of a comparable value to those older properties that enjoy protection; however, since there have been several rating revaluations since 1965, such properties may have entered the valuation roll for the first time at a level above £200. For such properties, therefore, it has been necessary to provide higher rateable value limits.

To sum up, therefore, a house will be within the rateable value limit for a protected tenancy in the following circumstances[1]:

(a) If it was already on the valuation roll on 23 March 1965 at a rateable value of under £200. As explained above, most protected tenancies are of older properties and will come under this heading.

(b) If it first appeared on the valuation roll between 23 March 1965 and 31 March 1978 with a rateable value under £200.

(c) If it first appeared on the valuation roll between 1 April 1978 and 31 March 1985 with a rateable value under £600.

(d) If it first appeared on the valuation roll after 1 April 1985 with a rateable value under £1,600.

In each of (b), (c) and (d), the relevant value is that when the property first appeared on the roll. The Secretary of State was given power under the 1984 Act to further raise the limit from time to time to allow for future rating revaluations[2]; and this happened in the case of category (d) above, in order to take account of the 1985 revaluation.

Since the introduction of the community charge and its successor the council tax, new rateable values are no longer entered in the valuation roll in respect of residential properties, either new or existing. However, since new regulated tenancies cannot normally now be created, and the exceptions are likely to relate to older properties, this fact is unlikely to create much difficulty.

There is no equivalent rateable value limit in respect of assured tenancies[3].

---

1 Rent (Scotland) Act 1984, s 1(1)(a), s 7; Protected Tenancies and Part VII Contracts (Rateable Value Limits) (Scotland) Order 1985, SI 1985/314.
2 Rent (Scotland) Act 1984, s 1(2).
3 See pt 2 above.

Further criteria for protection. Subject to the exceptions noted below, every tenancy will be a protected tenancy under the 1984 Act where a dwellinghouse within the appropriate rateable value limit is let as a separate dwelling. As long as there is a part that is held exclusively by the tenant, it does not matter if some of the accommodation is shared with other tenants[1]. For further discussion of the meaning of 'separate dwelling', see the relevant section above in relation to assured tenancies[2].

Subtenancies fall within the Act's definition of a tenancy, and so are also protected[3].

Excepted categories

The following categories of tenancy are *not* protected. Many of these exceptions (though there are important differences) are the same as or similar to those which apply to assured tenancies:

1. *Where no rent is payable or the rent is less than two-thirds of the appropriate rateable value limit*[4]. This refers to the historic rateable value that qualified the tenancy for protection[5]. In most cases this will be the rateable value in 1965.

2. *Where the house is bona fide let at a rent which includes payments for board or attendance*[6]. 'Board' means the provision of food and 'attendance' means personal services such as cleaning or laundry services. In the case of attendance, the amount of rent attributable to it must form a substantial part of the whole rent[7]. This provision was probably only intended to exclude from protection people like lodgers and residents of boarding houses or hotels. However, it has been exploited as a loophole by which landlords have attempted to exclude tenancies from protection by creating the notorious 'bed and breakfast lets', where tenants, as part of their lease terms, were supplied by their landlord with breakfast in some form[8]. This

---

1 Rent (Scotland) Act 1984, s 97(1).
2 See pt 2 above.
3 Rent (Scotland) Act 1984, s 115(1).
4 Ibid s 2 (1)(a); see also *Thomson v Lann* 1967 SLT (Sh Ct) 76 and *Fennel v Cameron* 1968 SLT (Sh Ct) 30.
5 Rent (Scotland) Act 1984, s 7(3).
6 Ibid s 2(1)(b).
7 Ibid s 2(4); see also *Marchant v Charters* [1977] 3 All ER 918, [1977] 1 WLR 1181, CA.
8 For a review of the case law on this see *Gavin v Lindsay* 1987 SLT (Sh Ct) 12; see also *Otter v Norman* (1987) 284 EG 372, (1988) 132 Sol Jo 52, CA.

exclusion does not apply to assured tenancies and is consequently now much less important.

3. *Student lets, where the landlord is the student's educational institution*[1]. This is identical to the equivalent exception for assured tenancies[2].

4. *Holiday lets*[3]. This is also identical to the assured tenancy provision.

5. *Where the house is let along with agricultural land exceeding two acres*[4]. Such tenancies, of course, are likely to enjoy the alternative protection of the Agricultural Holdings (Scotland) Act 1991[5].

6. *Public sector tenancies*[6]. These are mainly the same categories of public sector tenancy that are excluded from assured tenancies, and also include crown tenancies and shared ownership agreements.

7. *Where the landlord is resident*[7]. This is virtually the same as the equivalent provision relating to assured tenancies[8]. However, although this exception does not apply where the landlord and tenant occupy separate flats in a purpose-built block of flats, it *does* inadvertently apply where they occupy separate flats within a dwellinghouse that has been converted into flats. This loophole has been plugged in relation to assured tenancies[8].

8. *Business premises*[9]. Where a property is used exclusively for commercial purposes, it will not qualify as a dwellinghouse within the meaning of the 1984 Act. However, where it is used partly for business and partly for residential purposes, it may still be protected, provided that the residential element is substantial[10]. As with

---

1 Rent (Scotland) Act 1984, s 2(1)(c).
2 See pt 2 above.
3 Rent (Scotland) Act 1984, s 2(1)(d).
4 Ibid ss 1(3) and 2(1)(e).
5 See ch 12 above.
6 Rent (Scotland) Act 1984, s 5 (as amended *inter alia* by the Housing (Consequential Provisions) Act 1985, Sch 2, para 59, the Housing (Scotland) Act 1988, s 47(1) and the Local Government etc (Scotland) Act 1994, Sch 13, para 137); and s 4.
7 Rent (Scotland) Act 1984, s 6.
8 See pt 2 above.
9 Rent (Scotland) Act 1984, s 10.
10 *Cargill v Phillips* 1951 SC 67, 1951 SLT 110; *Cowan & Sons v Acton* 1952 SC 73, 1952 SLT 122. In these cases, however, the business element was in fact primary and the tenancies were *not* protected.

assured tenancies, public houses and shops are totally excluded from protection, even where there is a residential element. In the case of regulated (though not assured) tenancies there is an exception where the residential element of a shop tenancy is sublet[1].

7. REGULATED TENANCIES: SECURITY OF TENURE

Statutory tenancies

The result of a tenancy being a protected tenancy is, of course, that the tenant enjoys the benefits conferred by the Rent (Scotland) Act 1984. This means, in contrast to the situation with assured tenancies, that he has the right to have a fair rent registered with the rent officer and that the terms of his lease contract will generally only be effective to the extent that they are consistent with the terms of the 1984 Act. However, in common with assured tenancies, he has a right of security of tenure and his tenancy will become a statutory one when the landlord has served a notice to quit and the period of notice has expired[2]. And, once again, the landlord can only regain possession by court order, based on one of the relevant statutory grounds.

Terms of statutory tenancies

The terms and conditions of a statutory tenancy are the same as those in the original contract of tenancy, so far as they are consistent with the provisions of the 1984 Act[3]. The period of notice of termination by either party will be the same as in the lease contract except that (a) if no period of notice is stated, a tenant who wishes to terminate will require to give the landlord at least three months' notice and (b) in all cases, a landlord wishing repossession must give a minimum of four weeks' notice[4].

---

1 Rent (Scotland) Act 1984, s 10(4).
2 For the requirements and content of the notice to quit see the Rent (Scotland) Act 1984, s 112 and the Rent Regulation (Forms and Information etc) (Scotland) Regulations 1991, SI 1991/1521 (as amended by the Rent Regulation (Forms and Information etc) (Scotland) Amendment Regulations 1993, SI 1993/647), reg 4 and Sch 2.
3 Rent (Scotland) Act 1984, s 15(1).
4 Ibid s 15(3) and (4); s 112.

Assignations and sublets

A statutory tenant is entitled to assign his tenancy, provided that he obtains the landlord's consent, and the assignee will become a statutory tenant in his place[1]. Subletting is not allowed if it is against the terms of the original tenancy. Otherwise the tenancy may be sublet in whole or in part, and if the principal tenancy is terminated, the subtenant will be allowed to stay on as a statutory tenant[2].

Termination of statutory tenancies

The grounds of repossession by the landlord are contained in Schedule 2 of the 1984 Act and, as with assured tenancies, consist of both discretionary and mandatory grounds. Many of these are the same, or substantially similar, to the grounds for termination of an assured tenancy, though there are significant differences which will be noted below.

Discretionary grounds of repossession[3]

In these cases, the court will not grant a landlord an order for possession of the premises unless it considers that it is reasonable to do so and either (a) there is suitable alternative accommodation available or (b) there exists one or more of the grounds specified in Part I of Schedule 2 of the 1984 Act. In the case of these discretionary grounds (but not the mandatory ones) the court has power to delay the proceedings in various ways, including adjournment of the case[4]. This power would normally be used in cases of rent arrears in order to give the tenant time to pay.

The grounds for deciding whether or not suitable alternative accommodation is available are set out in Schedule 2, Part IV, and are virtually the same as in the case of assured tenancies[5].

A certificate of the housing authority for the district in which the house is situated, certifying that the authority will provide suitable alternative accommodation for the tenant by a particular date, is

---

1 Ibid s 17.
2 Ibid s 19; see also discretionary ground 6 below.
3 Rent (Scotland) Act 1984, s 11 and Sch 2, pt I.
4 Ibid s 12.
5 See pt 3 above.

conclusive evidence that suitable alternative accommodation will be available by that date[1].

The grounds specified in Part I of Schedule 2 are: (1) Rent arrears or other breach[2]; (2) Nuisance[3]; (3) Deterioration of house[4]; (4) Deterioration of furniture (if it is a furnished let[5]); (5) Tenant's notice to quit[6]; (6) Unauthorised assignation or subletting[7]; (7) House required for the landlord's employee[8]; (8) House required for occupancy by the landlord[9]; (9) Subletting at an excessive rent[10]; and (10) Overcrowding[11].

Mandatory grounds of repossession[12].

As with assured tenancies, these are situations where the court does not have discretion and must grant a repossession order if the ground is proved to exist. In the case of all these grounds (except number (8) below), the tenant must have been given advance written notice that the landlord might require possession on the ground in question; in the case of grounds (1), (2) and (9), however, the court has discretion to dispense with this notice[13]. The onus of proof that the ground exists is on the landlord.

The mandatory grounds are: (1) Requirement of the house by an owner who has formerly occupied it[14]; (2) Requirement of the house by the landlord as a retirement home[15]; (3) Off-season lets of holiday property not exceeding eight months[16]; (4) Lettings of student accommodation not exceeding twelve months[17]; (5) Short tenancies[18]; (6) Requirement of the house for a minister or a full-time lay

---

1 Rent (Scotland) Act 1984, Sch 2, pt IV, para 1.
2 Ibid Sch 2, pt I, case 1.
3 Ibid case 2.
4 Ibid case 3.
5 Ibid case 4.
6 Ibid case 5.
7 Ibid case 6.
8 Ibid case 7.
9 Ibid case 8.
10 Ibid case 9.
11 Ibid case 10.
12 Ibid s 11 and Sch 2, pt II.
13 *Bradshaw v Baldwin-Wiseman* (1985) 49 P & CR 382, (1985) 274 EG 285, CA.
14 Rent (Scotland) Act 1984, Sch 2, pt II, case 11.
15 Ibid case 12.
16 Ibid case 13.
17 Ibid case 14.
18 Ibid case 15.

missionary[1]; (7) Requirement of the house for the landlord's agricultural employee[2]; (8) In certain circumstances where the owner was a member of the British army[3].

Contrast with assured tenancies[4]

The above grounds of repossession were used as the basis for those applicable to assured tenancies, with the result that many of them are identical or substantially similar to the latter. In such cases the observations made above in relation to assured tenancies, as well as the case law (much of which is derived from regulated tenancies), will also be relevant here. However, there are important differences, the general effect of which is to make repossession more difficult for the landlord of a regulated tenancy than it is for the landlord of an assured tenancy.

Rent arrears. This is always a *discretionary* ground, and there is no equivalent of the assured tenancy ground of persistent late payment, or of the *mandatory* ground where three months rent is owing.

Occupation by owner. This is only a mandatory ground if the owner formerly occupied the house, or if he bought it as a retirement home, or was a member of the army when he bought it and when the lease was granted. Otherwise this ground is discretionary in the case of regulated tenancies, and in addition the landlord must have owned the house at the beginning of the tenancy, as opposed to having bought the property subject to the sitting tenancy[5]. In the case of assured tenancies, this ground is always mandatory (though it also does not apply at all if the landlord bought the property subject to the sitting tenancy).

Tenant's notice to quit. This ground only applies if the landlord has acted on the notice by contracting to sell or relet the house, or has taken some other step that would prejudice him if the tenant

---

1 Ibid case 16.
2 Ibid cases 17–19.
3 Ibid case 20.
4 See pt 2 above.
5 *Epps v Rothnie* [1945] KB 562, [1946] 1 All ER 146, CA; *Newton v Biggs* [1953] 2 QB 211, [1953] 1 All ER 99, CA. But see *Thomas v Fryer* [1970] 2 All ER 1, [1970] 1 WLR 845, CA.

changed his mind. In the case of assured tenancies there is no such requirement.

Service tenancies. As well as being let to a former employee, the house must now be 'reasonably required' for a current employee. The latter proviso does not apply to assured tenancies. The words 'reasonably required' mean more than just that the landlord desires the property, but something less than absolute necessity will do[1].

Short tenancies. This was a special type of regulated tenancy which was the predecessor of the short assured tenancy[2], and under which the landlord similarly had an absolute right to repossess at the end of the lease[3]. This is why the expiry of a short tenancy gives rise to a mandatory ground of repossession. However, because of the requirement that a fair rent be registered, short tenancies were never popular with landlords and so, considering that they had a maximum length of five years and that no new ones could be created after 1989, it seems unlikely that there are many left in existence; presumably this could only be the case in respect of tenancies now continuing by tacit relocation[4].

Similar grounds. The grounds which are identical or substantially similar for both regulated and assured tenancies are the availability of alternative accommodation, breach of the lease other than rent arrears, nuisance, deterioration of the house or furniture, off-season lets of holiday property and lets of student accommodation. Because of their temporary nature, it is unlikely that any regulated tenancies belonging to the last two categories are still in existence.

Other disparities. The right of the landlord in an assured tenancy to repossess the house for redevelopment and also from the successor of a deceased tenant have no equivalent in the case of regulated tenancies. On the other hand, other regulated tenancy grounds (for reasons not always obvious) have not survived into the new system: these are, overcrowding, subletting at an excessive rent and requirement of an adapted house for a person with special needs. Unauthorised assignation or subletting is only specifically mentioned as a ground in the case of regulated tenancies, although pre-

1 *Aitken v Shaw* 1933 SLT (Sh Ct) 21.
2 See pt 5 above.
3 See Rent (Scotland) Act 1984, ss 9, 13 and 14.
4 Rent (Scotland) Act 1984, s 14(3).

sumably, in the case of an assured tenancy, it could qualify under the general heading of breach of a tenancy obligation.

8. REGULATED TENANCIES: FAIR RENTS[1]

Rent regulation

As we saw at the beginning of the chapter, the present system of rent regulation was first introduced in 1965. The relevant Scottish provisions are now found in Parts IV and V of the Rent (Scotland) Act 1984. These allow for the fixing of fair rents for protected tenancies by local rent officers and rent assessment committees and for the registration of such rents. Rent officers are independent government officials appointed and paid by the Secretary of State. One or more rent officers normally serve for each registration area, which are the areas served by local authorities[2]. Rent assessment committees are drawn from a large panel of professional and lay people appointed by the Secretary of State, and a typical committee would consist of three members, one legally qualified, another a professionally qualified surveyor or valuer, and the third a lay member; it is, however, possible for a committee to have only two members and, in exceptional cases, the chairman may decide cases on his own[3]. Under the system of assured tenancies rent assessment committees also have a function, as we saw earlier[4]. Various forms relating to rent regulation and registration of fair rents, as well as the content of rent books, are prescribed by the Rent Regulation (Forms and Information etc) (Scotland) Regulations 1991, SI 1991/1521[5].

Registration of fair rent

Where a tenancy is a protected one, either the landlord or the tenant, or both, may apply to the local rent officer to fix a fair rent to be registered for the house[6]. This may be done either during the

---

1 See *Robson* pp 113–125.
2 Rent (Scotland) Act 1984, s 43 (as amended by the Local Government etc (Scotland) Act 1994, Sch 13, para 137(3)).
3 Ibid s 44.
4 See pt 4 above.
5 As amended by the Rent Regulation (Forms and Information etc) (Scotland) Amendment Regulations 1993, SI 1993/647.
6 Rent (Scotland) Act 1984, s 46.

contractual period of the tenancy, or after the lease has expired and it is continuing as a statutory tenancy. This means that, even if a tenant has already signed a lease at a particular rent, there is nothing to stop him going to the rent officer to have a fair rent registered if he thinks this will effect a reduction. After a fair rent has been registered, that rent will be the maximum that the landlord can charge, and if the tenant pays more he will be entitled to recover the difference from the landlord[1]. During the contractual period of the lease, however, the tenant can hold the landlord to the rent in the lease if it is less than the registered rent. The registration takes effect from the date of registration by the rent officer, except in the case of appeals, where it takes effect from the date of the decision of the rent assessment committee[2].

Any element of the registered rent which is attributable to the use of furniture, the provision of services, or the use of part of the premises as a shop or office or other business purpose must be noted separately on the register if it exceeds 5 per cent of the rent[3].

Either during the contractual or the statutory period of the tenancy, the landlord and tenant may enter into an agreement to increase the rent. However, such an agreement does not affect the tenant's right to have a fair rent registered, and unless the agreement draws the tenant's attention to his statutory rights it will be unenforceable[4]; thus the tenant is offered some protection from being persuaded to pay a higher rent than he needs to because he is ignorant of his rights.

If either the landlord or the tenant is dissatisfied with the figure arrived at by the rent officer, he can appeal to a rent assessment committee by lodging a written objection with the rent officer within 28 days[5]. The committee's decision is final on questions of fact, but not on questions of law.

Variation of rent

Once a fair rent has been determined for a property, it will remain fixed for a period of three years, unless there is a material change in the condition of the house (eg by the carrying out of a substantial

---

1 Ibid ss 28 and 37; see also *North v Allan Properties (Edinburgh)* 1987 SLT (Sh Ct) 141.
2 Rent (Scotland) Act 1984, s 50.
3 Ibid s 49(2) and (3).
4 Ibid ss 34 and 36.
5 Ibid s 46 and Sch 5, para 6.

improvement)[1], or in the terms of the tenancy or the quantity, quality or condition of the furniture[2]. After three years has elapsed since registration, either party can apply for re-registration; if an application is made before that, the registration will not take effect until after the three-year period has elapsed[3]. If the dwellinghouse in question ceases to be let under a regulated tenancy, the landlord can apply for a cancellation of the registration[4].

Phasing

When a rent is registered (or re-registered), the landlord may not be entitled to charge the new rent right away, but, depending on the size of the increase, may have to phase the increase over all or part of the three-year period. Following registration, the existing rent is increased annually by whichever is the greatest of the following amounts: (1) £104; (2) 25 per cent of the existing rent; or (3) half the difference between the existing rent and the new registered rent. At no point can the rent be raised above the level of the new registered rent, and so no increase can exceed the amount it takes to reach that level[5]. The same formula is applied at the end of each year to the rent being paid in order to determine the rent payable in the succeeding year. These limits may be changed in the future by a further order made by the Secretary of State[6].

Under the Housing (Scotland) Act 1988 the Secretary of State is given power to amend these provisions for phasing, or repeal them entirely[7].

Determination of fair rent

Fair rent formula. The fair rent formula is contained in s 48 of the 1984 Act:

1. In determining a fair rent, the rent officer or rent assessment committee must have regard to all the circumstances (other than

---

1 *London Housing & Commercial Properties v Cowan* [1977] QB 148, [1976] 2 All ER 385.
2 Rent (Scotland) Act 1984, s 46(3).
3 Ibid s 50(2).
4 Ibid s 52.
5 Ibid s 33; Limits on Rent Increases (Scotland) Order 1989, SI 1989/2469.
6 Rent (Scotland) Act 1984, s 33.
7 Housing (Scotland) Act 1988, s 41.

personal circumstances), and in particular apply their knowledge and experience of current rents of comparable property in the area, as well as have regard to the age, character and locality of the dwellinghouse in question and to its state of repair and, if any furniture is provided for use under the tenancy, to the quantity, quality and condition of the furniture.

2. It is to be assumed that the number of persons seeking to become tenants of similar houses in the locality is not substantially greater than the number of available houses.

3. There is to be disregarded:

(a) Any disrepair or defect of the property or furniture which is the fault of the tenant or his predecessor.

(b) Any improvements or replacements in respect of either the property or furniture by the tenant or his predecessor.

When it was first introduced, the fair rent formula was criticised as being too vague. This was a deliberate policy, however, in order to avoid the litigation and hair-splitting that might have resulted from a more detailed formula; instead a great deal was left to the professional discretion of the rent officers and rent assessment committees, and from this point of view the system seems to have worked reasonably well. However, the formula has been amplified to some extent by the decisions of the courts and we will now examine some of the ways in which its wording has been interpreted.

Interpretation of formula

1. (a) *All the circumstances.* Examples of relevant circumstances are: (1) the rents of comparable properties, especially those for which a fair rent has already been fixed[1]; (2) the capital value of the property[2]; and (3) the terms of the tenancy. In the last case, the fact that a let is a furnished one will normally mean that a higher rent can be fixed.

(b) *Other than personal circumstances.* The tenant's poverty or hardship are not factors that can be taken into account. Nor can the fact

---

1 *Learmonth Property Investment Co Ltd v Aitken* 1970 SC 223, 1971 SLT 349.
2 *Learmonth Property Investment Co Ltd* supra; *Skilling v Arcari's Exrx* 1974 SC (HL) 42, 1974 SLT 46, reversing sub nom *Mason v Skilling* [1974] 3 All ER 977, [1974] 1 WLR 1437, HL.

that the tenant is in possession of the property and enjoying security of tenure, as this is also considered to be a personal circumstance[1].

(c) *To apply their knowledge and experience of current rents of comparable properties in the area.* These words did not appear in the original fair rent formula and are still not in its English version; they were added to the Scottish version by the Tenants Rights Etc (Scotland) Act 1980, because the Scottish courts had been taking a different line from their English counterparts regarding the need for rent assessment committees to give reasons for their decisions[2]. The change in wording does not absolve rent assessment committees from the need to give reasons, but allows them to use their own judgment and skill in cases where there is insufficient evidence, eg of comparable properties.

(d) *The age, character and locality of the dwellinghouse and its state of repair.* 'Locality' in this context is thought to mean the immediate locality, as that is what is likely to affect the value of the property; in relation to the scarcity element 'locality' is thought to mean a much wider area[3].

(e) *The quantity, quality and condition of the furniture.* There are various ways in which this could be taken into account, but the method favoured seems to be one based on a return on the capital value of the furniture[4]. In *R v London Rent Assessment Panel ex p Mota*[5], it was held that, as long as the tenant was entitled to the use of the landlord's furniture, it could be taken into account in fixing the rent, even though the tenant, with the landlord's consent, had replaced it with her own furniture.

2. *The scarcity element.* This part of the formula, contained in s 48(2) of the 1984 Act, is arguably the single most important element that distinguishes a fair rent from a market rent. Effectively it means that any inflationary effect on rents from housing shortages in the locality should be disregarded. As noted above, 'locality'

---

1 *Skilling v Arcari's Exrx* 1974 SC (HL) 42, 1974 SLT 46, reversing sub nom *Mason v Skilling* [1974] 3 All ER 977, [1974] 1 WLR 1437, HL.
2 *Albyn Properties Ltd v Knox* 1977 SC 108, 1977 SLT 41.
3 See 'Calculating Fair Rents' by Paul Q Watchman, Journal of the Law Society of Scotland (Workshop Section) p 217 (July 1981).
4 *Mann v Cornella* (1980) 254 EG 403, CA.
5 (1988) 02 EG 66.

means not just the immediate area, but a fairly large one, ie 'the area within which persons likely to occupy this class of accommodation, having regard to their requirements and work, would be able to dwell'[1]. As there are very few, if any, areas where there is not some sort of housing shortage, it is normal for the rent to be reduced by a sizeable percentage to take account of scarcity[2].

3. *Tenant's improvements or disrepair caused by the tenant.* It would clearly be wrong if a tenant who added to the property's value by making improvements at his own expense was penalised by being charged a higher rent. Conversely, a tenant whose actions detracted from the property's value should not be able to gain from his actions. It is only improvements and not repairs carried out by the tenant that should be disregarded[3]. It should be noted that the word 'predecessor' in this context means predecessor in title under the same lease, eg where there has been an assignation, or where the tenant has died and has been succeeded in the tenancy by a member of his family. Where the property is being relet under a new lease, anything done to it by the previous tenant will be irrelevant.

9. PROVISIONS COMMON TO REGULATED AND ASSURED TENANCIES

Succession to tenancies

Prior to 2 January 1989, the widow or widower of a tenant under a regulated tenancy, failing which a member of the tenant's family who had resided with the tenant for six months prior to the tenant's death, had a right to succeed to the tenancy. Furthermore, there was a right to a second succession after the death of the first successor. This meant that in some cases security of tenure could span many years, covering two or even three generations of the same family.

The Housing (Scotland) Act 1988 gives much more limited

---

1 The Francis Committee and the London Rent Assessment Panel, quoted in 'Calculating Fair Rents' by Paul Q Watchman, Journal of the Law Society of Scotland (Workshop Section) p 217 (July 1981); *Metropolitan Property Holdings Ltd v Finegold* [1975] 1 All ER 389, [1975] 1 WLR 349, DC.

2 *Western Heritable Investment Co Ltd v Husband* [1983] 2 AC 849, 1983 SC (HL) 60.

3 *Stewart's Judicial Factor v Gallagher* 1967 SC 59, 1967 SLT 52.

succession rights to the tenant under an assured tenancy, basically confining the right of succession to the tenant's widow or widower who lived with the tenant at the time of his or her death[1]. Furthermore, there is no right of succession to a tenant who has already inherited the tenancy; this means, for example, that where a widow or widower succeeds to a tenancy and then remarries, the new spouse will have no succession right.

The 1988 Act similarly curtails succession rights in the case of existing regulated tenancies, so that only a widow or widower of the *original* tenant can now inherit a regulated tenancy[2]. In certain circumstances a member of the tenant's family may still succeed to the tenancy, but what he or she will get is an *assured* tenancy, *not* a regulated one. These circumstances are (1) on the death of the original tenant's spouse, where the original tenant died *after* 2 January 1989 and the spouse inherited a regulated tenancy; (2) on the death of the original tenant where he or she died after 2 January 1989 but did not leave a spouse, and (3) where the newly-deceased tenant was not the original tenant, but succeeded to a regulated tenancy under the old law prior to 2 January 1989. This means, for example, that where a tenant inherited a regulated tenancy from a parent prior to 2 January 1989, and he dies after that date, his widow can only inherit an assured tenancy; only the *original* tenant's spouse can now inherit a regulated tenancy. In order to qualify for succession to an assured tenancy, the member of the family must have resided with the tenant for two years prior to the tenant's death; to cover transitional cases, a lesser period will qualify, provided that the member of the family resided with the tenant for six months prior to 2 January 1989.

It should be emphasised that these rather complex provisions only apply where the original tenancy was a *regulated* tenancy. As mentioned above, where it started life as an assured tenancy (ie after 2 January 1989) the position is much simpler: only the spouse can inherit.

For the purpose of these provisions, a person who was living with the tenant as the tenant's wife or husband (even though they were not married) will qualify as widow or widower.

The main effect of these amendments will be to hasten the changeover from regulated to assured tenancies. Existing regulated tenancies will not now last beyond the lifetime of the existing tenant or his spouse.

---

1 Housing (Scotland) Act 1988, s 31.
2 Rent (Scotland) Act 1984, s 3 and Sch 1; s 3A, Sch 1A and Sch 1B (added by the Housing (Scotland) Act 1988, s 46 and Sch 6, pt I).

Protection from eviction and harassment

We saw in part 3 of chapter 7 that a tenant who is unlawfully evicted may have a claim of damages against the landlord at common law. In the case of dwellinghouses, this common law remedy has been greatly reinforced by the Rent (Scotland) Act 1984 and the Housing (Scotland) Act 1988, making the landlord, or other person responsible for the unlawful eviction, liable under both the criminal and the civil law. Moreover, these provisions apply very widely, to all residential occupiers. This means that they apply to *all* leases of dwellinghouses, not only those under regulated or assured tenancies. They also probably apply to residential occupation of property that is not strictly a dwellinghouse, eg a caravan or houseboat, and to forms of tenure other than a lease, eg where the property is occupied under a licence[1].

Criminal liability. The Rent (Scotland) Act 1984[2] makes unlawful eviction or harassment of a residential occupier a criminal offence. There has been unlawful eviction if the landlord, or anyone else, 'unlawfully deprives the residential occupier of any premises of his occupation of the premises or any part thereof or attempts to do so'[3]. The deprivation does not need to be permanent provided that it has the character of an eviction, but deprivation for one day and night only has been held not to be enough[4]. It is a defence if the person accused 'believed, and had reasonable cause to believe, that the residential occupier had ceased to reside in the premises'[5]. Harassment is where either the landlord or someone else, with the intention of getting the occupier to move out of the property, or relinquish any of his rights in connection with it, 'does acts likely to interfere with the peace or comfort of the residential occupier or members of his household, or persistently withdraws or withholds services reasonably required for the occupation of the premises as a residence'[6].

---

1 See ch 1, pt 3 above.
2 Rent (Scotland) Act 1984, s 22 (as amended by the Housing (Scotland) Act 1988, s 38 and the Housing Act 1988, Sch 17, para 87). The 1984 and 1988 Act provisions specify separate offences which are similar but not precisely identical (see *Robson* pp 198–199).
3 Rent (Scotland) Act 1984, s 22(1).
4 *R v Yuthiwattana* (1984) 80 Cr App R 55, 128 Sol Jo 661, CA. But see also *Schon v Camden London Borough Council* (1986) 279 EG 859; 53 P & CR 361.
5 Rent (Scotland) Act 1984, s 22(1).
6 Rent (Scotland) Act, 1984, s 22(2) (as amended by the Housing (Scotland) Act 1988, s 38 and the Housing Act 1988, Sch 17, para 87).

Civil liability. Under the 1988 Act, a landlord who unlawfully evicts or harasses a tenant or other residential occupier is liable in damages to him[1]. 'Eviction' and 'harassment' are given similar definitions to those in the 1984 Act. The liability is stated to be a delictual one[2], but an interesting feature of this provision is that the measure of damages is not the usual one in delict, ie the loss suffered by the claimant. Instead it is the difference in value between the landlord's interest subject to the sitting tenancy, and the value of his interest with vacant possession[3]. In other words, the landlord stands to forfeit any gain that evicting the tenant is likely to bring him. Without this provision, it might in some cases have been in the landlord's interest to unlawfully evict a tenant if damages based on the tenant's loss were likely to be less than what the landlord would gain by obtaining vacant possession.

Cases where the tenant's right to occupy has ended. The above provisions apply to situations where the tenant or other occupier still has the right to occupy the property, ie where his lease has not yet ended, or where he has the right to extended security of tenure as a regulated or assured tenant. However, the 1984 Act also makes provision for cases where the tenant's tenancy or right to use the property has come to an end, and he does not have extended security of tenure. In such cases, the owner of the property must obtain a court order before he can recover possession[4]. This reinforces the common law principle applicable to all leases[5]. This provision does not apply to lodgers, temporary occupants without title, occupiers under holiday lets or occupants of hostels owned by local authorities or other public sector landlords[6].

Rather curiously, section 23 of the 1984 Act does not specify the consequences incurred by a landlord for evicting without a court order in such circumstances. It might be thought that he would be liable to the civil and criminal sanctions for unlawful eviction referred to above, but the definition of a residential occupier whose eviction can give rise to such liability seems to be confined to those who have a contractual or other legal right to occupy, or a statutory

---

1 Housing (Scotland) Act 1988, s 36(1) and (2).
2 Ibid s 36(4).
3 Ibid s 37(1).
4 Rent (Scotland) Act 1984, s 23 (as amended by the Housing (Scotland) Act 1988, s 39).
5 See ch 7, pt 3 above.
6 Rent (Scotland) Act 1984, s 23A (added by the Housing (Scotland) Act 1988, s 40).

right to security of tenure under a regulated or assured tenancy[1]. Presumably, however, section 23 has the effect of reinforcing the civil right at common law to claim damages for unlawful eviction[2].

Prohibition of premiums[3]

These provisions, in relation to both regulated and assured tenancies, make it an offence for the landlord or anyone else to accept any additional payment as an inducement to grant a tenancy, or to grant a renewal or other continuance of it. Payments to obtain an assignation (which could be made either to the landlord or the existing tenant) are also an offence. In each case the person receiving the premium is liable to a fine and to repay the sum involved. The sale of furniture to an incoming tenant at an excessive price may be considered a premium.

It is also illegal for a landlord to charge rent for a rental period that has not yet started, or to demand an advance payment of rent for a period of more than six months[4]. Breach of this will render the landlord liable to a fine and the rent for the prohibited period will be irrecoverable from the tenant[5].

These provisions were originally introduced for regulated tenancies to prevent a possible method of evading rent control; for example, a landlord confined to charging a fair rent might have sought to compensate for this by charging a capital sum in addition to rent. There seems less need for this protection in the case of assured tenancies: since the landlord is allowed to charge a market rent anyway, presumably any housing shortage that might induce a tenant to pay a premium will now be reflected in the rent. Nevertheless, there may still be cases where these provisions will operate to protect a tenant from exploitation.

1 Rent (Scotland) Act 1984, s 22(5); Housing (Scotland) Act 1988, s 36(8)(a).
2 See ch 7, pt 2 above
3 Rent (Scotland) Act 1984, pt VIII; Housing (Scotland) Act 1988, s 27.
4 Rent (Scotland) Act 1984, s 89.
5 Ibid s 89(2) and (3).

14 Residential Leases: The Public Sector

1. INTRODUCTION

We saw in chapter 13 that under the various Rent Acts the tenants of most privately let dwellinghouses have enjoyed protection of one kind or another for about eighty years. At the beginning of that period, the private let was still the most common type of tenure for householders. Since the 1939–45 war, emphasis has increasingly been on the public sector, mainly in the form of council lets. And yet, until recently, public sector tenants did not have the legal protection from eviction enjoyed by their private sector counterparts. They might have felt in less need of protection, being in the hands of publicly accountable organisations rather than private landlords, but in strict law their tenure was very much at the discretion of their landlords. When the lease contract came to an end, the council, or other public sector landlord, could terminate the let if it chose[1].

This was changed by the Tenants Rights Etc (Scotland) Act 1980 which gave to public sector tenants a statutory right to security of tenure at the end of their leases, along with a number of other rights, collectively nicknamed 'the Tenants' Charter'. This right to security of tenure is similar, but not identical, to the right formerly enjoyed by most private tenants under regulated tenancies; paradoxically, the security of tenure rights under the system of assured tenancies introduced by the Housing (Scotland) Act 1988 are now less favourable than those enjoyed by public sector tenants. The first part of this chapter will be concerned with the rights of secure tenants.

Along with security of tenure, a public sector tenant was also for the first time given the right to buy the house he occupied, at a substantial discount. This was the most controversial aspect of the 1980 legislation – prior to that, local authorities did not even have

---

1 *City of Aberdeen District Council v Christie* 1983 SLT (Sh Ct) 57. But see also *Edinburgh District Council v Parnell* 1980 SLT (Sh Ct) 11.

the right to sell their houses if they wanted to, without the consent of the Secretary of State. The second part of this chapter will therefore be concerned with the current statutory rules relating to the right to buy.

Finally, the Housing (Scotland) Act 1988 introduced a machinery by which council and other public sector tenants have a right to transfer their tenancy to a new landlord, possibly a private one. This 'choose a landlord' scheme is described in the last part of the chapter.

The bulk of the present law is consolidated in the Housing (Scotland) Act 1987. There have since been a number of amendments to that Act which will be noted as we go along. The English provisions are similar, but are contained in different legislation.

2. SECURE TENANCIES

The provisions relating to secure tenancies are mainly contained in Part III of the Housing (Scotland) Act 1987, as amended. For the tenancy to be a secure tenancy, the landlord must be one of the following types of body: (1) a local authority; (2) a water or sewerage authority; (3) a new town or urban development corporation; (4) Scottish Homes; (5) a police authority; or (6) a fire authority[1].

The tenants of the following also have secure tenancies, but only if the tenancy was entered into prior to the commencement of Part II of the Housing (Scotland) Act 1988 (ie 2 January 1989) or in certain other limited circumstances[1]: (a) the Housing Corporation; (b) a registered housing association (with the exception of co-operative housing associations); (c) a housing co-operative; and (d) any housing trust which was in existence on 13 November 1953. In the case of a local authority the right will also apply where the landlord is not the council itself, but an associated body, such as a joint board or committee of two or more local authorities or the common good of a local authority or any trust under the control of a local authority[2].

Apart from the exceptions listed below, all tenants of the above

---

1 Housing (Scotland) Act 1987, s 44(2) and s 61(2)(a) (as amended by the Housing (Scotland) Act 1988, s 3(2) and the Local Government etc (Scotland) Act 1994, Sch 13, para 152(2))); Housing (Scotland) Act 1988, s 43(3). At the time of writing the relevant part of the 1994 Act is not yet in force, and category (1) still comprises district, islands and regional councils.
2 Housing (Scotland) Act 1987, s 61(2)(a) (i) and (ii), (as amended by the Local Government etc (Scotland) Act 1994, Sch 13, para 152(2)).

landlords are secure tenants provided that (a) the house is let as a separate dwelling and (b) the tenant is an individual (ie rather than a limited company or other corporate body), and the house is his only or principal home[1]. Joint tenancies will be secure tenancies as long as all the joint tenants of the house in question are individuals and at least one of them occupies the house as his only or principal residence[2]. In *Thomson v City of Glasgow District Council*[3], it was held that a tenant who occupied a bedroom in a council hostel, where all the other facilities were communal, was not occupying a house let as a separate dwelling. One can understand why the tenant might want to claim security of tenure, but in that particular case he had applied to purchase the property!

Excepted categories

Schedule 2 of the Housing (Scotland) Act 1987 contains eight categories of let that are not secure tenancies. The Lands Tribunal for Scotland has expressed the opinion that the underlying intention of the Act is to exclude only the minimum number of houses consistent with the particular authority's functions[4], which means that they should be interpreted fairly narrowly. The excepted cases are as follows:

(1) Where the tenant is the employee of the landlord, or of any local authority or development corporation, and he occupies the house under his contract of employment for the better performance of his duties. This last part need not be expressly stated in the employment contract, but may or may not be implied depending upon the circumstances[5].

(2) Lets made expressly on a temporary basis to people seeking accommodation in the area because they are taking up employ-

---

1 Housing (Scotland) Act 1987, s 44(1); *Miller v Falkirk District Council* 1990 SLT (Lands Tr) 111.
2 Ibid s 44(3).
3 1986 SLT (Lands Tr) 6.
4 *Barron v Borders Regional Council* 1987 SLT (Lands Tr) 36.
5 *Douglas v Falkirk District Council* 1983 SLT (Lands Tr) 21; *Kinghorn v City of Glasgow District Council* 1984 SLT (Lands Tr) 9. See also *Stevenson v West Lothian District Council* 1985 SLT (Lands Tr) 9, *Docherty v City of Edinburgh District Council* 1985 SLT (Lands Tr) 61, *Campbell v City of Edinburgh District Council* 1987 SLT 51, *Forbes v City of Glasgow District Council* 1988 GWD 31–1330; *Little v Borders Regional Council* 1990 SLT (Lands Tr) 2, and *McTurk v Fife Regional Council* 1990 SLT (Lands Tr) 49.

ment there. The effect of the word 'expressly' is that the lease must make it clear that the let is temporary, and it is not enough for it merely to refer to the appropriate schedule and paragraph of the Act[1].

(3) Temporary lets of houses that are due for development. Development could either be a building operation or a material change of use[2]. Again the situation must be expressly stated in the terms of the lease[3].

(4) Temporary lets of alternative accommodation while works are being carried out on the tenant's usual house, to which he has the right to return as a secure tenant. The tenant, however, does have the right to stay on in the temporary accommodation until his previous house is ready for occupation again[4].

(5) Temporary accommodation granted under the landlord's duty, as a local authority, to homeless persons.

(6) Where the house is let along with agricultural land[5] or business premises[6], ie along with more than two acres of land, or along with a shop, office or premises licensed to sell alcohol.

(7) Rent and rate free lets by police authorities to police constables, and lets by fire authorities to firemen in consequence of their need to live near a particular fire station. Also excluded are temporary lets to other people pending a let to a police constable or fireman.

(8) Where the house is within the curtilage of a building that is not used as housing accommodation. This means that it must be used for the comfortable enjoyment of the other building so as to form an integral part of it[7]. Where the house and the other building are separated by a public road, the house cannot be within the curtilage of that other building[8].

1 *Campbell v Western Isles Islands Council* 1988 SLT (Lands Tr) 4.
2 Town and Country Planning (Scotland) Act 1972, s 19.
3 *Shipman v Lothian Regional Council* 1989 SLT (Lands Tr) 82.
4 Housing (Scotland) Act 1987, s 46(2).
5 *Lamont v Glenrothes Development Corporation* 1993 SLT (Lands Tr) 2.
6 *Fleck v East Lothian District Council* 1992 SLT (Lands Tr) 80.
7 *Barron v Borders Regional Council* 1987 SLT (Lands Tr) 36. See also *Burns v Central Regional Council* 1988 SLT (Lands Tr) 46; *Allison v Tayside Regional Council* 1989 SLT (Lands Tr) 65 and *MacDonald v Strathclyde Regional Council* 1990 SLT (Lands Tr) 10.
8 *Fisher v Fife Regional Council* 1989 SLT (Lands Tr) 26.

Security of tenure

The effect of a tenancy being secure is essentially the same as with regulated and assured tenancies in the private sector. In other words, the tenant has the right to stay on in the property even though the contractual term stated in his lease has expired. The landlord has only very limited rights to bring the tenancy to an end. The tenant, on the other hand, can terminate the let at any time by giving the landlord four weeks' notice[1]. The tenancy may end on the tenant's death, but only where there is no relative entitled to succeed to the tenancy and who wishes to take it up[2]. Otherwise, the tenancy can only be terminated if the tenant abandons the property[3], or the landlord obtains a court order for possession.

Before it can raise court proceedings, the landlord must give the tenant at least four weeks' written notice, stating the ground of termination[4]. The notice will cease to be effective if not used by the landlord within six months[5]. The court will only grant the landlord a possession order on certain limited grounds which are specified below. These are not quite the same as the grounds of possession for regulated and assured tenancies, although there are similarities[6].

Grounds for termination

The grounds entitling the landlord to recovery of possession are set out in Part I of Schedule 3 of the Housing (Scotland) Act 1987. There are sixteen grounds in all. The first seven of these all relate to situations where the tenant could be said to be at fault in some respect. In these cases there is no requirement that other accommodation will be available to the tenant, but the court must be satisfied that it is reasonable to make the order[7]. This therefore gives the sheriff discretion, if he does not think that a landlord is acting reasonably, to refuse it possession even where a ground of termination exists. The onus is upon the landlord to show that the ground of termination exists and that it is reasonable for the tenant to be

---

1 Housing (Scotland) Act 1987, s 46(1)(f).
2 Ibid s 46(1) (a) and (b).
3 See section on 'Abandonment of tenancy' below.
4 Housing (Scotland) Act 1987, s 47(2) and (3).
5 Ibid s 47(4); *City of Edinburgh District Council v Davis* 1987 SLT (Sh Ct) 33.
6 See ch 13, pts 3 and 7 above.
7 Housing (Scotland) Act 1987, s 48(2)(a); *Second WVRS Housing Society v Blair* (1987) 19 HLR 104, CA.

evicted[1], even if the tenant does not defend the action[2]. It is preferable for the landlord's claim to expressly narrate that it is reasonable to grant an order of possession, but lack of this will not nullify the action if enough information is presented to the court to enable it to make a decision (eg that the rent for almost half of a ten-year tenancy had never been paid)[3].

The remaining grounds ((8)–(16)) do not involve any fault on the tenant's part, but there is other good reason for him to be moved out. In all of these cases the court, before it can grant an order, must be satisfied that suitable alternative accommodation is available to the tenant[4]. The criteria for suitability are set out in Part II of Schedule 3. The alternative accomodation need not be provided by the landlord itself, but *must* be either under another secure tenancy, or be a protected tenancy under the Rent (Scotland) Act 1984 or an assured tenancy under the Housing (Scotland) Act 1988[5]. The other criteria are not mandatory, but the sheriff must have regard to them in deciding whether or not the accommodation is reasonably suitable. They include the proximity of the new house to the tenant's or a member of his family's place of work, comparability with the tenant's existing house and any special needs of the tenant or his family[6].

The following are the sixteen grounds that may entitle the landlord to recover possession of the house[7].

(1) Rent arrears or breach of any other obligation of the tenancy.

(2) Use of the house for immoral or illegal purposes.

(3) Any deterioration in the condition of the property or its common parts caused by the neglect or default of the tenant. This will also be a ground if the deterioration was caused by a lodger or subtenant, unless the tenant has taken reasonable steps to have the person removed.

(4) In the case of furnished lets, deterioration of the furniture due to ill treatment. There is a similar provision to (3) in respect of lodgers or subtenants.

1 *Midlothian District Council v Drummond* 1991 SLT (Sh Ct) 67; see also *Midlothian District Council v Brown* 1991 SLT (Sh Ct) 80 and *Renfrew District Council v Inglis* 1991 SLT (Sh Ct) 83.
2 *Gordon District Council v Acutt* 1991 SLT (Sh Ct) 78.
3 *City of Glasgow District Council v Erhaiganoma* 1993 SCLR 592.
4 Housing (Scotland) Act 1987, s 48(2)(c).
5 Ibid Sch 3, pt II, para 1(a) (as amended by the Housing (Scotland) Act 1988, Sch 9, para 21); *Charing Cross & Kelvingrove Housing Association v Kraska* 1986 SLT (Sh Ct) 42.
6 Housing (Scotland) Act 1987, Sch 2, para 2.
7 Ibid Sch 3, pt I.

(5) Where the tenant and his spouse have been continuously absent from the house for more than six months without reasonable cause, or have ceased to occupy the house as their principal home. In the English case of *Crawley Borough Council v Sawyer*[1], the tenant left the house for about a year and a quarter to stay with his girl friend, then returned after he and his girl friend split up. During the period of his absence, he continued to pay the rent, visited the house about once a month and occasionally lived in it for periods of up to a week. It was held that the landlords were not entitled to repossess.

(6) Where the landlord was induced to grant the tenancy because of a false statement made knowingly or recklessly by the tenant.

(7) A nuisance committed in the neighbourhood by the tenant or someone living with him, in circumstances where it is not reasonable for the landlord to have to provide alternative accommodation[2].

(8) Same as (7) (ie nuisance), in circumstances where the landlord believes that it *is* appropriate for the tenant to be moved to other accommodation.

(9) Overcrowding amounting to an offence.

(10) Demolition of, or substantial work to, the house or the building of which it forms part. If the landlord intends that the tenant should return to the house afterwards, the court will make an order that he is entitled to do so[3]. The tenant will have security of tenure in the alternative house until such time as his original house is ready for occupation again[4]. In England it has been held that, before it can regain possession, the landlord must show a firm and settled intention to carry out the works and also to show that the works cannot be reasonably carried out without obtaining possession[5].

(11) Where the house has been designed or adapted for a person with special needs. This applies only if there is no longer anyone in the house with such needs and the landlord requires the house for someone who has.

(12) Where the house is part of a group of houses intended for persons in need of special social support. This is subject to a similar proviso to that in (11).

1 (1988) 20 HLR 98, CA.
2 *Scottish Special Housing Association v Lumsden* 1984 SLT (Sh Ct) 71.
3 Housing (Scotland) Act 1987, s 48(5).
4 See excepted category 4 above.
5 *Wansbeck District Council v Marley* (1987) Times, 30 November, 1987 CLY 2229.

(13) Where the landlord is a housing association that caters for the elderly, the infirm, the disabled or people in special social circumstances. Again, there is a similar proviso to that in (11).

(14) Where the landlord is itself a lessee under a lease that has terminated or is about to terminate.

(15) Where the landlord is the council for Orkney Islands, Shetland Islands or Western Isles[1] and the house is reasonably required for an employee of the council in the exercise of its function as education authority. This applies only if the existing tenancy was granted to a similar employee whose employment has now ended.

(16) Where the landlord wishes to transfer the tenancy to the tenant's spouse or former spouse or a person with whom the tenant has been living as husband and wife. This only applies if the other person has applied for the transfer of tenancy, and one of the parties (either the tenant or the other) no longer wishes them to live together. In respect of this ground only, the court has to be satisfied *both* that it is reasonable to make the repossession order *and* that other suitable accommodation is available.

Abandonment of tenancy

We saw above (termination ground (5)) that the tenant's absence from the house for more than six months can be a ground for a court order terminating the tenancy. However, if the landlord has reason to believe that the tenancy has been abandoned, it may be able to recover possession without waiting for six months or obtaining a court order. If it has reasonable grounds for believing that a house let under a secure tenancy is unoccupied and that the tenant does not intend to occupy it as his home, the landlord may take possession of it[2]. It must first serve four weeks' written notice on the tenant of its intention to repossess unless the tenant replies within that time that he intends to reoccupy the house[3]. If the tenant fails to reply, the landlord may, after making any necessary enquiries, serve another notice terminating the tenancy. After that it is entitled to take immediate possession without further proceedings[4]. Pending

---

1 Housing (Scotland) Act 1987, Sch 3, pt I, para 15 (as amended by the Local Government etc (Scotland) Act 1994, Sch 13, para 152(8)).
2 Housing (Scotland) Act 1987, s 49.
3 Ibid s 50(1).
4 Ibid s 50(2) and (3).

such termination, the landlord is entitled to enter the house, by force if necessary, to secure it against vandalism[1].

The tenant may appeal to the court within six months to have the tenancy restored, or be granted alternative accommodation. The grounds of appeal are that the landlord failed to carry out the prescribed procedure or that the tenant had good reason, such as illness, for not replying to the landlord's notice[2].

Succession to tenancy

On the death of a secure tenant, the tenancy will pass by operation of law to anyone qualified to succeed him[3]. Those qualified are (1) the tenant's spouse (2) anyone living with the tenant as husband and wife (3) a surviving joint tenant, if the house was his principal home at the time of the tenant's death and (4) if there is no-one in the above categories, a member of the tenant's family. In each of these cases the person succeeding must have lived in the house as his or her only or principal home at the time of the tenant's death; in number (4) the successor must have resided there for at least twelve months prior to the tenant's death and have attained the age of sixteen[4]. In *Roxburgh District Council v Collins*[5] the deceased tenant's son, during the year preceding his mother's death, had lived and worked in London, where he had accommodation in a lodging house. However, a bedroom had been kept in his mother's house for his exclusive use, he had kept clothes and other possessions there, and he had returned to live at the house every Christmas, Easter, during summer holiday periods and occasionally for weekends. It was held that this was sufficient to make the house his only or principal home during the relevant period. 'Family' is defined very widely, and includes parents, grandparents, aunts, uncles, brothers, sisters, relationships by marriage and relationships of half blood. As well as children of the tenant, there is included stepchildren and illegitimate children, and in England the equivalent definition has been held to include foster children[6].

In England, the Court of Appeal has held that two women living in a homosexual relationship should not be considered to be living

---

1 Ibid s 49(2) and (3).
2 Ibid s 51.
3 Ibid s 52.
4 Housing (Scotland) Act 1987, s 52(2).
5 1991 SLT (Sh Ct) 49.
6 Housing (Scotland) Act 1987, s 83; *Reading Borough Council v Ilsley* (1981) CLY 1323.

as husband and wife for the purpose of succession to a secure tenancy[1].

If more than one person is qualified to succeed to the tenancy (eg where there is no surviving spouse but two or more children), the tenancy may be transferred to any one of them, or to two or more of them as joint tenants. Who is to succeed will be decided by agreement of all the qualified people. If they cannot agree, the landlord will decide[2].

A person qualified to succeed is entitled to decline the tenancy[3].

A second succession is not allowed, unless it is to a joint tenant[4]. However, if there is someone who would otherwise have been entitled to succeed, he may stay on in the house for up to six months[5].

Fixing of rent levels

Although the 1987 Act confers security of tenure on public sector tenants analogous to that enjoyed under the Rent (Scotland) Act 1984 by tenants of private landlords, there is no general public sector equivalent of rent regulation and the fixing of fair rents. The landlord may increase the rent, without terminating the tenancy, by giving the tenant four weeks' notice of the increase[6].

Local authority landlords are free to charge 'such reasonable rents as they may determine'[7]. They are directed to review rents from time to time and, in fixing rent levels, must take no account of the personal circumstances of the tenants[8]. After the rent levels have been fixed, however, the latter may be taken into account in determining the eligibility of individual tenants for rent rebates.

Tenants of housing associations and the Housing Corporation were formerly in a special category. Under Part VI of the Rent (Scotland) Act 1984, it is provided that they may have fair rents registered and rent increases phased over three years in the same way as those under regulated tenancies from private landlords[9]. However, in the case of tenancies entered into after 2 January 1989 (with a few limited exceptions) there is no longer that right[10].

1 *Harrogate Borough Council v Simpson* [1986] 2 FLR 91, (1985) 25 RVR 10, CA.
2 Housing (Scotland) Act 1987, s 52(3).
3 Ibid s 52(4).
4 Ibid s 52(5).
5 Ibid s 52(6).
6 Ibid s 54(2).
7 Ibid s 210(1).
8 Ibid s 210(2) and (3).
9 See ch 13, pt 8 above.
10 Housing (Scotland) Act 1988, s 43(1) and (2).

Other tenancy terms

Every secure tenant is entitled to a written lease, subscribed by the parties in accordance with the Requirements of Writing (Scotland) Act 1995[1]. It is up to the landlord to draw up the lease, free of charge to the tenant, and to supply the tenant with a copy[2]. The parties may later agree to a variation of the terms, which the landlord must record in a similarly formal document[3].

If either the landlord or the tenant wishes to change any terms of the lease (other than rent), but cannot get the other to agree, the party wanting the change may apply to the sheriff court for a variation of the terms[4]. The sheriff may make such variation as he thinks reasonable, taking particularly into account the safety of any person or the likelihood of damage to the property[5].

Where it is the tenant who makes the application for a variation, there are additional criteria to be met, which are, incidentally, very similar to those required for the variation of land obligations by the Lands Tribunal for Scotland (ie that they are unreasonable, inappropriate or unduly burdensome)[6]. In *Taylor v Moray District Council*[7] it was held that it was not unreasonable, inappropriate or unduly burdensome for a lease to contain a prohibition against keeping animals without the landlord's consent, merely because a neighbour who had exercised the right to buy was not subject to a similar restriction. The tenant may be ordered to pay compensation to the landlord for any loss caused by the variation[8]. Also, he may be required to serve notice of his application on the owner or tenant of any land who benefits from the term in its existing form, or who would be adversely affected by the change[9].

Assignation and subletting

The landlord's written consent must be obtained before the tenant can assign, sublet or in any other way give up possession of the

1 Housing (Scotland) Act 1987, s 53(1) (as amended by the Requirements of Writing (Scotland) Act 1995, Sch 4, para 59).
2 Ibid s 53(2).
3 Ibid s 54(1) and (6) (as amended by the Requirements of Writing (Scotland) Act 1995, Sch 4, para 60).
4 Housing (Scotland) Act 1987, s 54(3).
5 Ibid s 54(4).
6 Ibid s 54(3); Conveyancing and Feudal Reform (Scotland) Act 1970, s 1.
7 1990 SCCR 55.
8 Housing (Scotland) Act 1987, s 54(4).
9 Ibid s 54(5).

house to another person, or before he can take in a lodger[1]. The landlord's consent, however, may not be unreasonably withheld. In order to obtain consent, the tenant must serve a written application on the landlord and, if the landlord fails to reply within a month, its consent will be deemed to have been given[2]. If the landlord refuses consent, the tenant may appeal to the sheriff[3].

It is stated that assignees and subtenants will not be entitled to protection under the Rent (Scotland) Act 1984 or to an assured tenancy under the Housing (Scotland) 1988[4]. This makes sense in relation to subtenants, as their immediate landlord will be a private individual and therefore potentially within the ambit of the 1984 or 1988 Acts. It is rather confusing in relation to assignees: as they will be tenants directly under the original public sector landlord, they could not be regulated or assured tenants anyway, and there seems no reason why they should not be regarded as secure tenants under the 1987 Act.

The landlord must be notified of any proposed increase in a subtenant's rent, and may object to it[5].

Repairs

Common law position. As with all types of tenancy, the landlord is under an obligation to keep the premises in a tenantable and habitable condition[6].

Statutory rights. In relation to dwellinghouses, these common law obligations of the landlord have been reinforced considerably by statute and generally cannot be contracted out of. The first two of the following categories apply (within certain limitations) to all residential tenancies, both within the public and private sectors; the third category only applies to certain types of secure tenancy.

(1) *Habitability*[7]. These provisions only apply to houses with a rent of less than £300 per week, though the Secretary of State has power to raise the limit from time to time. There is an implied condition that

1 Ibid s 55(1).
2 Ibid Sch 4, para 3(b).
3 Ibid Sch 4, para 4.
4 Ibid s 55(4) (as amended by the Housing (Scotland) Act 1988, Sch 9, para 10).
5 Housing (Scotland) Act 1987, s 56.
6 See ch 3, pt 2 above.
7 Housing (Scotland) Act 1987, s 113 and Sch 10, para 1 (as amended by the Housing (Scotland) Act 1988, Sch 8); Landlord's Repairing Obligations (Specified Rent)(Scotland)(No 2) Order SI 1988/2155.

the house is reasonably fit for human habitation at the commencement of the tenancy and will thereafter be kept so by the landlord during the tenancy. A house is considered unfit for human habitation if it falls short of local building regulations by reason of disrepair or sanitary defects; 'sanitary defects' includes lack of air space or ventilation, darkness, dampness, absence of adequate and readily accessible water supply or of sanitary arrangements or of other conveniences, and inadequate paving or drainage of courts, yards or passages[1]. There are certain exceptions where the obligation does not apply, eg where a house is let for a period of three years or more on condition that the lessee renders it fit for human habitation. Otherwise, this obligation of the landlord cannot be contracted out of.

(2) *External repairs and installations.* In respect of houses let *for less than seven years* (which probably includes most house lets) there is an implied condition that the landlord will (a) keep in repair the structure and exterior of the house (including drains, gutters and external pipes) and (b) keep in repair and working order the installations for *the supply of* water, gas and electricity, and for sanitation (including basins, sinks, baths and sanitary conveniences), as well as installations for space or water heating. Apart from the above, the landlord's liability does not extend to fixtures, fittings and appliances *for making use of* water, gas or electricity (eg a gas or electric cooker or fire).

In *Hastie v City of Edinburgh District Council*[2] it was held that the exterior of the building included windows and the tenant was entitled to recover from the landlord the cost of a window broken by vandals.

With regard to this category of obligation, a contracting-out provision in the lease is not normally allowed, but may exceptionally be included by permission of the sheriff where he considers it reasonable to include such a provision.

(3) *Secure tenants' right to repair*[3]. This right was introduced in 1994 and (unlike (1) and (2) above) does not apply generally, but

---

1 See *Fyfe v Scottish Homes* 1995 SCLR 209; *Quinn v Monklands District Council* 1995 SCLR 393.
2 1981 SLT (Sh Ct) 92; see also *City of Edinburgh District Council v Laurie* 1982 SLT (Sh Ct) 83.
3 Housing (Scotland) Act 1987, s 60 (as substituted by the Leasing Reform, Housing and Urban Development Act 1993, s 146); the Secure Tenants (Right to Repair) (Scotland) Regulations 1994, SI 1994/1046; see also 'Improved Rights for Public Sector Tenants?' by June Hyslop, SCOLAG Journal No 221 (March 1995).

only to certain types of secure tenancy, ie those of local authorities and associated bodies[1], new town and urban development corporations and Scottish Homes. Other secure tenancies are not included, eg those housing association tenancies (entered into prior to 2 January 1989) which still qualify as assured tenancies.

The right to repair does not add to the categories of repair which are the landlord's responsibility. Instead, it is designed to strengthen the mechanism for enforcing the landlord's obligations by allowing a tenant, if the landlord does not respond urgently, in certain cases to take the matter into his own hands by instructing the repair himself and charging it to the landlord.

The right only applies to a 'qualifying repair', ie repair of a defect specified in the regulations[2] which *is the responsibility of the landlord*. The latter proviso means that merely appearing on the list contained in the regulations is not enough to make a repair a qualifying repair, unless the repair is already the landlord's responsibility either in terms of the lease or under the statutory obligations in (1) and (2) above; in most cases, however, this will in fact be the case. The list of defects giving rise to a qualifying repair includes the following: loss (total or partial) of electricity, water or gas supply, or of space or water heating, blocked or defective sanitary facilities, various types of leak, insecure windows or doors, unsafe flooring, handrails, stairs or electrical facilities, and broken extractor fans[3].

When a tenant applies to his landlord to have a qualifying repair carried out, the landlord's contractor must carry out the repair within the maximum time allowed (either one, three or seven days, depending on the type of repair), unless the contractor is refused access or there are exceptional circumstances beyond his or the landlord's control. The time limit is calculated from the first working day after the landlord received notification, or when he carried out an inspection (if the latter was deemed necessary).

If the landlord's usual contractor fails to meet the time limit, the tenant may instruct another contractor from a list of alternative contractors which the landlord is obliged to provide. The landlord will be obliged to meet the alternative contractor's bill (up to a maximum of £250 per repair) and in addition the tenant can claim compensation from the landlord up to a maximum of £50, depending on the length of delay.

---

1 At the time of writing these are still the regional, district and islands' councils.
2 Secure Tenants (Right to Repair)(Scotland) Regulations 1994, SI 1994/1046, para 4 and Schedule.
3 Ibid, Schedule.

Alterations and improvements

Right to carry out work. A secure tenant is entitled to carry out alterations and improvements to the house, including the erection of garages or other outhouses[1]. The landlord's consent is required, but may not be unreasonably withheld. If the effect of the tenant's work is to add to the value of the house, he cannot be charged extra rent in respect of that increase[2].

Discretionary compensation. A landlord has a discretionary power to make a payment to the tenant at the end of his tenancy in respect of any value his improvements have made to the property[3].

Right to compensation. In addition to the landlord's discretionary power, tenants who carry out improvements have, since 1994, a *right* to compensation in certain circumstances[4]. However, this right is not enjoyed by all secure tenants, but only those of local authorities, new town and urban development corporations and Scottish Homes, ie the same ones that have the right to repair. Also, the right only applies to certain types of improvement, namely those which are qualifying improvements in terms of the relevant regulations[5]. These comprise a number of internal improvements (such as bathroom and kitchen installations, insulation work, window replacement and installation of space and water heating) but not external additions like garages or outhouses, in respect of which payment remains at the discretion of the landlord.

The amount of compensation will not be paid if it would be less than £50 and cannot exceed £3,000 per improvement. It is based on the cost of the improvement, less any grant received and an allowance for depreciation depending on the age of the improvement when the tenancy ends. This is worked out according to a formula laid down in the regulations[6]. Provision is made for the resolution of disputes[7].

1 Housing (Scotland) Act 1987, s 57 and Sch 5.
2 Ibid s 59.
3 Ibid s 58.
4 Ibid s 58A (added by the Leasehold Reform, Housing and Urban Development Act 1993, s 47); the Secure Tenants (Compensation for Improvements) (Scotland) Regulations 1994, SI 1994/632. See also 'Tenants' Improvements' by June Hyslop, SCOLAG Journal No 222 (April 1995).
5 Secure Tenants (Compensation for Improvements)(Scotland) Regulations 1994, SI 1994/632, Schedule.
6 Ibid reg 5.
7 Ibid reg 8.

The right to compensation does not apply in all cases where a tenancy comes to an end[1]. It is payable, for example, when there is a change of landlord or the tenancy is assigned, but not where the tenant has exercised his right to buy or the tenancy has been terminated by court order on one of the grounds of repossession stated in Part I of Schedule 3 of the 1987 Act[2].

3. RIGHT TO BUY

Who may buy

A tenant has the right to buy the house he lives in provided (a) he holds it under a secure tenancy[3] and (b) he has been a tenant for at least two years immediately prior to the application[4], which may partly consist of a period in occupation of another public sector tenancy[5]. There are some exceptions to this right to purchase:

(1) Where the house is one of a group designed or adapted for elderly or disabled persons and the facilities include a call service and a warden (ie sheltered housing)[6]. Provided that the house fits this description, there will be no right to buy, even if the tenant is not actually of pensionable age or disabled[7]. Where a house has been so designed or adapted, but does not fall within the above definition (eg because it is not part of a group of sheltered houses) there *is* a right to buy; however, if the house was first let prior to 1 January 1990 the Secretary of State has the power to authorise the landlord's refusal of the tenant's application[8].

---

1 Housing (Scotland) Act 1987, s 58A(1)(c) (added by the Leasehold Reform, Housing and Urban Development Act 1993, s 147); the Secure Tenants (Compensation for Improvements)(Scotland) Regulations 1994, SI 1994/632, reg 4.
2 See section on 'Grounds for termination' above.
3 See pt 2 above.
4 *Matheson v Western Isles Islands Council* 1992 SLT (Lands Tr) 107; but see *McLoughlin's Curator Bonis v Motherwell District Council* 1994 SLT (Lands Tr) 31.
5 Housing (Scotland) Act 1987, s 61(1), (2) and (11); Right to Purchase (Prescribed Persons) (Scotland) Order 1993, SI 1993/1625 (as amended by the Right to Purchase (Prescribed Persons) (Scotland) Amendment Order 1994, SI 1994/2097).
6 Housing (Scotland) Act 1987, s 61(4)(a). See *Crilly v Motherwell District Council* 1988 SLT (Lands Tr) 7; *Martin v Motherwell District Council* 1991 SLT (Lands Tr) 4; *Holloran v Dumbarton District Council* 1992 SLT (Lands Tr) 73; and *City of Dundee District Council v Anderson* 1994 SLT 46.
7 *Moonie v City of Dundee District Council* 1992 SLT (Lands Tr) 103.
8 Ibid s 69 (as amended by the Local Government and Housing Act 1989, s 177(1)).

(2) In certain cases where the landlord is a registered housing association. These include where the association has less than 100 dwellings for let, in some cases where it is a charity, or where it provides houses for people (such as the mentally ill or physically handicapped) who require a social service or special facilities[1]. As far as other housing association tenancies are concerned, there will of course only be a right to buy where the tenancy is a secure tenancy, ie entered into prior to 2 January 1989[2]. And there will be no right to buy in the case of the other excepted categories where there is no secure tenancy[3].

It is also a requirement that the landlord should either be the heritable proprietor of the house or the tenant under a registered lease[4].

The tenant may purchase the house jointly along with another member or members of his family[5]. The right to purchase may not be exercised by any tenant or joint tenant without the consent of his or her spouse where the spouse occupies the house as his or her only or principal home[6].

If the house is acquired by a private landlord, the right to buy is not lost, unless the transfer takes place under Part III of the Housing (Scotland) Act 1988 (the so-called 'choose a landlord' scheme)[7].

What is purchased

Section 62 merely gives a tenant the right to purchase 'the house' which he has on lease. 'House' is defined later in the Act to include any part of a building, including a flat, which is occupied or intended to be occupied as a separate dwelling. It is also stated to include 'any yard, garden, out-houses and pertinents belonging to the house or usually enjoyed therewith'[8]. In *Neave v City of Dundee District Council*[9], the landlord's offer excluded the garden ground at the front and back of the house, the reason given being that it was

---

1 Ibid s 61(4) (as amended by the Housing Act 1988, Sch 17, para 79 and Sch 18, and by the Housing (Scotland) Act 1988, Sch 2, para 9 and Sch 7, para 2).
2 See pt 1 above.
3 See section on 'Excepted categories' in pt 1 above.
4 Housing (Scotland) Act 1987, ss 61(2)(b) and 84A (inserted by the Local Government and Housing Act 1989, s 178(2)).
5 Ibid s 61(6).
6 Ibid s 61(5).
7 Housing (Preservation of Right to Buy) (Scotland) Regulations 1993, SI 1993/2164; see also pt 4 below.
8 Ibid s 338(1).
9 1986 SLT (Lands Tr) 18.

part of a communal area maintained by the district council. It was held that the tenant was entitled to buy the garden ground, but that the ground should be subject to the control of the district council, who could maintain it if they wished.

The position seems to be that the tenant is entitled to buy everything that is included in his lease and possessed by him. This applies even to parts that the council, perhaps inadvertently, have already disposed of. In *Morrison v Stirling District Council*[1], the purchaser was held entitled to a right in common to a mutual path and steps separating the house from the one next door, even though the tenant next door had already been sold his house with the whole steps and path included. In *Popescu v Banff and Buchan District Council*[2], the applicant was held entitled to buy his house free of a servitude right that had been granted in favour of the house next door. The reason was that the lease to him was free of any servitude rights. This produced the rather odd result that the council was compelled to modify its offer to include something that was no longer its to sell. But, said the Lands Tribunal, the problem was the council's. It would either have to obtain a discharge of the servitude or be liable in breach of contract for failing to implement its bargain. In contrast, in the case of *Hannon v Falkirk District Council*[3], the tenant was held not to be entitled to a lockup garage because it and his house were let to him under separate leases.

In *MacDonald v Strathclyde Regional Council*[4] it was held that a restrictive title condition was not a barrier to a sale going ahead and that it was up to the landlord to make the tenant's statutory right effectual by obtaining any necessary consents. However, in *Ross and Cromarty District Council v Patience*[5], it was held that a right of pre-emption in favour of the superior took precedence to the tenant's statutory right to buy.

The purchase price

The price is calculated as follows:

(a) The market price is determined either (i) by a qualified valuer nominated by the landlord and accepted by the tenant or (ii) by the

1 1987 SLT (Lands Tr) 22.
2 1987 SLT (Lands Tr) 20.
3 1987 SLT (Lands Tr) 18.
4 1990 SLT (Lands Tr) 10; see also *Walker v Strathclyde Regional Council* 1990 SLT (Lands Tr) 17.
5 1994 SCLR 779; see also articles on this decision by Douglas J Cusine in 1994 JLSS 331 and 1995 JLSS 234.

district valuer, the choice of which being up to the landlord. It is to be calculated as if the dwellinghouse were available for sale on the open market with vacant possession[1].

(b) No account is to be taken of any element in the market value of the house which would qualify as an improvements reimbursement at the end of a secure tenancy[2]. Otherwise the tenant would be paying for this element in the value twice.

(c) A discount is deducted from the market value. The discount for houses is 32 per cent of the market value plus an additional 1 per cent of the market value for every year beyond two of the tenant's occupation, up to a maximum discount of 60 per cent. In the case of flats, there is a higher discount; for them, the minimum discount is 44 per cent and rises at a rate of 2 per cent per year, up to a maximum of 70 per cent[3]. The Secretary of State has the right by statutory instrument to vary the minimum and maximum discounts and the annual percentage increases[4]. Where the tenant wishing to buy has succeeded to the tenancy (eg from his father) the period when he occupied the house as the tenant's child will be taken into account in calculating the discount, both in relation to his present and previous houses[5]. However, those years before the child reached the age of sixteen will be excluded[6]. In *Kelly v City of Dundee District Council*[7] it was held that the tenant could not include the years spent living in another house, which had been tenanted by his father and later by his mother, when both of them had died and that earlier tenancy had terminated before the right to buy was introduced in 1980.

(d) The tenant's earlier occupation of another public sector house or houses can be taken into account in ascertaining the relevant number of years for calculating the discount. The earlier tenancies which may be used for this purpose include those where there is a right to buy – ie those which qualify as secure tenancies in Scotland – but extend to a number of other public sector tenancies as well. These include tenancies from English local authorities and govern-

---

1 Housing (Scotland) Act 1987, s 62(2) (as amended by the Housing (Scotland) Act 1988, Sch 8, para 2).
2 Housing (Scotland) Act 1987, s 62(2); see also pt 2 above.
3 Housing (Scotland) Act 1987, s 62(3).
4 Ibid s 62(5).
5 *Motherwell District Council v Gliori* 1986 SLT 444.
6 Housing (Scotland) Act 1987, s 61(10)(a).
7 1994 SLT 1268.

ment lets to prison officers or members of the armed forces[1]. Thus, for example, a tenant may buy a Scottish council house with a discount partly calculated from his previous occupation of a council house in England. Likewise, a member of the armed forces may not have a right to buy the house let to him by the Crown, but his period of occupation there may be taken into account if he later exercises his right to buy another public sector house. There was formerly a requirement that (for the purpose of calculating the discount) the tenant's periods of occupation should be continuous and have occurred immediately prior to the application. This requirement has now been dropped[2]. However, in order to qualify for the right to buy in the first place (as opposed to calculating the discount) it is still necessary for the tenant to have occupied the house for two years *immediately* prior to the date of application[3], which partly frustrates the effect of the above amendment.

(e) The person whose period of occupation is taken into account need not be the tenant but, if this would produce a higher discount, may be either the tenant's spouse (if living with him at the date of the application), a deceased spouse (if living with the tenant at the time of death), or any joint tenant who is a joint purchaser[4]. However, if the person whose period of occupation is selected has received a discount from a previous public sector house purchase, this will be deducted from the discount now payable[5]. The purpose of this is to exclude the benefit of a second discount within the same family.

(f) *Cost floor provision.* If the house is a fairly new one, or the landlord has in the recent past spent substantial sums in improving it, a situation could arise where selling it at a large discount might result in the landlord incurring a loss. In other words, the amount spent on building or improving the house could exceed the sale price after deduction of the discount. This is more likely to happen if the costs were incurred recently; if they were incurred some years before, the effect of inflation is likely to have brought the price

---

1 Ibid s 61(11); Right to Purchase (Prescribed Persons) (Scotland) Order 1993, SI 1993/1625 (as amended by the Right to Purchase (Prescribed Persons) (Scotland) Amendment Order 1994, SI 1994/2097).
2 Housing (Scotland) Act 1987, s 62(3)(b) (as amended by the Leasehold Reform, Housing and Urban Development Act 1993, s 157(3)).
3 Housing (Scotland) Act 1987, s 61(2)(c).
4 Ibid s 62(4) (as amended by the Leasehold Reform, Housing and Urban Development Act 1993, s 157(3)(c)).
5 Housing (Scotland) Act 1987, s 62(3A) (added by the Leasehold Reform, Housing and Urban Development Act 1993, s 157(3)(b)).

above any outstanding costs, even after deducting the discount. In order to minimise the chance of a loss occurring, it is provided that the price may not be less than any outstanding costs incurred within the landlord's five previous financial years. If, however, the market value before deduction of discount is itself less than the outstanding costs, then that market value is what will be paid[1]. If the purchaser bought through the rent to loan scheme (see below), the purchaser's deferred financial commitment may also be affected.

These provisions were introduced by the Housing (Scotland) Act 1988 in place of those in the earlier legislation which performed a similar function, the relevant figure then being known as the 'outstanding debt' on the house. Where a landlord in its offer erroneously deducted the full discount, overlooking the fact that the outstanding debt was higher, it was held that the contract of sale was void and that the landlord could not be held by the tenant to the lower figure[2].

If any of the costs are not known, the landlord should make an estimate of them[3]. In *Wingate v Clydebank District Council*[4], where the cost of improvements was difficult to disentangle from repair and maintenance work that had been carried out as part of the same package, it was held that it was up to the council as landlord to quantify the amount attributable to improvements.

The Secretary of State also has power to make an order substituting a different period for the five years stated, and to make different provisions in relation to different cases or circumstances, or different areas[5].

(g) *Abatement of price.* If the purchase transaction is prolonged because of delays by the landlord either during the application procedure or after conclusion of the contract of sale, some of the rent paid by the tenant during that period may be deducted from the purchase price[6].

---

1 Ibid s 62; and ss 6A and 6B (added by the Housing (Scotland) Act 1988, s 65); see also *Murdoch v Gordon District Council* 1985 SLT (Lands Tr) 42.
2 *McGroarty v Stirling District Council* 1987 SLT 85.
3 Housing (Scotland) Act 1987, s 62(10).
4 1990 SLT (Lands Tr) 71.
5 Housing (Scotland) Act 1987, ss 6A and 6B (added by the Housing (Scotland) Act 1988, s 65(2)).
6 Housing (Scotland) Act 1987, ss 66A–C (inserted by the Leasehold Reform, Housing and Urban Development Act 1993, s 144).

Purchase procedure

The tenant must submit to the landlord an application to purchase, including a statement of his relevant period of occupancy and the name of any joint purchaser[1]. The form of the application to purchase is prescribed by statutory instrument[2]. The landlord must make the tenant an offer within two months[3] after which, within one month, the tenant may request the landlord to alter any terms he considers unreasonable or have a new term added[4]. The Secretary of State has power to direct either landlords in general or particular landlords that certain types of term are unreasonable[5].

The landlord may not include a pre-emption provision, ie one giving the landlord first option to buy if the house is ever resold by the tenant[6]. The reason for this is to prevent landlords who were reluctant to sell (probably for political reasons) using a pre-emption provision in order to regain ownership of the property at a later date. There is an exception to this rule in the case of houses adapted or designed for elderly or disabled persons[7]. Also, the Secretary of State has power to sanction pre-emption provisions in certain rural areas, if it appears necessary to stop houses purchased by sitting tenants being resold as holiday houses[8].

If the landlord refuses the offer or fails to amend its offer when requested, the tenant may within one month appeal to the Lands Tribunal[9]. The Lands Tribunal is not restricted in its consideration to grounds which were stated in the landlord's notice of refusal[10]. Where the tenant is seeking to vary a condition of a landlord's offer, this does not entitle him to challenge the market value[11]. The landlord is entitled to refuse if it believes that the tenant's application contains incorrect information[12], and also if the house is reasonably required for someone employed by a local authority for

1 Housing (Scotland) Act 1987, s 63(1).
2 Right to Purchase (Application Form) (Scotland) Order 1993, SI 1993/2182.
3 Ibid s 63(2).
4 Ibid s 65(1); see also *Forsyth v Scottish Homes* 1990 SLT (Lands Tr) 37 and *McLuskey v Scottish Homes* 1993 SLT (Lands Tr) 17.
5 Ibid s 78.
6 Ibid s 64(4).
7 Ibid s 64(4).
8 Ibid s 64(6) and (7) (as amended by the Housing (Scotland) Act 1988, Sch 9, para 11); see also *Pollock v Dumbarton District Council* 1983 SLT (Lands Tr) 17.
9 Housing (Scotland) Act 1987, ss 68(4) and 65(2); see also *Keay v Renfrew District Council* 1982 SLT (Lands Tr) 33.
10 *Fernie v Strathclyde Regional Council* 1994 SLT (Lands Tr) 11.
11 *Macleod v Ross and Cromarty District Council* 1983 SLT (Lands Tr) 5.
12 Housing (Scotland) Act 1987, s 68(2).

Orkney Islands, Shetland Islands or Western Isles as part of its educational function[1]. The Secretary of State may also give the landlord permission to refuse where the house is designed or adapted for the needs of an elderly person[2], though only in the case of houses first let on a secure tenancy prior to 1 January 1990[3]. As we saw above, where the house is part of a group of sheltered housing, there is no right to buy at all.

The tenant is entitled to a loan in order to purchase the house. Where the landlord is a new town or urban development corporation, the Housing Corporation or a district or islands council, the landlord is obliged to grant the loan if applied for; where the landlord is a registered housing association, the loan is to be granted by the Housing Corporation or Scottish Homes (depending upon which one of them the association is registered with); in all other cases the loan is to be granted by the relevant local authority. In the event of a refusal, the tenant may appeal to the sheriff court[4].

If the tenant enters any proceedings against the landlord in connection with his right to sell, he may be able to obtain financial or other assistance from the Secretary of State in order to fight his case[5].

In England, a situation arose where a tenant submitted an application to buy and then, after the application but before the sale had been concluded, the landlord raised an action to terminate the tenancy. It was held that the landlord was entitled to do so, provided that there was a statutory ground of termination[6].

In *Cooper's Exrs v City of Edinburgh District Council*[7] a tenant died after exercising his right to buy and concluding missives, but before delivery of the disposition. The House of Lords held that the tenant's executors could compel the landlords to complete the transaction.

Clawback on resale

It would be an obvious abuse of the Act if a tenant were to purchase at a substantial discount and immediately, or very soon thereafter,

1 Ibid s 70 (as amended by the Local Government etc (Scotland) Act 1994, Sch 13, para 152(4)).
2 Housing (Scotland) Act 1987, s 69.
3 Ibid s 69 (1A) (added by the Local Government and Housing Act 1989, s 177(1)).
4 Ibid s 216 (as amended by the Housing (Scotland) Act 1988, Sch 2, para 13).
5 Housing (Scotland) Act 1987, s 79.
6 *Enfield London Borough Council v McKeon* [1986] 2 All ER 730, [1986] 1 WLR 1007, CA.
7 1991 SLT 518 (HL).

resell the house at the full market value. Accordingly, if a tenant sells within three years, the discount, or a proportion of it, is recoverable by the landlord at the following rate:

Within the 1st year:	100 per cent
Within the 2nd year:	66 per cent
Within the 3rd year:	33 per cent[1]

There is no liability to repay the discount where: (a) the house is being sold by the executor of a deceased owner[2]; (b) the house is being compulsorily purchased, or (c) the house is being transferred free of charge to a member of the owner's family who has lived with him or her for the previous twelve months[3].

If the house is sold for a second time within the three year period, there will be no liability to repay discount on that second occasion[4].

Rent to loan scheme[5]

Nature of scheme. The rent to loan scheme was introduced by the Leasehold Reform, Housing and Urban Development Act 1993 in order to make it easier for tenants with limited financial means to exercise their right to buy. The essence of the scheme is that the tenant, when he buys the house, is only required to pay a certain proportion of the purchase price (the initial capital payment) for which he can obtain a mortgage in the usual way. While he remains owner he is not liable for the remainder of the price, but when he eventually sells he becomes liable to the landlord for a payment known as the deferred financial commitment. The advantage to the tenant is that his loan repayments need be no more than he was previously paying in rent. The disadvantages are that he is entitled to a lower level of discount than a tenant who buys in the usual way and that, when the house is eventually resold, the former tenant's liability is not merely to pay the proportion of the purchase price that was deferred. Instead the landlord is entitled to a percentage of the sale price, thereby sharing in any capital appreciation of the property.

---

1 Housing (Scotland) Act 1987, s 72.
2 See *Clydebank District Council v Keeper of the Registers of Scotland* 1994 SLT (Lands Tr) 2. But see also *Jack's Exrx v Falkirk District Council* 1992 SLT 5.
3 Housing (Scotland) Act 1987, s 73.
4 Ibid s 72(4).
5 Housing (Scotland) 1987, s 62A and ss 73A-73D (inserted by the Leasehold Reform, Housing and Urban Development Act 1993, ss 141 and 142); Leasehold Reform, Housing and Urban Development Act 1993, s 143.

Eligibility for scheme[1]. All tenants who are entitled to buy their house are also eligible for the rent to loan scheme, with two exceptions: (1) tenants of houses designated as 'defective' under Part XIV of the 1987 Act; and (2) tenants claiming housing benefit; to be more precise, the scheme is denied to tenants who have been held entitled to housing benefit during the period from twelve months prior to the application date up until conclusion of the sale contract, or who have claimed housing benefit, but the claim has not yet been determined or withdrawn.

Price. The purchase price is calculated in the usual way, except that the discount is reduced across the board, so that it is 15 per cent less of the purchase price than it would otherwise have been. The minimum discount for houses therefore becomes 17 per cent and the maximum 45 per cent, and for flats the minimum will be 29 per cent and the maximum 55 per cent[2]. If the discount is limited because of outstanding costs incurred within the previous five years[3] this will sometimes also affect the deferred financial commitment[4].

Initial capital payment. The minimum figure is a sum which, if repaid as a loan repayment, would come to not less than 90 per cent of the rent. This is assuming an interest payment at the statutory rate[5] and a repayment period of 25 years; if the latter would take the purchaser beyond pensionable age (presently 60 for women and 65 for men), the repayment period assumed will be the number of years until the applicant reaches that age, subject to a minimum of 10 years.

The purchaser may, if he wants, make a higher initial capital payment.

Deferred financial commitment. The formula for calculating this is somewhat complex, but basically (subject to certain adjustments) it works out as a percentage of the resale value of the property. This percentage is worked out by taking the difference between the initial capital payment and the purchase price (after deduction of discount), and expressing that difference as a percentage of the *market*

---

1 Housing Scotland Act 1987, s 62A (inserted by the Leasehold Reform, Housing and Urban Development Act 1993, s 141).
2 Housing (Scotland) Act 1987, s 73A(2).
3 See section on 'Purchase price' above.
4 Housing (Scotland) Act 1987, s 73D(5) and (6).
5 Ibid s 73B(2)(a).

value of the property at the time of purchase[1]. The resulting figure
is then reduced by 7 to reach the final percentage. No interest is
payable on the deferred financial commitment, presumably
because the landlord is sharing in any capital appreciation[2]. The
resale value is the actual amount received by a sale on the open
market with vacant possession or, if the purchaser has died, the
value for the purpose of the confirmation to his estate[3]. However, if
ownership passes on the owner's death to someone for whom the
house was his only or principal home for at least twelve months
prior to the owner's death, the deferred financial commitment will
not have to be paid at that time. The same is the case if the successor is a joint purchaser, or if the owner sells or otherwise disposes
of the house during his lifetime to his spouse or anyone else with
whom he was living as if they were husband and wife, provided that
in each case the house was the recipient's only or principal home[4].

Interim payments. The purchaser is entitled to make contributions
towards the deferred financial commitment at an earlier stage, or even
pay it off entirely, provided that any such payments are at least a year
apart and no payment is less than £1,500 or (in the case of a partial
payment) it exceeds the statutory maximum. The statutory maximum
is the sum that would reduce the deferred financial commitment to
less than 7.5 per cent of the resale value; in such a case the owner
would either have to keep his payment within the limit or pay off the
whole amount. Any such payments will be calculated as a percentage
of a notional resale value at the time of payment, as agreed by the parties or, failing agreement, as fixed by an independent valuer.

Legal status. An offer to sell to the tenant under the rent to loan
scheme must include a condition that the tenant will be entitled to
ownership of the house in exchange for the initial capital payment[5].
The deferred financial commitment is secured by a standard security over the house; however, any such standard security will rank
after any standard security securing a loan by a recognised lending
institution if it is to enable payment of (1) the initial capital payment; (2) any interim payment of the deferred financial commitment; (3) the improvement of the house; or (4) for any
combination of these purposes[6].

1 Ibid s 73C(1).
2 Ibid s 73C(2).
3 Ibid s 73C(8)(a).
4 Ibid s 73D(1) and (2).
5 Ibid s 73A(3).
6 Ibid s 73A(4) and s 73C(7).

4. RIGHT TO TRANSFER TO NEW LANDLORD

General

Part III of the Housing (Scotland) Act 1988 provides the legal machinery by which a public sector tenant may have his tenancy transferred to a new landlord. The latter may be Scottish Homes or may be a housing association or a private landlord. It is also suggested that tenants might form co-operatives with their neighbours to purchase their homes[1]. The choice of landlord has to be approved by Scottish Homes, unless they themselves have been chosen as landlords.

The stated aim of the government is that tenants who are not content with their housing conditions or the standard of management offered by their public sector landlord should have the right to choose to transfer their tenancy to a landlord who might be able to do a better job[2]. This suggests that the initiative in seeking the transfer will normally be taken by the tenant (or perhaps by a group of tenants). However, the procedure laid down by the Act is for the prospective new landlord to apply to the existing public sector landlord to purchase the property, in very much the same way as a tenant may apply to them under the right to buy provisions. Presumably this formal application by the new landlord might happen because an informal approach has been made to it by the tenant. It seems equally possible, however, that a commercial landlord might approach a tenant (or, more probably a group of tenants) proposing a transfer. In any case, a transfer cannot proceed without the tenant's consent.

This process (like a tenant's right to buy) can be carried out against an unwilling public sector landlord. In other words, provided that the proposed new landlord has been given the necessary approval, and the tenant's consent has been obtained, the existing landlord does not normally have the right to refuse an application. This should be distinguished from a situation where a local authority or other public sector landlord may want *voluntarily* to sell a house or group of houses with sitting tenants to a new owner; for that the tenants' consent is not necessary, though they have to be consulted and the Secretary of State's consent is required[3].

The procedure laid down is for applications to be made on an

---

1 Housing: The Government's Proposals for Scotland (Nov 1987) (Cmnd 242), para 6.10.
2 Ibid para 6.9.
3 Housing (Scotland) Act 1987, s 13(2) (inserted by the Housing Act 1988).

individual basis, so that it would be possible for even a single flat in a block to be transferred to a new landlord. However, private land-lords are more likely to be interested in buying houses in a group, and the Act makes provision for Scottish Homes to give its general consent for a new landlord to buy all the houses within a particular category, eg all those in a particular area[1].

As we saw in the early part of this chapter, public sector tenants generally enjoy security of tenure under a secure tenancy, in terms of the Housing (Scotland) Act 1987. It should be noted that ten-ants transferring out of the public sector to a private landlord, or to a housing association, will cease to have secure tenancies[2]. This will be the case, not only where the transfer occurs as a result of the 'choose a landlord' provisions described in this section, but also in any other situation where a tenancy is transferred out of the public sector. Although s 45 does not actually say so, such tenancies would normally qualify as assured tenancies instead[3]. A tenant transferring to Scottish Homes would normally continue to enjoy a *secure* tenancy[4].

There are several factors that a tenant thinking about transfer-ring to the private sector should keep in mind: (1) the security of tenure provisions are less favourable under assured tenancies than they are with secure tenancies[5]; (2) the Act makes no provision for a tenant to be transferred back to the public sector should he want to, so a transfer to a private landlord may be an irrevocable step; (3) the landlord chosen by the tenant can dispose of his interest to yet another landlord, and although the consent of Scottish Homes will be required for this, the tenant's consent is not necessary for any such subsequent transfer (though Scottish Homes has to be satis-fied that the tenant has been consulted and must have regard to his views)[6]. However, no consent or consultation is required for future transfers after that. The tenant, therefore, has no guarantee that he will remain with the landlord whom he has chosen; and (4) unlike the situations with other transfers to a private landlord, the tenant will lose his right to buy[7].

---

1 Housing (Scotland) Act 1988, s 57(2).
2 Ibid s 45.
3 See ch 13, pt 2 above.
4 See pt 2 above.
5 See ch 13, pt 2, and this chapter, pt 2 above.
6 Housing (Scotland) Act 1988, s 63 (as amended by the Housing Act 1988, Sch 17, para 89).
7 Housing (Preservation of Right to Buy) (Scotland) Regulations 1993, SI 1993/2164; see also pt 3 above.

Acquisition procedure

The public sector landlords to whom an application can be made are: (a) a local authority; (b) a development corporation, including an urban development corporation; (c) the Housing Corporation, and (d) Scottish Homes[1]. As with the right to buy, there are exceptions in respect of special categories of properties, eg those adapted for persons with special needs, or those situated in designated rural areas[2]. The applicant may be either Scottish Homes or a person or body approved by them[3].

The application must contain a statement that the applicant seeks to exercise the right conferred on him under the Act and be accompanied by the written consent of the tenant[4]. Unless the landlord disputes the applicant's right, the landlord must reply with an offer to sell containing the market value of the house and other conditions of the sale.[5] The applicant must send a notice of acceptance within two months, which will have no effect unless he has already entered into a lease with the tenant, conditional upon the sale proceeding[6].

Price

The price is to be the market value of the house as determined either by a qualified valuer nominated by the landlord and accepted by the applicant, or by the district valuer, the choice of which being up to the landlord[7]. The market value is to be the price which the house would realise if sold on the open market by a willing seller, but subject to a number of assumptions, including that the only prospective purchasers are Scottish Homes or the approved applicant, and also that the applicant will, within a reasonable time carry out any repairs required to fulfil the landlord's repairing obligations. Provision is also made for the price to be nil, or even a negative amount. This means that a public sector landlord could in some circumstances be compelled to pay a prospective private landlord to acquire a particular house or houses[8].

1 Housing (Scotland) Act 1988, s 56(3) (as amended by the Local Government etc (Scotland) Act 1994, Sch 13, para 157).
2 Housing (Scotland) Act 1988, s 56(5).
3 Ibid s 57.
4 Ibid s 58(1).
5 Ibid s 58(5).
6 Ibid s 60.
7 Ibid s 58(6).
8 Ibid s 58(8).

It is clear from these provisions that the government contemplates situations where run-down properties, of little or no market value, will pass into the hands of private landlords and be upgraded. However, this need not be so, in which case the first of the two valuation assumptions mentioned above seems rather strange. It would seem to mean, for example, that a well-maintained house in a good area, for which there might be considerable market demand, would still have its price calculated on the assumption that no-one was interested in it apart from the applicant or Scottish Homes. This could have the effect of producing a price that was well below the real market value, giving private landlord applicants a considerable bargain. It would, of course, be open to Scottish Homes to refuse consent to a transfer in such cases.

Reference to Lands Tribunal

As with the right to buy, the Lands Tribunal for Scotland has been given jurisdiction to settle disputes that may arise at different stages of the process:

(1) Where a landlord served with an application fails to issue timeously either an offer to sell or a notice of refusal[1].

(2) Where the landlord has refused to strike out or vary any condition which the applicant thinks unreasonable[2].

(3) Where the landlord has served a notice of refusal on the applicant[3].

(4) Where the landlord has served an offer to sell which does not comply with a requirement of Part III of the 1988 Act[4].

The Lands Tribunal, if it considers the applicant's complaint to be justified, has the power to serve an offer to sell, or take any other appropriate action in the landlord's place[5].

---

1 Ibid s 62(1)(a).
2 Ibid s 59(3) and s 62(1)(b); see *Waverley Housing Trust v Roxburgh District Council* 1995 SLT (Lands Tr) 2 (inclusion of a right of pre-emption).
3 Housing (Scotland) Act 1988, s 61(3) and s 62(1)(c).
4 Ibid s 62(1)(d).
5 Ibid s 62(2).

Index

Additions. *See also* IMPROVEMENTS,
    TENANT'S
clause in lease, 107
Agricultural holdings. *See also*
    CROFTS AND SMALL
    LANDHOLDINGS
arbitration—
    appeal against arbiter's decision,
      190–191
    procedure, 189–190
    rent referred to, 174, 190–191
    statutory provisions for, 170, 189
assured tenancy, not, 209–213
compensation rights of tenants—
    damage by game, for, 188
    disturbance, for, 169, 186–187
    early resumption, for, 188
    generally, 183–184
    improvements, for—
      drainage and associated
        improvements, 184
      generally, 95, 169, 184–186
      permanent improvements, 185
      temporary improvements, 186
    reorganisation of tenant's affairs, for,
      187
contracting out prohibited, where,
    170–171, 184
definition of, 171–172
delectus personae in, 67
English and Scottish law compared, 170
fixtures—
    provision and maintenance of, by
      landlord, 173–174, 175
    record of, 175–176
    tenant's right to remove, 175
hypothec, most not subject to, 60
improvements to—
    compensation rights for. *See*
      compensation rights of tenants,
      above

Agricultural holdings—*continued*
improvements to—*continued*
    encouragment for, 169
leases generally, 7
less than a year, leases of, 171–172
notice to quit—
    counter notice by tenant, 181, 183
    grounds where landlord has absolute
      right of removal, must expressly
      state, 179
    part of holding, 182–183
    period of, 91
    referral to Land Court, 181–182, 183
    requirement for, 178–179
    statutory period of notice, 178
protected tenancy, not, 228
purposes of statutory control, 169–171
rent—
    appeals relating to, 190–191
    non-payment of, removal for, 176,
      179–180
    reviews, 174–175
Scottish Land Court—
    jurisdiction excluded, where,
      179–181
    landlord's objection to succession,
      referral of, 193, 193–194
    rent review appeals to, 190–191
    role of generally, 170–171
    tenant's referral to, following notice
      to quit, 181–182
security of tenure—
    counter-notice served by tenant,
      181–182
    exceptions to, 179–181
    notice to quit. *See* notice to quit,
      above
    onus of proof where tenant serves
      counter-notice, 181–182
    rights of, generally, 169–170,
      177–178